Digital Culture Unplugged

Digital Culture Unplugged

Probing the Native Cyborg's Multiple Locations

Editor

Nalini Rajan

Routledge
Taylor & Francis Group

LONDON AND NEW YORK

First published 2007 by Routledge

2 Park Square, Milton Park, Abingdon, Oxfordshire OX14 4RN
711 Third Avenue, New York, NY 10017

Routledge is an imprint of the Taylor & Francis Group, an informa business

First issued in paperback 2018

Transferred to Digital Printing 2007

Typeset by
Bukprint India
B-180A, Guru Nanak Pura, Laxmi Nagar,
Delhi 110 092.

British Library Cataloguing in Publication Data
A catalogue record of this book is available from the British Library

ISBN 978-0-415-44545-0 (hbk)
ISBN 978-1-138-38024-0 (pbk)

Contents

Acknowledgements

This book would not be possible without the constant encouragement and cooperation extended to me by Omita Goyal. I also wish to thank all my contributors for their excellent and well-researched articles on an admittedly difficult topic like the interface of culture and digital technology.

I am grateful to the organisers of the seminar on 'Information Technology and Social Science Research' organised under the Malcolm Adiseshiah Chair on Policy Studies, Madras Institute of Development Studies, in Chennai, on September 18, 2004, for readily giving me permission to rework my paper presentation, *The New Technologies and the Constitution of Theft*, for this volume.

A radically modified version of Charlene Rajendran's article in this collection was earlier published as *Viewing the Necessary Stage Screen on Stage: a Flat Look at its Character*. The article appeared in a book entitled *Ask Not: The Necessary Stage in Singapore Theatre*, edited by Tan Chong Kee and Tisa Ng, published by Marshall Cavendish International Asia Pte Ltd, Singapore, 2004.

Finally, as always, working on this edited volume has considerably expanded my knowledge of digital technology—for that I am thankful.

Nalini Rajan

Introduction

Nalini Rajan

When they weren't playing [seriously old-fashioned computer] games they'd surf the Net—drop in on old favourites, see what was new. They'd watch open-heart surgery in live time, or else the Noodie News. ... Or they'd watch animal snuff sites, Felicia's Frog Squash and the like. ... Or they'd watch dirtysockpuppets.com, a current-affairs show about world political leaders. ... Or they might watch hedsoff.com, which played live coverage of executions. ... Shortcircuit.com, brainfrizz.com, and deathrowlive.com were the best; they showed electrocutions and lethal injections...(Atwood 2004).

Margaret Atwood's apocalyptic vision of warfare, genetic engineering and mind control, exemplified in the quotation given above, reminds us of the horrors of unbridled technophilia. Thus 'technophobia' among women is understandable as a response to military and scientific abuses within a patriarchal system. Television warfare—as the reporting on the Indo-Pakistan Kargil war reporting or that on the two Gulf wars is called—is supposed to be a depiction of a war to end all wars. It has a panoptic effect, as acts of warfare are subjected to television audiences' gaze and nationalist or patriotic frenzy acquires the garb of normality.

Are We All Cyborgs?

However, not everyone shares Atwood's morbid perspective on science and technology. From Mary Wollstonecraft Shelley's 19th-century Frankenstein figure[1] to Donna Haraway's feminist cyborg manifesto in the mid 1980s, we have come a long way—and not just in chronological terms. The 'cyborg' concept has found expression in the arts, but it is an originally scientific concept first seen in a speculative 1960 article by Clynes and Kline on how human bodies can manage to survive space travel (1960: 26–27; 74–76). Later, the cyborg came to mean anyone with artificial or animal implants. Metaphorically, Roland Barthes dubbed Albert Einstein a cyborg—namely, a mind producing thoughts just as a mill churned out flour (1972).

An excellent example of a contemporary cyborg is the cyclist champion and former cancer patient Lance Armstrong, who has been profiled in the *New Yorker* magazine by Michael Specter: 'Referring to the gulf that now exists between the race and the racers, the French philosopher Robert Redeker has written, "The athletic type represented by Lance Armstrong, unlike Fausto Coppi or Jean Robic"—two cycling heroes from a generation ago—"is coming closer to Lara Croft, the virtually fabricated cyber-heroine. Cycling is becoming a video game; the onetime prisoners of the road have become virtual human beings . . . Robocop on wheels, someone no fan can relate to or identify with"'(2002).

The feminist Shulamith Firestone (1970) had already anticipated the promise of a female cyborg in 1970. She referred to a feminist revolution when women seize control of the means of production and reproduction. Firestone's grim optimism in the 1970s was countered within feminist discourse by the demonisation of science and technology, stemming from a fear of the link between technology and militarism. In particular, post-modern feminists have since sustained a critique of science and technology as being an intrinsic part of the dominant patriarchal discourse. (My own efforts in persuading my feminist academic friends to contribute to this volume have been largely fruitless, with most of them professing an aversion to linking technology to gender issues!)

Nevertheless post-modernism is a chameleon discourse, with no stable shape, form or location. Earlier, it has theorised with respect to the arts or literature, but now it cuts across disciplinary boundaries between the arts and the sciences and touches on artificial intelligence, quantum mechanics and information technology. Judith Halberstam, to cite an example, has a fascinating take on the Apple Computer Logo: 'A post-modern reading of the apple finds that the subject has always sinned, has never not bitten the apple. The female cyborg replaces Eve in this myth with a figure who severs once and for all the assumed connection between woman and nature upon which entire patriarchal structures rest' (1991).

Recent essays on the cyborg wish to get past the dualisms of self and other, person and machine, nature and technology, even gender and science. The post-modern sensibility now lies not in techno-avoidance, but in multiple, decentred locations in techno-celebratory popular culture, like television talk shows and soap operas, sacred music like *bhajans* based on Bollywood music, Nicole Kidman worship page on the Internet,[2] or religious sites and *puja* or prayer rooms on the Internet. All this gives credence to theatre analyst Brook's argument (1976) that melodrama provides audiences with the necessary emotional excesses, in a post-sacred age, in order to make ethical and moral decisions. When Haraway claims, 'we are all cyborgs', she implies positive attributes like hybridism, playfulness, and creativity. This is in sharp contrast to what Haraway calls Artificial Intelligence-inspired technofascism: 'The cyborgs dreamed up by the A.I. boys tend to be technofascist celebrations of invulnerability'.[3]

Gandhi and Digital Technology

It is important to resist the patriarchal gendering of technology, and to counter the patriarchal story of the goddess, who is morally superior to men and given the right to give birth to children. This is the mission of the new 'automated feminism' that Haraway endorses. All the same, automated feminism is a terrifying cultural icon because it calls to mind the fusion of femininity and intelligence. A female cyborg is artificial in flesh and in mind—as much machine as woman, as close to science as to nature. Haraway's cyborg radically destabilises nature. Admittedly, it is difficult to envisage the cyborg in the nuclear age, and ecofeminism is an inevitable counter response to technophilia. Nevertheless, the new form of ecofeminism does not allow for sops like victimisation or motherhood; it envisages woman and nature not as passive victims, but as active agents in a mutual struggle. By breaking down the nature–culture divide, the new ecofeminism calls for artifactualism, rather than a simplistic pro-nature stance.

Is digital technology more favourable to the people in the first world who can indulge in an explosion of the self and of self-expression? By contrast, are people in the third world likely to find their selves annexed to machines? The truth is that the 'native' is not necessarily naïve and can be empowered with technology, and is likely to find radically new ways of empowerment. I like to imagine that Mohandas Karamchand Gandhi, if he were alive today, would not have been averse to digital technology and would have discovered some new form of radical technological empowerment, even while eschewing the Western model of technological invulnerability. This would be possible, not *despite* Gandhi's commitment to an ecological worldview, but *because* of it. After all, Gandhi is remembered today as the mass communicator par excellence of the 20th century, and his famous Dandi March or salt *satyagraha* of the early 1930s is a testimony to the power of symbolism, media technology and tele-communications.

The Gandhian viewpoint is quite different from the deep ecology of Aldo Leopold, which is a value-based ideal that pits itself against people or human-based ideals. Deep ecology is concerned with the preservation of the ecosystem above all else, even the welfare of human beings. In other words, deep ecology posits the indistinguishability of all things within the ecosystem. The indistinguishability thesis is exemplified variously as the Indian tribal notion of *sanatana dharma* or universal harmony, and as the *nishkama karma* or disinterested action in the early part of the Hindu sacred text, the *Bhagavad Gita*.

What is new about the Gandhian ecocentric perspective, however, is that it applies the standard ecological pro-nature model in the context of a broader and more encompassing pattern of layered inter-relationships that extend beyond personal and societal relations to include the different members of the non-human community. The latter are appreciated as important in their own terms, and as possessing varying degrees of relative autonomy—which, in some cases, may be superior to humans like infants and the brain damaged. The Gandhian environmental theory of the transcended or transpersonal self, for its part, allows for the expression of love and compassion for all things outside oneself. This is the quintessential Gandhian *bhakti* or devotional ideal, and is present in the later chapters of the *Bhagavad Gita*. It is essentially a humane, compassionate perspective, and leads more by practical example than by theoretical argument. Gandhian ecocentric practitioners—like those involved in the *Narmada Bachao Andolan* like Medha Patkar—are attempting to revitalise philosophy by offering a more integrated, non-anthropocentric approach than the application of instrumental rationality with respect to nature. More importantly, it calls for the erosion of the boundary between nature and culture.

The Gandhian form of empowerment lies in vulnerability, in the yogic reduction of one's self to zero or *sunyata*. There is even a cyborgian dimension to the Indian tradition of *yoga*, which Gandhi had recommended for his satyagrahis or followers in the first half of the 20th century. Perhaps the most contemporary expression of treating the body as part machine, part human, is in the daily exercise regimen of yogic breathing by the charismatic Baba Ramdev—belonging to the 'subaltern' *yadav* or shepherd caste—on the *Aastha* satellite television channel that has captured the imagination of the growing health-conscious middle and upper classes and castes in India. The idea here is not to learn to survive in outer space, but within our own planet replete with carcinogens and cholesterol.

Luddite Anxieties

In theory, of course, the ecocentric perspective and the cyborgian vision have been at opposite ends of the ideological spectrum. In reality, as we have noted from the Gandhian campaigns in India and elsewhere, they are crucially interdependent. Without media technology, there can be no mass environmental movement. In other words, we inhabit—and have inhabited down the ages—a 'multimedia' world. The instrument that facilitates the understanding of multimedia is dubbed as 'the creative interlocutor' (Traub and Lipkin 2000). Throughout history, this instrument has varied—from the pyramids of ancient Egypt that combined the scientific technology of preserving human remains with religious rituals, to the medieval Christian cathedral or Hindu temple that hosted an entire township of activity within its geographical limits, to the modern computer, which facilitates virtual museums or travel tours, religious pilgrimages, or research work pertaining to the life of the mind.

Multimedia preceded the computer; still, the computer is the modern cathedral of the creative interlocutor, simply because it achieves similar goals in a far more democratic and universal way. However, the anxiety persists: will the computer wipe out the book? This Luddite anxiety was rephrased in different ways, according to the historical context, in every age. For example, in Victor Hugo's novel, *The Hunchback of Notre Dame*, a Catholic priest of 15th century France compares the newly invented book to the cathedral and states, 'This will kill that' (2001). That is to say, the book will kill the cathedral. Needless to add, this has not happened. Again, more recently, Marshall McLuhan in his magnum opus, *The Gutenberg Galaxy* (1962), wrongly foresaw the decline of the written word and the rise of the visual image. The truth is that all these can and will coexist—the modal imagery of the church, the textual mode of representation in the book, the visual power of the photograph, and the non-linear digital technology of the computer. All these may change in terms of function and meaning, much as did painting, with the advent of photography, but they are unlikely to be 'killed'.

This, then, summarises A. R. Venkatachalapathy's opening essay in this volume. Venkatachalapathy's point is that there is no universal history of the book; consequently, there is no single future for it. As far as the Tamil language publishing goes, it is all set to have a great future with its continued engagement with computerised digital technology.

For all this, the spectacular power of the computer often reinforces the power of the technocrat, who is believed to design, implement and direct technology for technology's sake. I reproduce below one of my favourite passages, written in the 1980s, on this obsessive modern imperative to adopt 'the new and the improved' at any cost:

'The digital watch is a perfect example of the reductivist aesthetic of modernism: We now look at the time instead of reading it. The early method, internalised in childhood, of reading the time from a clockface has been supplanted by a sidelong glance at liquid crystal display (L.C.D.). This economy of intellectually learned skills has come about with the change in technology, from flywheel to liquid crystal microelectronics. Along with this change in technology has come a vastly higher level of timepiece accuracy and efficiency. Do we really need such split-level accuracy in our daily activities? Or do we think so, simply because the technology makes it available and advertising tells us we do? Does the advent of the digital watch mean that unpunctuality has been abolished? Now that people have apparently infallible timekeeping machines on their wrists, are they somehow more scrupulous about keeping to life's schedules? ... I miss the old Swiss timepieces because they were not universal in appearance. They looked by turn expensive, macho, kitsch, or just plain cheap. What they almost never looked like were futuristic identification bracelets, imposed on us by an alien race, who wanted cruelly to remind us with split-second accuracy just how much time humans really waste' (Porch 1985: 46–47).

Indeed, one of the ironies of digital technologies like the computer is that—in an attempt to discover newer and more efficient time-saving devices—we are losing sight of leisurely, reflective activities like reading or writing books or discussing ideas with friends. No doubt, we continue to read, but there is a difference between 'deep reading and personal appropriation of an author's vision' and the more mediated 'hypertextual' reading that comprises our online activity on the Internet (Rud 1997). Hypertext refers to the arrangement of non-linear texts made possible by computers and virtual space. Here, unlike what happens with the use of paper, references can be expanded on and the interconnectedness of information made manifest without their taking up physical space.

The point is that the advent of the computer, as mentioned earlier, does not imply the disappearance of the book. This is especially relevant in the field of education and the constitution or formation of the self therein. The ideal pedagogical situation is one where both book and (computer) screen are decentred, and the focus is on the construction of the student's moral self through dialogue and discussion.

Dissecting the Digital Self

There are those, however, that do believe that technology has its discontents. Discussing the basic difference between the self involved in 'deep reading' of a book and that involved in the mediated reading that happens online, Anthony Rud comments: 'This type of interior relation within the self, using a single author book as the occasion for self-reflection, is at odds with the gathering or "retrieval" of information more typical in a digital environment' (1997: 30).

There are at least three problems, claims Rud, with online mediated reading. One is that web-based writing tends to erode linguistic complexity by employing a simplistic, 'prefabricated' vocabulary. The requirements of easy and quick communication squeeze out more subtle uses of language, such as irony and ambiguity. Second, as language becomes more fragmented, and as hypertextual information is arranged in an equally accessible, weightless order, the narrative's historical perspective will be attenuated. Third, this has adverse repercussions on the constitution of the self, especially in the context of education. 'Deep reading' expands the private, interior self; the shallow reading on the Internet shrinks the private self.

What, then, are the implications of digital technologies for religious reflections on the self? Here is a contemporary analyst's considered viewpoint on the interface of religion and technology: 'For the world's traditional religions cyborg identities raise profound issues. Foremost, they broach questions of normative human identity and social ethics, given the problematic public and private values entailed in their development. A notable measure of the internal cohesion of the world's major religions derives from concrete texts that represent layers of oral traditions that were the products of pastoralist and agrarian people. These texts provide shared stories for believers that set out norms for human–to–human relationships as well as for human relationships to the divine. The religious message they contain and convey assume embodied human existence as a given but, for cyborgs, universal embodiment is not the defining situation. A focal religious idea of Christianity is incarnational theology. In all of its diverse manifestations Christianity pivots around the idea of the embodiment of the divine in human form; however, this notion is problematised by the coupling now underway of human and machine. The technologisation of daily life appears to be undermining the ability of religious institutions to fulfil cultural functions like responding to the existential questions of their age or to proffer a symbol system that welds together a description of the world and prescriptions for action within it' (Brasher 1996: 817).

In his illuminating article on cyber-religion, Felix Wilfred points out that religion has generally been preoccupied with the misrepre-sentation of the 'original'. Nevertheless the imaginary world has become the real one, with changes in our perception of spatiality, owing to the rise of computer-mediated communication, which, in turn, offers the possibility of 'bringing out many layers of the self'. This, in itself, is no cause for alarm, because theology was never meant to navigate on safe waters. The task of the future is to ensure that the benefits of information technology percolate to the most deprived in society.

Picking on the notion of digital technology and the notion of self-formation, R. Radhakrishnan discusses the following question: If indeed technology is the radical 'other' that determines the existence of the post-humanist subject, what does it mean for this all-too-human and finite subject to be interpellated by the radical experiential possibilities of technology? Since Radhakrishnan envisages digital technology as the nightmare creation of the 'A.I. boys',[4] his answer to this question lies in the recognition of technology's susceptibility to ideological control and manipulation. In an ironic tone reminiscent of Richard Porch's commentary on the digital watch (1985), Radhakrishnan wonders whether modern gadgets like the mobile phone have increased in any way the epistemological worth of our conversations with others.

We may look back with a trace of regret to what we have lost with these technological changes; perhaps it is much more fruitful to look to the future to realise what we have gained in terms of our ability to organise disparate fields of knowledge in ways that were previously unimaginable. As against cultural theorists, who discuss 'aura' as a Platonic ideal, or mystics, who refer to 'aura' as emanating from within the human self, A. Srivathsan articulates some of the obfuscated processes of technology and focuses on one, namely, the concept of 'aura computing' or 'personal information field' as constitutive of the human self in the age of information technology and mobile telephony. According to Srivathsan, tools have made us as much as we have made them. As mobile phones seamlessly adjust themselves to human bodies, the consumption experience today—regardless of location—aids our psychological self-determination.

Another obscure process unfolding in our age is the withering away of the state. Has digital technology eroded the concept of the nation–state? We no longer talk of nation states, but of urban spaces and cityscapes. These are spaces, constituted in terms of discontinuities between localities or neighbourhoods, forging new localised political subjects. It is easier to be a political actor in the city than in a nation. Local initiatives, especially on the Internet, can and do add up to global initiatives. In a comprehensive article on the urban cybercultural phenomenon, our Brazilian contributors, André Lemos and Julio Valentim, probe the fantastic world of the mobile Internet, facilitated by wireless communications technology today, and peopled by thumb tribes and smart mobs. It is not surprising that digital technology has many takers in a country like Brazil, as Lemos and Valentim inform us, given its dominant mode of urban cities and urbanisation.

The unbounded optimism with which urbanised Latin Americans greet the new technology resonates in many parts of Asia. This phenomenon demonstrates the notion that we could be at the threshold of a new constructive modernisation rather than being burdened by a post-modern deconstruction. A couple of years ago, when HP iPAQ launched its 6500 series, with integrated GSM/GPRS/EDGE technologies to deliver the broadest range of high-speed data and voice connectivity, with a built-in HP Photosmart camera, GPS Navigation and attached keyboard, I chanced upon an Internet chatroom, where the Singaporean and Malaysian teenage members discussed the product and asked one another in awe: 'Is this God?' A. Vishnu's article informs us exactly why all manner of digital gadgets are so popular with young people in India and elsewhere.

The excitement generated by some forms of digital technology like the computer owes a lot to its amazing speed, flexibility and retention power. Studies (Benson *et al.* 2002) have shown that increased use of digital technologies in education can have positive results like enhanced cognitive development when socialising agents—like teachers and instructors—support their use. In the absence of such support, and in the case of unsupervised internet use like email usage, there can be negative results like a sharp decline in reading comprehension. There is a dazzling gold mine of information out there on the Internet, which needs to be skilfully navigated in order to provide coherence to what we say or write.

Computer-mediated interaction, say, in the form of the televised classroom or online education, lacks the spatial, physical and temporal dimensions of the face–to–face classroom in conventional educational institutions. Such discipline exists only because of boundaries and divisions artificially imposed on students by the establishment. The goal of education should be as much to help us understand the commonality of disciplines, as to recognise their differences.

Despite our understanding that technology is related to common-law where the resource is not depleted, but endlessly renewed, the harsh truth is that very few people, especially in the southern hemisphere of our planet, have access to this marvel. Most schools in rural India, for example, consider themselves lucky if they have two classrooms with blackboards and chalk pieces for the entire primary section. That by itself may not be a major setback in pedagogical terms. After all, what we need is not more information, but imaginative instructors who can guide students to acquire a more integrated and authentic view of life, as Rahul Srivatsava informs us. This can happen with or without digital technologies. Sandhya Rao's contribution reminds us why—despite the growing fascination with digital technology—the narrative, as a process of remembering, will continue to be an important part of a child's world. The question that remains unanswered is: to what extent do digital technologies create opportunities for accomplishing new pedagogical objectives that might not be possible without them?

In a comprehensive article on the advantages and disadvantages of digital technology, Ashok Panikkar poses a few questions that he claims all creators and consumers of this technology should ask themselves. Ultimately, we all need to know *what is going on*. The obvious reason for this is that the ideological processes that shape and are shaped by the new technology are generally hidden; these need to be uncovered.

An important question related to technological worth is relevant to children as well as adults. What does digital technology do to our belief systems? We normally experience the world through our senses, and give meaning or provide order to the chaos around us. Techno-logies that shape the way we see and sense the world, and which produce and interpret images, inevitably determine our cultural perspective. Dilip D'Souza's engaging article discusses the strange case of bloggers, who love power, hate responsibility, crave intellectua-lism, detest editors, nevertheless emerge as top-class watchdog–scribes when it comes to reporting on crisis situations like the tsunami.

Digital technology affects us more than its analogue counterpart, because it can be far more interactive—this certainly explains the popularity blogging is gaining. Although digital technology can mimic analogue technology, its functionality is far more diverse. All digital media can be reproduced endlessly, not by transcription or by making imprints of imprints, as in the case of analogue technology, but by reading the numbers and inscribing afresh each time. Thus each copy, even if it is several generations away from the 'original', is still an original inscription of information. This is possible because the role of digital technology lies in abstract numbers, say, in virtual space, not in concrete material, as in the case of a book or painting or sculpture.

Mimesis to Mathematics

This is not to say that error is completely eliminated in works of digital technology. It merely means that the error is of a different type from that of transcription, namely, of reading and writing abstract numbers. Information is less easily lost in digital than in analogue format. A book or painting can be marred or destroyed, whereas the ledger of numbers on the hard disk of a computer does not lose its utility or functionality completely owing to physical damage, because its information is cognitively conveyed and consumed with the senses. Data files can be stored and moved from silicon circuits to copper wires and optical fibres, or even printed and displayed on paper. The shift from analogue to digital is the shift from product to process, from mimesis to mathematics.

At another level, digital information is far more vulnerable than analogue transcriptions. Bugs, viruses, or human error can completely undermine or destroy its basic representational structure. By changing a small bit in a database, it is possible to corrupt or render nonsensical an entire database. While analogue media are somewhat hierarchical, digital media are more democratic and interactive. In my article, I discuss the fact that viruses tend to be selective, since virus writers are political entities that attack the big corporations rather than the small fry. Even while digital technology has become more democratic than its analogue counterpart, efforts are afoot to enforce the writ of copyright in the virtual world. I try to demonstrate the philosophical vacuity of a concept like private property, and end with the claim that the present attempt to copyright the cultures of traditional communities is equally misguided.

The principle of copyright is perhaps the most violated in the world of music recordings. The schizophrenic quality of sound recordings— where sound is separated from its originating source—becomes quite pathological with innovations in digital technology. Remixed and resequenced sound recordings are true simulacra—'perfect copies whose originals never existed' (Lysloff 1997: 216). In good Platonic terminology, a recording transcribes an original, but it is not that original; it is a remove from the original or from authenticity. When the stored information is decoded to produce sound, it is a *reproduction*, not a *representation* of the so-called original sound.

In a way, all technologies distort. They give expression to—and also diminish—our consciousness. This is true of digitally produced images in photography and cinematography, on the one hand, and television news, on the other. The subjectivity that is inherent in these image productions is determined by connotative strategies of content selection, framing, camera angles, and vantage points. In an image-saturated society like ours, competence in reading imagery is hard to come by and is an acquired skill like learning a new language in order to understand the users' cultural symbolism. In order to truly comprehend the ideological construction of our visual culture, we must know how to read images by looking at the technology that informs them:

'Photographs and video imagery consist of minute indeterminably arranged components such as the chemically generated grain in film and the variation of light intensities in video. While the digital photograph looks like its conventional counterpart, it reveals itself, when examined very closely, to be composed of discrete elements called pixels, which are assigned precise numerical values. Each pixel in the image has a determined Cartesian horizontal and vertical location value and a specific colour-intensity value. It is this relationship of modular units with definite values that makes it totally controllable' (Legrady 1990: 267).

With computer technology and improved scanning techniques, the fabrication or manipulation of photographs through mathematical processing becomes alarmingly easy. The digital photograph, while appearing to represent objective reality 'out there', is actually the product of a choice exercised by the photographer, who is faced with multiple virtual or simulated 'realities'. There is a new value and meaning attached to this digital photograph, which has no referent in the real world. Such manipulation is threatening because it undermines our confidence in the photographic image as a representation of reality.

Pixels, originating from the computer term 'picture elements', are computer data that translate the subtle, continuous tones of an image into a complex series of ones and zeros, the basis of computer language. Could we say that 19th-century photography, with its mechanical characteristic of reproduction, is the modernist transformation of art, while digital photography is the post-modernist transformation of making images?

Oddly enough, digital technology cannot sustain a post-modern perspective—perhaps owing to its ineluctable link to technology. Digital photography or art, for instance, calls for greater, not less, mimesis or conformity to a literal reality. High-resolution computer graphics are expected to render images exactly as they are in the real world. As Adi Shamir Zion puts it: 'While modernism rejected perspective drawings as imposing constructs, the developers of cyberspace imagery seem, despite the powerful arguments of postmodern fracture, to have inherited a "Renaissance" worldview that places the eye of the viewer in a singularly, centrally privileged position' (1998).

In a fascinating analysis of 'The Necessary Stage', a politically radical theatre company in Singapore, Charlene Rajendran refers to the theatrical art of making images for subversive reasons. In a context where there is persistent policing of the public space, 'The Necessary Stage' draws from the puppeteer tradition in South-East Asia and attempts a fusion of the proscenium stage with the television or computer screen, so that live performances co-exist with (often political) screened messages. As Rajendran points out, 'Interventions from digitised reality are often woven into performance by creating a range of screens (conventional and otherwise) on stage and deploying them as "performers" in the process. At times, the live performance is peripheral and the screen becomes a central site for expression and articulation, not simply a means of refraction. The screen can then become a "player" in the production.'

Digital imaging has produced special effects and animation forms that were unimaginable before computer technology. Radio and television are perhaps less responsive to digital technology, but cinema audiences are enthralled by special effects-driven action spectacles, even in the case of pedestrian blockbusters, that have little room for plot or character development. Our view of pleasure affects technology; at the same time, technology has an impact on what we find entertaining or pleasurable. The flip side of virtual reality is that it is non-detectable deception.

The new blockbuster is a stage-managed multimedia marketing event. Only a small part of the revenue comes from the actual screening of the film. The rest comes from multi-pronged advertising strategies involving book publishing, music CD releases, as well as commodity supplements like computer games, videos, fashion garments and fast food. According to K. Hariharan, Bollywood cinema is perhaps in a better position than Hollywood to usher in the new digital era, signalling both change and uncertainty, owing to its inherent capacity to derive order from disorder. As Hariharan explains, in the typical commercial Indian film, the 'seemingly disconnected random experience gets integrated into a "proper sequence" of events, largely due to an amazing socio-cultural interface with memories, legends and assorted folktales'.

What about the other media and their relationship to the native cyborg? While the radio and television may be dismissed in the West as alienating and consumer-driven media, they have an entirely different signification in traditional and developing societies. For Islamic communities in South-East Asia, for example, these media play the role of the *muezzin* by broadcasting calls to prayer, thereby maintaining traditional practice in urbanised settings. The unintended consequence of the introduction of technology in religious practice has been the shift of sacred space from the mosque to the household, resulting in women's increased participation in worship. Bindu Bhaskar points out, 'no form of the media can afford to maintain a singular identity. Degrees of separation are becoming unspecified and flux within specified spaces unstoppable, making descriptions hazy and definitions harder.' Discussing the role of radio, especially in developing countries, Bhaskar informs us that Latin American initiatives have been far ahead of those in India, given the Indian government's penchant to crush local media initiatives with the weight of bureaucratic red tape.

The new digital technology or gadget is not God—but it could well serve as your shrink! This is the thrust of the final contribution to this book by Valerie Kaye. In a humane narrative about a woman haunted by childhood trauma, Kaye describes the therapeutic value of the Internet that can be harnessed to heal psychological wounds and help renew contact with estranged friends and acquaintances.

To sum up: neither technophilia nor technophobia need be the order of the digital age. The location of the interface of the human and the machine should reside somewhere in between.

Notes

1. See *http://www.classicreader.com/booktoc.php/-sid.1/bookid.88/*.
2. See *http://www.geocities.com/Athens/Troy/9078/index_nicole.html/*.
3. See the Donna Haraway interview with Constance Penley and Andrew Ross (1990) on the subject of Artificial Intelligence.
4. *Ibid*.

References

Atwood, Margaret. 2004. *Oryx and Crake*. USA: Virago Press.
Barthes, Roland. 1972. *Mythologies*. Trans. by Annette Lavers. New York: Hill and Wang.
Benson, Denzel E. *et al.* 2002. 'Digital Technologies and the Scholarship of Teaching and Learning in Sociology', *Teaching Sociology,* 30(2): 140–57.

Brasher, Brenda. 1996. 'Thoughts on the Status of the Cyborg on Technological Socialization and its Link to the Religious Function of Popular Culture', *Journal of the American Academy of Religion*, (Special Issue on 'Religion and American Popular Culture'), 64(4): 809–30.

Brook, Peter. 1976. *The Melodramatic Imagination: Balzac, Henry James, Melodrama, and the Mode of Excess.* New Haven: Yale University Press.

Clynes, Manfred and Nathan S. Kline. 1960. 'Cyborgs and Space', *Astronautics*, 14(9).

Firestone, Shulasmith. 1970. *The Dialectic of Sex: The Case for Feminist Revolution.* New York: Morrow.

Halberstam, Judith. 1991. 'Automating Gender: Postmodern Feminism in the Age of the Intelligent Machine', *Feminist Studies*, 17(3): 439–60.

Hugo, Victor. 2001. *The Hunchback of Notre Dame.* Trans. by Walter J. Cobb. USA: Penguin.

Legrady, George. 1990. 'Image, Language and Belief in Synthesis', *Art Journal*, 49(3): 266–71.

Lysloff, René T. A. 1997. 'Mozart in Mirrorshades: Ethnomusicology, Technology, and the Politics of Representation', *Ethnomusicology*, 41(2).

McLuhan, Marshall. 1962. *The Gutenberg Galaxy.* Toronto: University of Toronto Press.

Penley, Constance and Andrew Ross. 1990. 'Cyborgs at Large: Interview with Donna Haraway', *Social Text*, 25/26: 8–23.

Porch, Richard. 1985. 'The Digital Watch: Tribal Bracelet of the Consumer Society', *Design Issues*, 2(2): 46–49.

Rud, G. Anthony Jr. 1997. 'Musty Paper, Blinking Cursors: Print and Digital Cultures', *Educational Researcher*, 26(7).

Specter, Michael. 2002. 'The Long Ride: How Did Lance Armstrong Manage the Greatest Comeback in Sports History?'. *http://www.newyorker.com/fact/content/?020715fa_fact1/.*

Traub, Charles and Jonathan Lipkin. 2000. 'Creative Interlocutor and Multimedia Dialog', *Design Issues*, 16(2): 25–35.

Zion, Adi Shamir. 1998. 'New Modern: Architecture in the Age of Digital Technology', *Assemblage*, 35: 62–79.

1

Exaggerated Obituaries:
The Tamil Book in the Age of
Electronic Reproduction

A. R. Venkatachalapathy

The death of the book, in the wake of the digital onslaught that was predicted, anticipated or feared—depending on one's ideological and cultural position—in the 1990s seems exceedingly alarmist now in the mid-decade of the 21st century. Following Mark Twain we could say that the obituaries for the book appear to have been somewhat exaggerated. However, even though Marshall McLuhan prophesied the disintegration of the Gutenberg galaxy as early as in the 1960s, there is no mistaking the anxiety occasioned in the 1990s.

> Over the past few decades, in the blink of the eye of history, our culture has begun to go through what promises to be a total metamorphosis [...]. The stable hierarchies of the printed page [...] are being superseded by the rush of impulses through freshly minted circuits.
>
> —(Birkets 1994: 3)

Even though, in hindsight, Sven Birkerts' anxiety seems unfounded there is no mistaking the palpable nature of such fears. But one should be conscious of the fact that the culture that Birkerts mentions is Western culture, which is predicated on the Enlightenment notion of self and knowledge, and the possible disappearance of an artefact that has been valued in that culture for over half a millennium. Given Roger Chartier's perceptive statement of its centrality in Western culture that 'the book has been one of the most powerful metaphors used for conceiving of the cosmos, nature and the human body' (1993: 49) one can understand and even empathise with such fears and anxieties.

However, such insights from the specialisation that has come to be called 'the history of the book' also point to the fact that there is no one universal history of the book. If there is no one universal history of the book, it does indeed follow that there need be no one single future for the book. If books have specific and contingent histories, it would thus follow that the advent of digital technologies will have its own differential impacts. The thrust of this essay is therefore to make a specific argument for the case of Tamil books and track how Tamil book publishing has fared in its engagement with digital technology.

I

First, a few preliminaries: about 70 million people the world over now speak the Tamil language. Though this population is concentrated in the state of Tamilnadu in the Indian Union and in Sri Lanka, it is also dispersed across all continents especially due to the colonial policy of indentured labour (to offset the abolition of slavery) in the mid-19th century, the Tamil diaspora in the wake of the civil war in Sri Lanka, and the boom in immigration as a result of the explosion in the global software industry. Further, Tamil is a classical language with an unbroken literary tradition of some 2,000 years.

Tamil is the first non-European language, not to speak of Indian languages, to see moveable types and printed books. *Thampiran Vanakkam (Doctrina Christinam)*, the first printed Tamil book, was published in 1577, barely a century from Gutenberg's 42-line Bible. The first complete translation of the New Testament (by Bartholomaeus Ziegenbalg in 1714), the first full translation of the Bible (by Fabricius, in 1796), and the first extended lexicon and the first modern encyclopedia constitute some other 'firsts' that printed Tamil can claim in relation to other Indian languages.

Such justifiably proud claims, however, conceal a host of congenital problems and weaknesses that characterise the Tamil publishing world. By common consent, Bengali and Malayalam, two modern Indian languages, whose engagement with printing begins some 200 years after *Thampiran Vanakkam* are way ahead of Tamil publishing.

Despite the early origins of print in Tamil, until the mid-19th century, printing was a European preserve with missionaries dominating the scene. From the later half of the 19th century, print made some inroads into Tamil society and developed organic links with indigenous society. The recovery of ancient Tamil classics and their canonisation through the mediation of print had far-reaching social and political consequences. Until the end of the 19th century, Tamil publishing was largely sustained by forms of traditional patronage derived from zamindars, native princes, religious monasteries, landlords and caste leaders. However, the establishment of Western-type schools and the expansion of a modern, bureaucratic administration had its implications for publishing. Apart from the demand for printed materials that this created, the emergence of new social classes based on education and colonial occupations and professions disrupted the material foundations of Tamil publishing. And by the time of World War I Tamil publishing was breaking away from patronage forms of publishing and inching towards a faceless and impersonal market.

In the inter-War period Tamil publishing showed vitality and growth, a trend that became more pronounced during World War II. The inflationary war economy ignited Tamil publishing, a process further fuelled by the influx of Chettiar capital fleeing Burma, Indo-China and South-East Asia from both Japanese invasion and local resistance. Many of the characteristic features of Tamil books until the advent of the digital technology—layout, typography, cover design, etc.—took shape during this period.

The process of state takeover of textbook publishing, which started in the mid-1960s and reached a head in 1971, exposed the real foundations of Tamil publishing: the bedrock of assured textbook sales had subsidised trade books. Once again, with characteristic myopia, publishers looked to the state without exploring ways and means to expand and reach out to a market. The outcome was the establishment of the Local Library Authority[1], which almost as a matter of routine, bought a certain number of copies—as much as 50 per cent of the actual print run. Even if this ensured the bread and butter for publishers, it effectively killed creativity and innovation.[2]

II

This was the backdrop in which digital technology announced its entry into Tamil publishing. The deepest impact of digital technology in Tamil publishing has been in the field of text composition. Until the mid-1990s the technology of print had remained unchanged. For nearly a century movable types, cut and cast in local foundries, were used for composition in establishments that were little more than sweatshops. Even though hot metal technologies such as monotype, linotype and rotary were certainly available throughout the 20th century—and widely employed for publishing in English even in Chennai—these were rarely resorted to in the case of Tamil publishing. The primary reason was the low print run—the average print run of Tamil books hovered at the 1,000 mark. (In fact, in the shrewd manner of cost-cutting in which Tamil publishers are adept, they made printers print 1,200 copies for the price of 1,000 as they claimed that 200 copies were meant for free distribution to authors, reviewers and promotion!) The rare occasion when the rotary was used was when C. Rajagopalachariar's popular prose renditions of Mahabharata and Ramayana were published by *Sakti Karyalayam* and printed at the daily Dinamani press in the 1950s. Or when the periodical magazine press occasionally dabbled in book publishing they pressed their rotary machines into service. Given that the dimensions of the paper rolls used for these machines were different from the sheets that were ordinarily used for Tamil books such books were often in 'unsize' as popular publishing parlance went. The only major publisher to use hot metal technology—monotype in this case—was Poompuhar Prasuram, established in the mid-1970s by the owners of Eagle Press, the market leaders in the publication of diaries. Printing establishments such as Maruthi Press which had its own foundry would employ this luxury to occasionally use only freshly cast types for printing.

Another major impediment to the adoption of hot metal technology was the unwieldy nature of Tamil characters, which necessitated a vast number of types difficult to accommodate on a keyboard (a difficulty digital technology also had to encounter at the outset). Even when photo typesetting (with bromide print-outs) had made its entry in the 1980s—apart from the prohibitive costs involved both due to the process itself as well as the compulsory recourse to offset printing it necessitated—it was only rarely used (for instance by Cre-A publishers. Kanthalakam was one of the few firms to provide photo typesetting facilities in Tamil). Even when big publishers went in for offset printing they often preferred to do typesetting in letterpresses and took out an 'art pull' on the machine which was then filmed.

By the beginning of the 1990s the PC revolution was very much at the Indian doorstep. In the initial years progress in Tamil typesetting was tardy as good DTP software with WYSIWYG was still sometime in the future. Only with its advent did DTP become entrenched. This meant the gradual folding up of type foundries, such as Nelson Type Foundry and Modern Type Foundry, which were reduced to casting a limited amount to types for small letterpresses doing job work, especially in the mofussil or outlying areas.

Computer typesetting made it imperative to go for offset printing. Well, until the mid-1990s offset printing cost twice as much as regular mechanical printing. In a very inelastic book market this posed an insurmountable problem.

In the first instance, therefore, publishers took to offset printing only for printing of wrappers and jackets. Earlier, artists and illustrators had designed wrappers and covers printed in two or three colours using metal blocks. Emphasis was usually on stylistic and calligraphic writing. This simply did not work when offset printing could be done. Given the then prohibitive costs of scanning, plate making and printing, the pioneers in this field used single-colour wrappers, which were quite a novelty. They used elegant black and white photographs with un-stylised typefaces. It would take a decade before multi-colour wrappers made their entry into Tamil book wrappers. (Even then, book wrappers are printed four at a time to cut down on costs—it would be no exaggeration to say that printing single wrappers is still commercially unviable for Tamil books. Initially, many publishers instead of generating original wrapper designs used pictures from the *National Geographic* without acknowledgement—whether they were relevant to the contents of the book or not. The dominant trend now is to download images from the World Wide Web!)

Composing text using digital technology had its more than fair share of teething problems. The prime problem was the availability of suitable word-processing and DTP software. Despite various governmental and non-state initiatives Tamil digital technology is still faced with a multiplicity of keyboards (typewriter, phonetic and standard)—the standard keyboard 'accepted' in an international Tamil computing conference being one of the many available options. A Unicode is yet to gain acceptance in Tamil even though it seems inevitable in the foreseeable future. Presently there is a plethora of encoding systems: TAM, TAB, TSCII with each DTP software developer opting for their own encoding system. If the efforts of the Indian government's Pune-based C-DAC for Indian languages was too Devanagari-centred and impervious to Tamil needs, efforts by the Tamils themselves have taken two different trajectories. Though the pioneering efforts by Tamils abroad (especially in Singapore; the name of N. Govindasamy, who developed the Murasu software, will remain immortal in the history of Tamil computing) were techno-savvy in keeping with the demands of technology and the net, the fonts developed were far from aesthetic. On the other hand, the development of DTP software in Tamilnadu was almost exclusively propelled by publishing needs where the elegance of fonts was given priority. After a certain stage of development, interests had become so entrenched that no compromise could be effected between the two.

The long history of the Tamil fonts from the days when the earliest types were cut in Halle was forgotten and in the first instance the new fonts in Tamil DTP software, to which Tamil readers had been socialised to over more than half a century, did not gel with existing fonts in the letterpress. Even some first lessons were forgotten. The character of Tamil orthography lends itself to a slight tilt to the right, unlike the roman letters, and straight typefaces do not work well. (A corollary, given this natural tendency to the right, has been the still persistent difficulty of fashioning suitable and workable italics for Tamil fonts.) In the initial stages there was a medley of inelegant and unreadable fonts in use, a problem that has subsided only recently. Another outcome of the evolving digital typefaces was its independent development in Tamilnadu and Sri Lanka, not to speak of Malaysia and Singapore. While an almost universal set of typefaces had evolved in the movable type era, fonts diverged again. So much so, books produced in Tamilnadu and Sri Lanka have come to have distinct appearances, a situation further accentuated by the wider variety of paper available in Sri Lanka due to their open policy on the import of printing paper.

The other set of problems that cropped up with the advent of DTP was the redundancy of compositors and the resultant new recruitment of keying-in personnel. Though traditionally composition was a skilled manual job, which was pursued by people with little formal education, compositors acquired skills through long years of apprenticeship and training. (There are legendary stories about Ma.Po. Sivagnanam and Vindhan who started their lives as compositors and later emerged as not insignificant writers. There are many instances of compositors gaining political consciousness by simply reading the material they composed.) Through such a training process compositors produced decent galley and page proofs even when the authors (as they were often wont to) did not submit acceptable press copies. (In any case Tamil publishers do not usually have formal editorial staff.) Well-versed in standard page layouts and elementary proofing skills, some compositors could well make a page even without going through the galley stage. They were well-versed in em and en dashes, leading, etc.

Such training was virtually absent in the case of the new generation of computer typesetters. Basically they got trained only in the quick keying-in of text. The falling standards of school and even college education in Tamilnadu from 1980s to the present are evident in the mess they made of the copies they keyed in. The absence of even elementary, useable spell-checking software for the Tamil language (a still persistent problem) only compounded the confusion. Apart from the limited number of fonts that could be used for text composition, the non-standardisation of leading, inter-word pacing, hyphenation (being an agglutinative language with a syllabary rather than a phonetic alphabet, Tamil words do not require hyphenation), etc. made for some grotesque books in the 1990s. The entire aesthetics of the Tamil books, which had evolved over a period of about a century (from about the time of World War I when Tamil books began to be produced for a larger, impersonal market), very nearly collapsed. The almost innumerable ways in which fonts could be manipulated created confusion rather than being put to effective use. A new aesthetic based on the new digital technology emerged only by the turn of the new millennium and is far from being well entrenched even now.

If the new digital technology played such havoc in printing protocols, it also provided a variety of conveniences. Theoretically at least, it made proofreading a more effective and less time- and place-bound activity. Given the magnitude of the publishing industry, letterpress printing establishments were small and had very little type. Consequently, it was nearly impossible for the printers to keep the types locked up for long. The customary practice was to set the page (the galleys being read at the press itself, usually by the owner) at the end of the day, and to deliver the page proofs to the proofreaders' home at night, and to collect the corrected proofs in the morning before the press opened for the day. Few presses had the wherewithal to compose more than, say, ten formes of matter. Legendary printing presses such as Kabeer Printing Works, Progressive Printers or Diocesan Press which could deliver the entire manuscript in proof were few and invariably too expensive. Over the last century Tamil book publishing and printing had converged in the city of Chennai. Not only U.V. Swaminatha Iyer, the great editor of Tamil classics, but Veeresalingam Pantulu, the Telugu reformer, had preferred to move to *fin-de-siècle* Chennai so that their publishing activities could be carried on more effectively. That the centrality was Chennai began to be somewhat eroded with the rise of digital technology, as publishers did not have to flock to Chennai to meet their printing needs.

With digital technology practically any number of pages could be composed without worrying about locked-up types. Further, the proofs of a single book were handled not in instalments but in full. Consequently, the practice of proofreading is not bound by place or time (the contingency of the computer system crashing is of course a different matter). Even though many have been like the sorcerer's apprentice in the handling of this convenience there is no doubting its usefulness for serious pursuits such as critical editions. In my own experience, the chronological and variorum edition of the complete works of Pudumaippithan, which I have been producing through Kalachuvadu Pathippagam, would have been virtually impossible without digital technology, which makes slow accretions to the quality of the text possible.

This also had a very perceptible impact in the average size of books. While until the advent of digital technology the publishing of tomes was dreaded by Tamil publishers, they have more easily taken to it since. Combined with a perceived if not an actual expansion in the book market, more bulky volumes are being published in Tamil than ever before. This has also exposed the paucity of real content for the books. How much can even a society, which is fast changing and throwing up new talent, produce? One could take recourse to offsetting the dearth by republishing old and out of print books with cultural value. The bane of Tamil publishing—that very few books got reprinted—was almost wiped out overnight. In fact, there are some publishers who print only out of print and out of copyright books. This process has been strengthened by the peculiar Tamil tradition of the state taking over the copyright of the works of many cultural icons and putting them in the public domain thus unleashing a huge corpus of texts for unrestricted and even irresponsible use.

Offset printing for text matter became a norm only after it had become a normal procedure for wrappers. With offset printing the cylinder machines became completely redundant and from the late 1990s many printing presses disposed of their machines for scrap value. (The opportunity this afforded for the setting up for a printing museum was missed. One hopes that it may not be too late even now.)

As a result of all these changes not only the face of Tamil publishing, but also the physical aspect of the book, has changed perceptibly if not drastically. John B. Thompson, in his comprehensive study of books in the digital age, has established that the digital revolution at least in the West is 'not so much *a revolution in the product* as *a revolution in the process*' (2005: 405, emphasis in original). This is evidently untrue in the Tamil context. The Tamil book, in its physical aspect—bulk, layout, typeface, etc—has irrevocably changed.

This has gone hand in hand with an explosion in the number of books published. Unfortunately, there is no data, reliable or unreliable, on the volume of book production in India.[3] No bibliometric analysis is therefore possible. But the phenomenal growth in Tamil publishing is unmistakeable.

A major trend in international publishing over the last two decades has been the rise of huge publishing conglomerations, which have with gargantuan appetite gobbled up many independent publishing houses or have gone in for huge corporate mergers. As a result, many venerable publishing houses had become little more than imprints of huge corporations.[4] Even though Tamil publishing is marked by the very palpable absence of corporate organisation, the trend in the last decade has been the proliferation of dozens of independent publishing houses that have ridden over the digital wave and in the process brought in fresh talent and consolidated earlier gains.

The spatial rupture between typesetting establishments and printing shops first led to the mushrooming of DTP firms all over Tamilnadu. (Considering the relative cheapness of typesetting there was a major boom in such establishments in the late 1980s; Pondicherry, for instance, catered to international publishing to a great extent. That's a different story.)

Ultimately, this also paved the way for the launching of publishing houses all over Tamilnadu rather than being clustered in Chennai, especially in Broadway until the early 1980s and then in Pondy Bazaar since. Until then Mercury Puthaka Nilaiyam based in Coimbatore and Annam based in Sivagangai were the major exceptions. But in the late 1990s, a publishing house not in Chennai but in far-off Nagercoil, Kalachuvadu Pathippagam, spearheaded trend setting publishing in Tamil.

Another sign of growth is the entry of major media companies into what could be called 'quasi book publishing'. There was, of course, a trend in the 1970s and 1980s for the periodical press to publish monthly novels in newsprint. There was even a 'crime novel revolution' in the later half of the 1980s when there was a surfeit of pulp novels. The qualitative difference in the last few years has been the publication of well-produced products, printed on mechanical glazed newsprint, but recognisable as books and marketed as books. The major players in this field are: Nakkeeran, Ananda Vikatan and Kumudam.

The attempt of some publishers to negotiate rights for publication, a virtually non-existent practice, also shows the growing maturity of Tamil publishing as well as the impact of globalisation. If some publishers have negotiated the translation rights of their books Adayalam publishers have, in a major coup, launched the Tamil translation of the 'very short introduction' series of the Oxford University Press.

The maturity and confidence of Tamil publishers is also materially premised on the growth and expansion of the market. Even though the expansion is somewhat exaggerated it is not to be discounted. The crowds that have thronged the annual Chennai Book Fair is only one indication of growing reader interest as well as the expansion of the market. Even though physical network of bookselling is still weak, digital technology has undoubtedly extended the book market. As indicated earlier, the Tamil diaspora in the wake of the political violence in Sri Lanka and the software boom have meant that readers for Tamil books—with significant disposable income—are now spread across the world. There are now a few online booksellers catering to their needs such as *kamadenu.com*, *anyindian.com*, *intamm.com*, *kanthalakam.com*, and so on.

III

The book scene in Tamilnadu thus presents not a picture of gloom but of great promise. Tamil publishing—producers and consumers—

have never had it so good. Undoubtedly, digital technology has been an enabling factor. This is, of course, not to push forward a mono-causal explanation for a very complex phenomenon that has to take into account the effects of globalisation, the structural adjustment of the Indian economy, a burgeoning middle class with a considerable amount of cultural anxiety, and the unleashing of fresh talent from hitherto marginal social groups. The book, certainly its Tamil avatar, is far from dead. The next decade would prove to be crucial to its future.

Notes

1. Local Library Authority is the agency of the Government of Tamilnadu which administers the network of about 2,000 libraries all over the state. The network is constituted of the 'branch libraries' at the bottom, 'circle libraries' and district central libraries and an apex state central library. This authority annually acquires about 600 copies of each published book in the Tamil language at a certain fixed price (offering a low, but assured, margin of profit to the publishers).
2. This section summarises two of my works (Venkatachalapathy (1998; 2003). For an extended analysis of the culture of print in colonial Tamilnadu, see Venkatachalapathy (1995).
3. All publishers in India are legally mandated, under the Registration of Books Act, 1867, to submit one copy of every publication to the four national deposit libraries including the National Library, Kolkata. (This is a provision which is observed more in the breach.) The National library is expected to register the books and prepare annual bibliographies which would also provide statistics regarding books published in India. These bibliographies are woefully behind schedule.
4. See Schiffrin (2000), Preface and passim.

References

Birkets, Sven. 1994. *The Gutenberg Elegies: The Fate of Reading in an Electronic Age.* Boston: Faber & Faber.

Chartier, Roger. 1993. 'Libraries Without Walls', *Representations*, 42: 38–52.

Schiffrin, Andre. 2000. *The Business of Books: How International Conglomerates Took over Publishing and Changed the Way We Read.* London: Verso.

Thompson, John B. 2005. *Books in the Digital Age: The Transformation of Academic and Higher Education in Britain and United States.* Cambridge: Polity Press.

Venkatachalapathy, A. R. 1995. 'A Social History of Tamil-Book Publishing, c. 1850–1938', unpublished Ph. D. diss., New Delhi: Jawaharlal Nehru University.

—————.1998. 'Almanacs and Railway Timetables: A Brief History of Tamil Book-Publishing', in A. R. Venkatachalapathy and Cyrille Desombre (eds), *Gum and Calico: Libraries of India*. New Delhi: Alliance Française.

—————.2003. 'Panchangamum Railway Guideum: Naveena Tamilaga Pathippulagam', *Kalachuvadu*, January–February.

2

Religion and Theology in the Information Society

Felix Wilfred

Recently, during a brief visit to the United States for a board meeting, I asked one of the immigrant Indians whether and to what extent the image of India has changed in that country. His response was picturesque: 'Not long ago', he said, 'in American homes, mothers used to tell children at mealtimes, "Don't waste food; in India children are starving"'. Today the parents are telling their teenagers, 'Study hard; otherwise Indians will come and take away your jobs!' No doubt, at the root of this dramatic change of perception of India is the computer-mediated Information Technology.

No one will deny the fact that the advent of a new technology shapes the society in ways that are not predictable, and brings about transformations in the manner people live, resulting in a 'transformation of consciousness'. Information Technology is not simply a matter of communication and economy. It transforms society and culture and impacts upon our lifestyle. History attests to the fact that every time there was a shift in the means of communication, there took place profound changes in the society, and more importantly, in the way people perceive themselves and the society (cf. Marvin 1999). The most obvious example is the change from the oral mode of communication to the culture of the text or written word, and from this to the culture of print.

In the past, social theorists have employed different analytical keys to interpret the society and its dynamics. Karl Marx used 'political economy' and Max Weber employed 'instrumental rationality' as explanatory frameworks. Neither of them, however, took into account the change of communication in a society as contributing decisively to mould it in novel ways.

Religion Today: The Imaginary is Real

The question about religion in the Information Age needs to be placed against the backdrop of the profound cultural and social transformation that has been effected by digital technology and computer-mediated communication.[1] As historians tell us, every time a new mode of communication came into existence, the shape of religion and the mode of practising it changed. The change from the oral to the textual, and from the textual to print, brought about significant changes in religion, giving rise to new attitudes and practices. Today, we observe the emerging of new cultural patterns and social practices as a result of the communication revolution. Our question is: what kind of changes is the new mode of communication bringing about in the field of religious practice?[2] Obviously, with the advent of a new communication situation, the traditional beliefs and practices stand challenged. There is, for example, a crisis today in the understanding of and approach to symbol, authority, and community, which are all bound to affect the practice of religion in the age of digital communication.

Besides, this situation also seems to give rise to the emergence of a computer-mediated religion, known as 'cyber-religion' or virtual religion. This has been made possible because, communication technologies have led to a blurring of the real and the imaginary, to adopt a classical idealist adage for today, 'the imaginary is real'. Traditionally, religions have abounded in symbols and these have been amply made use of in religious communication; however, one knew when one was in the symbolic realm, as in the case of rituals, and when out of it. With the progressive elimination of the distinction between the real and the imaginary, people today inhabit and interact with the virtual world created by the various forms of computer-mediated communication, and for many, this imaginary world has become the real one.

Closely connected with this collapse of the real and imaginary is the transformation that is occurring in the perception of spatiality. There is, of course, the simultaneity of space in our experiences made possible through the means of digital technology, whereby we could participate instantaneously in events at the other end of the world. What is meant here is something more: Whereas real space is something *given*, the virtual space is something *created*. This being the case, the question whether the virtual or imaginary space represents reality is not the real point. The very question of representation is becoming meaningless.

Now, we shall delve into these two aspects of the question, namely, how and why changes are taking place in the approach to traditional religions, and what sense it makes to speak of a virtual religion or cyber-religion.[3]

In the second part of the article we shall explore the challenges the new situation poses to theology. The role of theology in the Information Age will be analysed not only in terms of what the new mode of communication has brought about to religion, but also in terms of the changes and transformations created in the social and cultural domains.

From Interpretation of Symbols to Play of Symbols

Religion is a realm dense with symbolism. The lack of any one single precise meaning lets the symbol be multivalent. Traditional religions, by and large, do not have any difficulty regarding the evocative character of symbols and their polysemic trajectory. Our concern here is a new dimension and approach to symbols characterising computer-mediated religiosity; and what is at stake is the way signifier and signified are related. In the new approach, symbols have no point of reference outside them, like in any game: here the signifiers become self-referential and religious experience becomes a play of signifiers without any reference to outside reality, rather the signifiers themselves become the reality. Speaking of this characteristic of Information Society, Frank Webster (1999) notes:

> Finally, though culture is quintessentially about meanings, about how and why people live as they do, it is striking that with the celebration of non-referential character of symbols...we have congruence with communications theory and the economic approach to information. Here too we have a fascination with the profusion of information, an expansion so prodigious that it has lost its hold semantically. Symbols are now everywhere and generated all of the time, so much so that their meanings have imploded, hence ceasing to signify.
>
> —(1999: 161)

Religious symbolism through the digital media dovetails with the emerging general culture in other spheres created and sustained by the same media. The culture that is created by the digital media inclines towards what Baudrillard has called '*simulacra*'. Commenting upon the new type of religious experience, Dawson notes:

> For them [those practicing religiosity through cyberspace] the sacred need not be a real other, not even in the reduced sense of the power of sociality itself. They are content to work with a simulacrum. In true postmodernist manner the 'appearance' can stand in for the reality if it generates the desired experience ...The experience itself though ill-defined, has been sacralized.
>
> —(2005: 29)

All this leads us to our next point—that is, about an important transformation that challenges the traditional religious conceptions and practices.

When Facsimile Becomes the Real...

Analysts characterise the modern world as a world of machines and calculations. In fact, the computer itself was viewed as a large machine meant for computation, as its very name indicates, and for storing data. Correspondingly, modernity is described as a period of calculative rationality. Computer and communication through digital technology exemplify the mechanical and calculative paradigm of modernity.

But the new thing about computer-mediated communication is that, while it still continues with its calculative functions, it has led us to a type of experience in which we enter into many virtual worlds, societies and persons. Increasingly, there is a blurring of the boundaries between reality and appearance, similar to the one between the real and the imaginary. People do not seem to question the real man or woman behind the acting, for acting is the 'real thing'. The identification with the flow of images on the screen congeals into a real world in which one begins to inhabit. The reification of appearance into reality happens constantly through the computer-mediated communications; it is the world of simulation. In other words, the cultural situation created by digital technology is such that people deal with facsimile and the original is not a matter of any serious consideration or interest. The facsimile becomes the real, obscuring the very idea of the real or the original.

Paradoxically, everyday life becomes an extension of the screen, and not the other way round. No wonder, today people are attaching more and more importance to how they appear. Since appearing is important—because it is the reality—there is understandably, growing interest in the care for the human body in its aesthetic dimension, in dress and fashion. It is interesting to note that with the growing computer-mediated communications, garment designs and fashion shows are on the increase in China and India, the two fast growing economies in the world.

A Radical Approach to Self and Identity

All major religious traditions have concerned themselves with the question of the human self and its relation to God, or the ultimate reality. The Self, which was defined in relation to the Ultimate, underwent a horizontalisation and self-affirmation, ever since the autonomous ego was proclaimed in the Western Enlightenment. The Enlightenment questioned the definition of the Self with reference to God, and made freedom the point of reference for the constitution of the ego. This trend, though it challenged the religiously inspired explanation of the self, however, did not prove incompatible with religious concerns, for human autonomy and freedom do not go against the authentic understanding of religion.

Today, the fluidity in the understanding of the Self as a result of computer-mediated communications is something very radical. We are in the face of not a single unitary self, which for many is becoming more and more of an illusion. Computer-mediated communication, especially the Internet, offers the possibility of bringing out many layers of the self, and indeed many 'selves' of the same person. This is because the virtual reality, world and society, which digital communication creates, is such that a person may assume many selves and enter into communication with a wide variety of virtual contexts, situations and persons (cf. Turkle 1995). The noteworthy point is that this multiplicity of selves is not something like acting out many roles made possible by the performing arts: here a person does not return to her real self after taking on other roles, rather each of those selves is real, which means that a person exists with multiple selves. The answer to the question—'Who am I'—is found in the aggregation of the many avatars computer-mediated communication makes possible for the self.

What happens with many windows in the computer-mediated communication can be viewed as a symbol of what multiple selves mean: a person assumes new flexible selves as he/she shifts from one window of life to the other. Interestingly, there is a certain convergence between the post-modern thought on self as de-centred, and dispersed, and the multiple selves in the computer-mediated communication. The problem of multiple selves in the experience of computer-mediated communication leads us to the thoughts of Michel Foucault, Gilles Deleuze, Jacques Lacan and Felix Guattari, and one cannot but note close resemblance between their theories and computer-related practices.

To be able to understand better the emergence of a multiple selfhood in relation to computer-mediated communication, we could contrast it with the constitution of the self in the print culture. In the print culture, there is the reader and the text. The reader is an autonomously constituted subject with his/her fixed identity, and he/she stands in relation to the text as the subject stands in relation to an objectively given reality. On the other hand, computer-mediated communication is creating a multiple selfhood. The social, political and cultural consequences of a multiple selfhood still need to be worked out.

We need to take note of yet another emerging aspect of the identity of the self through computer-mediated communication. In modernity, under the influence of the Enlightenment, the affirmation of the autonomous subject also implies the constitution of a well-defined private sphere zealously guarded from the public gaze. The new communication situation has brought about a significant transformation in this respect. On the surface, it may appear that each individual operating through computer-mediated communication is an impregnable individual. In reality, the modern networking or communication is such that people cannot conceal their identities. The system of registering and recording of personal data gives every person an electronic identity that can be retrieved at the click of the mouse at any time in any part of the world. The erosion of private identity and the control exerted by networking remind us about the *panopticon* of Jeremy Bentham.

What is important for us here is to note that the kind of social and cultural situation the present mode of communication presents has deeper consequences for religion, its belief system and practices. If such is the case of the Self in computer-mediated communication, it follows that the traditional Christian understanding of sin, guilt and redemption stands challenged. To recall the extent of the religious implication of the new approach to the Self, we need to ask: Who is the Self that is supposed to sin and feel guilty? Who is the Self spoken about in relation to redemption? Who is the Self that bears personal responsibility for commissions and omissions? These are very uneasy questions pertaining to the traditional religious conception of self and identity.

Critique of Traditional Religious Symbols and Authority

The present cultural shift, to simulation and a new perception of self and identity, have their consequences. The progressive use of digital technology creates a mutation of interest in religion from some of its traditional concerns to new areas. For example, the new mode of communication challenges the exaggerated importance accorded to orthodoxy. In a text-based culture, religions, in varying degrees, will concentrate on reproducing exactly their doctrines and belief systems. The preoccupation that the original should not be misrepresented was so great in certain religious traditions that they forbade any iconic representation of divinity. The fear was that the copy could eventually replace the original—a situation that we are experiencing precisely with the culture of the computer-mediated communication. Given this background of traditional religions, it is understandable that this new mode of communication is bound to cause a crisis in religions and in their practices.

As a result of this new mode of communication, the form of authority religions maintained in oral, textual and print communications too stands challenged (cf. Barker 2005). People enter into communication with each other on serious religious matters without being inhibited by the religious authorities as in the case of the traditional mode of religious beliefs and practices. In these earlier forms of communication, religious agents and authorities still retained an aura of sacredness and authority. They were viewed as mediators in the transmission of religious knowledge, and not seldom, as the representatives of the divinity itself.

Symptomatic of the levelling effect of modern communication can be seen in the erosion of 'secrecy' which in the past played an important role in enhancing the authority of religious agents. For example, today pontifical secrets are to be found in the Internet for anyone to access! Secrets and mantras communicated solely to selected disciples by gurus can be availed of by anyone through these media. Thus, the above examples illustrate that the traditional institution of religion and its structures are challenged to rethink the mode of authority and other symbols that were part of a different mode of communication.[4] This need not surprise us when we know that similar things happen in other fields. To cite an example, in the past, in the medical field the prescription of experts went unquestioned. Today, the doctors and medical experts have to take into account the influence of television and Internet over the patient's self-diagnosis, which, in its turn, will affect the way he or she takes the expertise and authority of doctors (cf. Horsefield 1993: 45).

Alternative Social and Religious Space

Like the construction of self-identity, which has serious implications for religious conceptions and practice, there is also a construction of community through digital communication i.e., computer-mediated communication has opened up the possibility of virtual religious communities through the Internet and other digital media. According to a broad definition, the kind of communities that can be created through Internet and digital communication are 'social aggregations that emerge from the net when enough people carry on public discussions long enough with sufficient human feeling to form webs of personal relationships in cyberspace' (cf. Rheingold 1993: 5).[5] When the creation of such communities is centred on religion and religious experience, we could speak of virtual religious communities. This needs to be distinguished from religious groups who make available on cyberspace material and information about themselves, and which are then shared by its members through the Internet and other computer-mediated means. Hence, there is a difference between 'religion on cyber space' and 'cyber-religion'(Højsgaard 2005: 50). Consequently, the nature of communities in these two modes is also different.

Sceptics would question the seriousness of such virtual religious communities and ask to what extent they could be real. However, we will be able to assess the significance of a virtual religious community if we look at it not as a substitute for a real community, but as an *alternative* space for social and religious communication. As an alternative it appears to overcome certain limitations of traditional religious communities and present at the same time challenges to these forms of community identities. If meditations and prayers could be undertaken online, there should be no serious difficulty in forming via Internet a group of people who share similar religious concerns and meet regularly on the net and form a virtual religious community.[6] Many participants in these virtual religious communities seem to benefit from it—by overcoming their loneliness and isolation, by creating a sense of solidarity and even 'affectivity' with others with whom they communicate online. But it would be a tall claim that the practice of religious communities congregating together in places of worship for rituals, festivals and celebrations could be substituted with computer-mediated communication.

This brings us to the broader issue of cyber-religion and its possibilities.

The Case of Cyber-Religion

Today, one may order Tirupathi temple *prasadam* in the form of a *laddu* and participate in the religious rituals of Vailankanni Church through computer-mediated communication. Hindu Indians away from their country and hometowns may welcome, for example, participation online in a *puja* in one of their preferred temples, and receive also a virtual *prasadam*, or undertake a virtual pilgrimage to Kasi or to Sabarimala. In this case, digital communication makes present and enables association with a physically-absent reality. But this is not yet 'cyber-religion'. What we are probing here is cyber-religion that exists online, creating in the process a virtual community. Cyber-religion can be understood best by contrasting it with the use made by established religion to reach out through the Internet and other means:

> Religion *on* cyberspace…thus refers to the information uploaded by *any* religion, church, individual or organisation which also exists and can be reached in the off-line world…Contrarily 'religion *in* cyberspace' refers to religion which is created and exists exclusively in cyberspace, where it enjoys a considerable degree of 'virtual reality'. In the first case, the primary function of

the Internet is to mediate information on religious contents and activities that has already been established or defined by various religious traditions outside cyberspace. In the second case, the Internet rather functions as a creative or formative environment fostering new religious contents and activities online.
—(Højsgaard 2005: 50–51)

If in the past, as we saw, the mode of communication transformed the nature of religious practices, we ask what is strange if we have a new mode of religion corresponding to the new modes of digital technology. This would constitute virtual or cyber-religion.[7] The religious experience here is not, so to say, a fast-food version of established religion, packaged for quick and easy consumption. We are at the threshold of an altogether new genre of religiosity where people meet and celebrate their religions by means of digital technology.[8]

The new genre of virtual religion has different presuppositions about the individual and society and needs to be studied on its own, and should not be mixed up with other forms of connecting religion and digital technology. In its creation, this particular form of religiosity is a matter of 'bricolage', assembling bits and pieces from a variety of sources. It is a kind of virtual syncretism that may not be compared with the kind of syncretism spoken of in traditional religions. Finally, this religiosity of the Internet may have religious aspirations other than traditional ones, as well as a different understanding of the sacred. This is an area which requires more empirical study and research. One of the things this type of religiosity has done is to challenge the theory of secularisation (Aupers and Houtman 2005: 87).

The Other Side of Virtual Religiosity

It may be further argued that virtual religiosity through computer-mediated communication can be very distracting and may not be conducive to reflection, and much less to meditation and contemplation. By highlighting the visual sense, as is the case with computer meditation, the virtual religiosity could be even an obstacle to deeper spirituality. As one author put it,

> Net is not very compatible with the demands for solitary contemplation and social disengagement that most religious traditions prescribe for true spiritual development. Rather the Internet tends

to involve its users in an endless and distracting series of addictive
facsimiles of life experiences.

—(Dawson 2005: 8)

If that is the case, such an objection could be raised against elaborate religious rituals and narratives in traditional religious practices,
which pander to the visual and auditory senses and prove to be a
distraction from deeper spiritual practices.

Yet another difficulty could be that virtual religion, disassociated
from physical space and from the community, may not respond to
the collective and communitarian character that is required of religion.
But those who practice virtual religion attest to the fact that they are
able to enter into communion and fellowship with other members
and feel as part and parcel of a community, (cf. Mitchell 2005)
which, though virtual, seems true and effective as far as they are
concerned.[9]

Going by the above reasoning, it would appear that virtual religion
is not only a legitimate form of religious means, but could also be
effective. Unlike traditional religious expression, where people are
passive while the religious agent performs rituals, in virtual religion,
there is ample scope for people to be active and interactive. Moreover,
some of the objections made against the practice of virtual community
and religiosity, derive from the criteria used to judge the traditional
forms and expressions of religion. The new virtual religious reality
needs to be judged on its own terms, and not in relation to the canons
of traditional religiosity.

The traditional forms of religiosity and cyber-religion may not be
opposed to each other. Cyber-religion need not replace traditional
religion; it may be more suitable for some than for others. History
tells us that the print media did not supplant the expressions of religion
through the oral medium. Even when the textual tradition came into
existence, the oral continued, which makes us speak of 'oral aspects
of scripture in the history of religion' (Graham 1987).

To conclude our discussion on cyber-religion: first of all, it
would be quite unrealistic and utopian to claim that cyber-religion is
going to be the religion of the future. No such claim is made here.
The type of cyber-religion described above with enthusiastic followers
does exist today, and will continue to exist. But that need not characterise the general situation of religion in the future. However, the
experience of cyber-religion and, more basically, computer-mediated

communication has brought to the fore certain issues and questions that must be addressed as these undermine old certainities and practices.

Second, one of the questions about the computer-mediated religion is whether and to what extent it is able to relate to the sacred, which is a fundamental dimension of religious experience. Unless we want to reduce religiosity to a reality of human solidarity and find sacredness in it (Durkheim 1965), we need to question people's interpretation of the transcendental dimension of religion—not only as something that happens in inter-human relationships—as something given, or as a gift. This argument is not meant to deny sacredness to the religious experience through the Internet and the other media. That may well be possible, even if the sacred as portrayed in the digital medium will have other features distinguishing it from the traditional characterisation of the sacred. We need to respect the experience of people who claim that through cyber-religion they have gained spiritual benefit and have encountered the sacred.

New Theological Questions and Tasks

The above analyses and reflections have thrown up a lot of challenges to theology. Besides, like religion, theological understanding itself needs to undergo profound changes. In the following pages, we shall consider the task of theology in the computer-mediated society from two basic angles. In the first place, certain tasks for theology derive from the need to accommodate the culture of modernity. Second, the computer-mediated communication takes us beyond the culture of modernity to a new way of life and experience, to which theology needs to respond creatively.

A retrospective look will attest that Christianity found itself in a situation of struggle every time a different culture appeared on the horizon as the result of a new mode of communication. This can be most clearly discerned from early Christianity, especially in its differentiation with respect to the mode of communication in Judaism and in classical culture (cf. Boomershine 1989). Heir to the Jewish culture, Christianity found it extremely difficult, for example, to accommodate itself to the culture of the Greco–Roman world characterised by strong visual expressions in statues, public altars, or in Roman imperial architecture. The temptation was to turn

Christianity into an *iconic religion* and in the process condemn the visual world of the classics. The history of this struggle brought out new insights into symbols and icons.

The Crisis of the Dogmatic Mode of Religious Communication

Communication through digital technology calls for a radical rethinking about the ways in which Christian faith has been communicated in the past. To take digital technology merely as an instrument or vehicle for more effective communication of Christian truths is to remain at the surface level. In fact, exaggerated attention to this way of looking at the relation of faith and communication could obscure the deeper issues and real challenges posed by digital communication.

The predominant model of communication we find in mainline Christianity is that of the written text, by which is meant not the Scriptures alone. The transmission of faith and its communication on the whole has been too strongly text and formula-bound. The rigidly fixed formulas anchored in dogmatic spirit found concrete expression in the production of catechisms. This mode of communication of religious truths by its very nature makes the people passive recipients rather than active agents. The fact that catechisms are an important vehicle of faith-communication can be inferred from numerous catechisms that have appeared and the impressive number of copies printed. For example, copies of Luther's *Kleiner Katechismus* (small catechism) of 1529 saw the printing of 100,000 copies, something quite astounding in that age when printing was in its infancy and literacy substantially low. Even more striking is the fact that the catechism by Peter Canisius, written in 1554, saw 233 editions by the time of his death in 1597 (Babin 1991: 26). Catechisms ensured uniformity, assisted by the new communication mode of print that helped reproduce identical copies of the same. With such a practice of communication, it was easy to create conceptual stereotypes and standardisation in the transmission of faith. The existence of identical copies also created the possibility of a rigorous control over deviations from the text. Contrary to the mode of communication implied in the transmission of dogmatic texts and catechisms, the new mode of computer-mediated communication is interactive and involves the subject in the appropriation of faith.

The dogmatic mode of religious communication is based on the dated and rather simplistic theory of sender, message and recipient. Obviously, the sender becomes a centre of religious power. But today, the digital communication challenges such forms of religious communication by highlighting a semantic model in which there is interaction and a certain construction in the process of communication, which goes beyond the role of simply decoding and translating the message. This is true of all communication, including religious communication. All this needs to be taken into account by a theology that is sensitive to the developing situation.

Theological education today is confined to the models of communication centred on oral traditions, text or print. There is even an assumption that the study of religion connected with texts and documents is superior to computer-mediated communication, which is at the most a means to convey the truths laid down in texts and documents. There is the colossal failure to see that a different mode of communication creates a different shape of society with its own modes of thought, behaviour and culture. For theology to fulfil its vocation and tasks today, it needs to critically rethink its methods and approaches in the light of the Information Society being created by digital technology. For many in the Church, cultural issues have come to be identified with the issue of 'enculturation' which is a relatively small field and which has societies of the oral, textual and print cultures as points of reference, and not the Information Society created through digital technology.

The Challenge of Computer-mediated Culture

Theology would not be playing a helpful role if its critique is unenlightened about the nature and dynamics of computer-mediated communication and its functioning. A moralising strategy will not enable us to face the new cultural situation. Hence, we cannot but sufficiently underline the importance of present-day cultural studies for theology. The culture that computer-mediated communication creates needs to be understood on its own terms and cannot be made an object of condemnation from a moral standpoint completely divorced from present-day experiences. What Douglas Kellner and others call 'counterpedagogy' could become a concrete programme for theology today and help inculcate 'critical thinking and the art of interpretation'. Theological hermeneutics today is not only the engagement with sacred texts and faith formulas; it needs to expand to include the critical reading and interpretation of cultural texts.

> [F]resh critical strategies are needed to read cultural texts, to interpret the conjunctions of sight and sound, words and images that are producing seductive cultural spaces, form and experiences. This undertaking also involves exploration of the emergent cyberspaces and modes of identities, interaction, and production that is taking place in the rapidly exploding computer culture...
> —(2001: 29)

A Critical Task

Recognition of digital technology and computer-mediated communication is to acknowledge two important truths: God's creation and human capacity to transform nature. However, there are many critical areas of the present-day information society which faith and theology need to examine.

There is a prophetic task ahead for a theology sensitive to the culture and society that emerges as a result of Information Technology and communication. Part of this prophetic task is to raise questions about the power and control the system of computer-mediated communication today represents. First of all, things are so vague and amorphous that one may tend to forget that the system behind the new digital technologies is a strongly centralised and controlled one, despite the appearance to the contrary. If hegemony is defined as the rule through forced consent of the subjugated, much of it is true about the situation of power operative in the networking and centralisation of communication. A theology that is concerned about the human condition cannot but raise the question whether the computer-mediated communication is truly a liberating activity.

Critique of Knowledge-Control in the Informational Capitalism

Since every technology and every new form of communication has a particular social context, theology needs to interrogate the social implications of the information technology. This is something that tends to be overlooked.

In all societies there has been a certain form of control of know-ledge, which gave power to certain groups of people. Among many civilizations, the control of knowledge by the priestly class helped to maintain their hold over the society. In medieval Europe the impor-tance of monastic institutions derived from the fact that the monks were gatekeepers of knowledge. At a time when there was no print media, the monks spent day and night copying texts and preserving them, sometimes even chaining them together—because they were so precious. The extent of present-day control of knowledge, strangely in an information society, has no parallel.

Second, producing enormous quantities of information on the Internet does not guarantee that conditions are created for people to be *critical* and *creative*. In fact, the opposite seems to be happening. Social and critical consciousness is drowned in the plethora of infor-mation. Moreover, the Information Society does not seem to facilitate greater participation of people in public affairs, as it should. In fact, the availability of information could create conditions for greater involvement in public affairs and to formulate policies that benefit the people. There is a deeper reason for inhibiting social conscious-ness and engagement, and that leads us to the next point.

There is such overwhelming attention given to the engineering and quantitative aspect of communication that one easily forgets that information has to do with *quality*. This is another area of critical theological reflection we need to undertake. A genuine theology will be concerned about the enhancement of the quality of human life today. Such a goal, evidently, cannot be achieved by simply increasing the volume of information. Precisely because we are unaware of the social implications of information technology, we tend to oversee the fact that virtual texts lose their meaning and operate in a decontextualised and dehistoricised vacuum, losing in meaning and quality. Creation of public libraries in the past had the goal of providing the means for the public to inform themselves. To what extent does the present information society have social goals and ideals? Similar critical questions need to be raised about the origin, purpose and consequence of information.

Commodity in the Informational Capitalist System

Information is today turned into a marketable *commodity,* so much so, that we could speak of 'informational capitalism', which through connectivity and strategic alliances turns information into a profitable capital for investment and trade. Its functions, in many respects, are similar to industrial capitalism. Information is not produced and circulated in a neutral atmosphere. Thanks to the flow of information, there has come into existence an 'intellectual and social organisation of the sciences' (Whitley 2000). The domination inscribed into the networking gets reproduced also in the circulation of information, favouring the powerful. As in the colonial times, rail-links were built for better exploitation of resources, similarly the connectivity and networking serve the cause of economic exploitation. Drawing a parallel to today's situation, Ien Ang comments critically on the 'global village'.

> In this respect, McLuhan's 'global village', a world turned into a single community through the annihilation of space in time, represents nothing other than (the fantasy) of the universal culmination of capitalist modernity.
>
> —(1999: 36)

Everything is done for a price. This strong economic and market angle to information explains why—despite being in an information society—people are deprived of vital information that is necessary for their life. Like other commodities, information is produced, stored and exchanged. Money and the market are involved in each of these processes. Institutions and structures, that will serve this economic end, are created and, what is more, the existing institutions are transformed and steered to this goal. The most obvious case is the institutions of higher education—universities, research institutions and colleges, which are all turned into factories of knowledge. This trend is observable everywhere—both in developed and developing countries. There is clear evidence for the neglect of the humanities and social sciences in the institutions of higher learning, and the privileging of those science subjects that produce marketable knowledge and application skills.

Recently, while listening to a talk by a very highly placed official in charge of higher education in the country, I was appalled at the lack of any social thrust in the educational policies for the country he was trying to present in managerial jargon. The impression was inevitable that higher education is a system of efficient knowledge management—production, distribution and consumption. The strategies and funding are all oriented in this direction. The underlying assumption in such educational orientation is one that sees progress and development as enabling rational choices through the furnishing of information, and it is in this sense that educational institutions are viewed and interpreted (cf. Elliott 1995: 261).

Transformative Knowledge and Wisdom

Knowledge has other purposes. It is the failure to pay attention to these purposes that contributes to the amnesias of social realities. Knowledge has a transformative power and that is why education is connected with the formation of the person and the development of the total personality. Moreover, there has been a strong conviction in all religious traditions that knowledge has a sacred character like nature itself. Even if it is acquired through human effort, there is a character of *givenness* in all knowledge in which human beings partake. This transcendent character of knowledge is also behind the respect traditionally given to *gurus* as a source of knowledge, and to veneration of knowledge in the Hindu tradition, for example, through S*araswati puja* or the worship of the goddess of learning, and the personification and veneration of knowledge as *Sophia* or wisdom in the Christian tradition. Possessing knowledge for enhancing one's power, while depriving others of it, is reprehensible. Hence, the sacred character of knowledge needs to be related to the social and service aspect of this form of power. Concretising this goal means turning communication from a vertical and centralised practice into a horizontal and participative process. Like in other areas of life, participative communication will help overcome the risks and dangers involved in a dominating mode of communication. This form of communication will stir the critical sense in the people regarding the generation and channelling of knowledge.

We are here in a very different realm from the cult of information, about which Theodore Roszak observes,

> People who have no clear idea of what they mean by information or why they should want so much of it are nonetheless prepared to believe that we live in an information Age, which makes every computer around us what relics of the True Cross were in the age of Faith: Emblems of salvation.
>
> —(1988: 10)

Accountability of Knowledge Experts

Experts and professionals of knowledge are accountable to the society. There seems to be greater consciousness about this, especially among the poor. Recently, on the eve of the tsunami anniversary on December 26, 2004, a journalist, who wanted to assess the mood of the people, interviewed individuals on the badly hit coastal villages of Tamilnadu. There was widespread belief that the tsunami will be there again exactly one year after on the same day of December 26. People were even booking rooms in lodges away from the shore in view of what they believed would be the repeat of the tsunami! When the journalist pointed out that their view was not scientific, there came the retort: 'But where was science when our dear ones were swallowed up by tsunami? Why did not science predict and inform us about tsunami?' These are disturbing questions coming from the simple suffering folk as a challenge to science and technology and directed to know-ledge experts and professionals. They are questions that remind us about the social purpose of information and knowledge. It is this that is lacking, because information and knowledge, as we noted earlier, have clear economic goals. The mask of legitimacy science and technology wear are ripped open by the public fury incensed by disappointment and suspicion that knowledge is stored and shared for making profits.

Popular demands for information concerning health and environmental protection must be fulfilled. Moreover, there is general scepticism about knowledge transmitted to people regarding environ-mental and health issues, particularly if the experts are associated with profit-making institutions like the multinationals (cf. Leiss 1994: 134). Here I think a meaningful theology will find stimulus for a critique of the information society and an opportunity to strengthen the resolve of the people to challenge a knowledge system and communication that only serves the elite.

This whole unfolding scenario tells us that communication is not simply a matter of culture and society today; it has a crucial economic function, which allows us to speak legitimately about an 'informational economy'. If power is conditioned by economy, it is information that qualifies to be a great power since it has become an indispensable ingredient in the structure and functioning of the present-day economy.

Heightened Uncertainty

A critical question theology needs to ask is whether the Information Age has contributed to lessen the uncertainty and ambivalence that have marked the life of humanity since the advent of modern science and technology (Ang 1994; Bauman 1996). Experience tells us that, with every advancement, and with growing accumulation of information, uncertainty gets heightened rather than reduced. As Baudrillard (see Smart 1999) has pointed out,

> What is constant is an immense uncertainty...The revolution of our time is the uncertainty revolution. We are not ready to accept this. Paradoxically, however, we attempt to escape from uncertainty by relying even more on information and communications systems, so merely aggravating the uncertainty itself.
>
> —(1999)

Informational increase and uncertainty work in tandem with each other. The uncertainty is nurtured in our times by the fragmentation and atomisation of knowledge. Specialisation and atomisation of knowledge apparently serve to solve problems. But we also observe that they are the sources of new problems, something that makes us seriously doubt whether uncertainty can be reduced through specialisation. The flow of information, instead of lessening the uncertainty, has heightened it.

The contribution of theology is not through specialisation. Rather in a world of fragmentation, it needs to instil more than ever a sense of the whole. This holistic approach to life will bring about greater sense of security and peace to humanity. Now that the multiplying of information is not a solution to the uncertainty that has gripped the world and our societies, theology will also pay attention to instilling a qualitative dimension in our Information Society.

Theology for an Inclusive Information Society

Like in other fields, in the field of communication too there has taken place a scandalous divide between those who are digitally powerful and those who are left behind. Given the fact that communication technology is increasingly becoming a central element in the organisation of the society, its governance, mobilisation and control of resources, it is highly important that the benefits of the communication serve holistic developmental goals and objectives. Here is a field in which theology needs to involve itself, so that greater digital justice is ensured, and those in rural areas and at the margins of the society have access to communication.

The struggle for liberation and justice needs to be fought today in the communication field given its crucial importance, and theology should assist in this process. At the global level, greater consciousness for an inclusive information society has been created by the World Summit on Information Society held at Geneva in 2003, and more recently a follow-up summit in Tunis 2005 (cf. Capurro 2005). The declaration of principle made in Geneva, calling for a people-centred Information Society, and the reiteration of the same in Tunis will serve as a stimulus for theology to engage itself both at the macro level and at the local level for the cause of justice. The call to commitment to justice today is a call to transform the field of communication in such a way that the poor and the marginalised have greater access to it, and that they and their concerns are included in creating policies and infrastructures relating to communication. Governments, private sector, NGOs, civil society—all these need to concur towards the goal of greater digital justice. Theology could become an important source of inspiration in this important common project.

Conclusion

With information society and computer-mediated communication, we are at the bottom dealing with the question whether technology 'determines' our lives, or whether it 'serves' our lives.[10] In other words, should technological facts and possibilities become automatically the defining elements of human and social life? It is these larger questions which offer us clues as to how to go along with religion in this Information Age. Digital technology offers new possibilities in the exercise of religion that need to be considered on their own and not be judged by traditional forms of religiosity, which themselves are expressions of particular modes of communication. There is then a set of questions that relate to how theology needs to adapt to the change of society caused by the new mode of communication. In its broader sense, these questions would fall under faith and modernity, of which technology is a very crucial element.

For religion and theology, the information society presents a challenging task because this society is characterised by ambiguity and contradictions. The nature of this situation is well-captured by Manuel Castells when he observes:

> The implicit logic of the Network Society appears to end history, by enclosing it into the circulation of recurrent patterns of flow. Yet, as with any other social form, in fact it opens up a new realm of contradiction and conflict, as people around the world refuse to become shadows of global flows and project their dreams, and sometimes their nightmares, into the light of new history making.
> —(1999: 410)

Theology is not meant to navigate on safe waters or to be anchored securely close to *terra firma*. It needs to assist the people and society in making sense of the contradictions and help transform the situation. The critical role of theology will consist in examining whether and to what extent the Information Society is equitable and just. It will go into the domination, control and commodification of information, and interrogate whether Information Society brings knowledge closer to the people and acts for their well-being. Hence, questions like access to information, and availability of resources for the weaker sections in the society will form part of the critical agenda of theology.

On its part, theology will undergo a thorough transformation, since communication through digital technology and the attendant values and cultural practices raises questions on certain crucial aspects of the traditional practices of faith and the institutions and structures and mode of thought connected with it. Taking up these new challenges and rethinking theology in the context of information society is important for it to play effectively its critical and transformative role in our times.

Notes

1. For an overview of theories relating to cultural transformations resulting from new technologies, see Durham and Kellner (2001: 1–29). See also Curran *et al*. (1982: 11–29); Poster (1998: 611–24).

2. This is different from the question of how various religions are making use of digital technology. This point is simple enough and I am not going to dwell on it. Religious traditions find in digital technology a very effective means to propagate their religious beliefs world-wide by opening up websites and networks. This is true of Hinduism, Buddhism, Islam, Judaism, Christianity, and other religious traditions. These traditional religions are joined by new religious groups and sects who try to bring their faith to others by taking advantage of the digital technology. Thousands

of pages of materials could be found in the World Wide Web. Among some Christian groups and religious sects, digital technology has been made ample use of the work of evangelicalism. Whereas several religious groups are disdainful of modernity, which is perceived as undermining the religious universe, they accommodate themselves perfectly to digital technology.

3. These questions represent the new situation created by the computer-mediated communication, which has thrown up new sets of issues and problems not covered under the general consideration of religion and media. For the various aspects of this latter question, see Arthur (1993).

4. Secrecy as a means of control for the authorities went along with social mores of the past which attached much importance to it. This stands in contrast to our age which is 'fascinated by exposure. Indeed the *act* of exposure itself now seems to excite us more than the content of the secrets exposed' Meyrowitz (1999: 103). One more factor that creates this situation is the collapse of the traditional demarcation of the private and the public. The merging of the two has its consequences also in the religious domain.

5. See also Rheingold (1999: 273–85) and Morley and Robbins (1999: 336–51).

6. Mun-Cho Kim reports the existence of Buddhist religious communities online. Cf. Kim (2005: 138–48).

7. It may be interesting to recall in this connection that in the Christian tradition, the physical absence of a person in the ritual mode did not hinder him or her from participating in another religious mode. This is the case, for example, with 'communion of desire' where, even though the person is not physically present, he or she is virtually made a participant in the eucharistic celebration.

8. The cyber religious experience has gone through three different 'waves' ever since the studies on the relationship of internet and religion started in the 1990s. See Højsgaard and Warburg (2005: 1–11). Also other relevant articles in the volume, especially Dawson (2005: 15–37); Højsgaard (2005: 50–63); O'Leary (2005: 38–49).

9. That having been acknowledged, we need to also pay attention to the danger of isolation from the larger society. There is the danger of net-mediated virtual religious communities turning into sects and ghettos, fostering esoteric beliefs and arcane cults bordering on fanaticism with disastrous consequences.

10. According to some, the technological euphoria which depicts the present age has led to dramatic changes in the society. Here, I think, there is some exaggeration of issues. We would have a more realistic assessment of the general condition created by computer-mediated technologies, if we viewed the present state not as something totally new, but in continuity with the past. Let us take the case of the 'information society'—a characterisation of the present-day world. The way the matter is portrayed is such that almost every occupation is viewed as belonging to the knowledge industry. By these standards, even a mason and carpenter would be workers in knowledge industry, since they cannot do what they do without the 'know-how'!

References

Ang, Ien. 1994. 'In the Realm of Uncertainty: The Global Village and Capitalist Modernity', in David Crowley and David Mitchell (eds), *Communication Theory Today*, pp. 193–213. Cambridge: Polity Press.
————. 1999. 'In the Realm of Uncertainty', in Hugh Mackay and Tim O' Sullivan (eds), *The Media Reader: Continuity and Transformation*. London: Sage Publications.
Arthur, Chris (ed.). 1993. *Religion and the Media: An Introductory Reader*. Cardiff: University of Wales Press.
Aupers, Stef and Dick Houtman. 2005. 'Reality Sucks: On Alienation and Cybergnosis', *Concilium: International Journal of Theology*, (Special Issue on 'Cyberspace-Cyber Ethics-Cyber Theology', (eds) E. Borgman, Van S. Erp and H. Haker), 1: 81–89.
Babin, Pierre. 1991. *The New Era in Religious Communication*. Minneapolis: Fortress Press.
Barker, Eileen. 2005. 'Crossing the Boundary: New Challenges to Religious Authority and Control as a Consequence of Access to Internet', in Morten T. Højsgaard and Margit Warburg (eds), *Religion and Cyberspace*, pp. 67–85. London: Routledge.
Bauman, Zygmunt. 1996. *Moderne und Ambivalenz*. Frankfurt am Main: Taschenbuch Verlag.
Boomershine, Thomas E. 1989. 'Christian Community and Technologies of the Word', in James Mcdonnell and Frances Trampiets (eds), *Communicating Faith in a Technological Age*, pp. 56–77. Middlegreen: St Paul Publications.
Capurro, Raphael. 2005. 'Does Digital Globalization Lead to a Global Information Ethic?', *Concilium: International Journal of Theology*, (Special Issue on 'Cyberspace-Cyber Ethics-Cyber Theology', (eds) E. Borgman, Van S. Erp and H. Haker), 1: 36–45.
Castells, Manuel. 1999. 'An Introduction to the Information Age', in Hugh Mackay and Tim O' Sullivan (eds), *The Media Reader: Continuity and Transformation*. London: Sage Publications.
Curran, James, Michael Gurevitch, Tony Bennett and Janet Woollacott (eds.). 1982. *Culture, Society and Media*. London: Routledge.
Dawson, Lornel. 2005. 'The Mediation of Religious Experience in Cyberspace', in Morten T. Højsgaard and Margit Warburg (eds), *Religion and Cyberspace*. London: Routledge.
Durham, Meenakshi Gigi and Douglas M. Kellner (eds). 2001. *Media and Cultural Studies: KeyWorks*. Oxford: Blackwell Publishers.
Durkheim, Emile. 1965. *The Elementary Forms of the Religious Life*. Trans. by Joseph Swain. New York: Free Press.
Elliott, Philip. 1995. 'Intellectuals, the Information Society and the Disappearance of Public Sphere', in Oliver Boyd-Barrett and Chris Newbold (eds), *Approaches to Media: A Reader*. New York: E. Arnold.

Graham, William A. 1987. *Beyond the Written Word: Oral Aspects of Scripture in the History of Religion*. Cambridge: Cambridge University Press.

Højsgaard, Morten T. 2005. 'Cyber-Religion: On the Cutting Edge Between the Virtual and the Real', in Morten T. Højsgaard and Margit Warburg (eds), *Religion and Cyberspace*. London: Routledge.

————— and Margit Warburg (eds). 2005. *Religion and Cyberspace*. London: Routledge.

Horsefield, Peter. 1993. 'Teaching Theology in a Cultural Environment', in Chris Arthur (ed.), *Religion and the Media: An Introductory Reader*. Cardiff: University of Wales Press.

Kellner, Douglas M. and Meenakshi Gigi Durham. 2001. 'Adventures in Media and Cultural Studies: Introducing the KeyWorks', in Meenakshi Gigi Durham and Douglas M. Kellner (eds), *Media and Cultural Studies: KeyWorks*. Oxford: Blackwell Publishers.

Kim, Mun-Cho. 2005. 'Online Buddhist Community: An Alternative Religious Organization in the Information Age', in Morten T. Højsgaard and Margit Warburg (eds), *Religion and Cyberspace*, pp. 138–48. London: Routledge.

Leiss, William. 1994. 'Risk Communication and Public Knowledge', in David Crowley and David Mitchell (eds), *Communication Theory Today*. Cambridge: Polity Press.

Marvin, Carolyn. 1999. 'When Old Technologies were New: Implementing the Future', in Hugh Mackay and Tim O' Sullivan (eds), *The Media Reader: Continuity and Transformation*, pp. 58–72. London: Sage Publications.

Meyrowitz, Joshua. 1999. 'No Sense of Place: The Impact of Electronic Media on Social Behaviour', in Hugh Mackay and Tim O' Sullivan (eds), *The Media Reader: Continuity and Transformation*. London: Sage Publications.

Mitchell, Nathan D. 2005. 'Ritual and New Media', *Concilium: International Journal of Theology*, (Special Issue on 'Cyber Space-Cyber Ethics-Cyber Theology', (eds) E. Borgman, Van S. Erp and H. Haker), 1: 90–98.

Morley, David and Kevin Robins. 1999. 'Reimagined Communities? New Media, New Possibilities', in Hugh Mackay and Tim O' Sullivan (eds), *The Media Reader: Continuity and Transformation*, pp. 336–51. London: Sage Publications.

O'Leary, Stephen D. 2005. 'Utopian and Dystopian Possibilities of Networked Religion in the New Millennium', in Morten T. Højsgaard and Margit Warburg (eds), *The Media Reader: Continuity and Transformation*, pp. 38–49. London: Routledge.

Poster, Mark. 1998. 'Postmodern Virtualities', in Arthur Asa Berger (ed.), *The Postmodern Presence: Readings on Postmodernism in American Culture and Society*. Walnut Creek: AltaMira Press.

Rheingold, H. 1993. *The Virtual Community: Homesteading on the Electronic Frontier*. Massachusetts: Addison–Wesley Publishing Company.

Rheingold, H. 1999. 'The Virtual Community: Finding Connection in a Computerized World', in Hugh Mackay and Tim O' Sullivan (eds), *The Media Reader: Continuity and Transformation*, pp. 273–85. London: Sage Publications.

Roszak, Theodore. 1988. *The Cult of Information: The Folklore of Computers and the True Art of Thinking*. London: Grafton Books.

Smart, Barry. 1999. *Facing Modernity: Ambivalence, Reflexivity, and Modernity*. London: Sage Publications.

Turkle, Sherry. 1995. *Life on the Screen: Identities in the Age of Internet*. New York: Simon and Schuster.

Webster, Frank. 1999. 'What Information Society?', in Hugh Mackay and Tim O' Sullivan (eds), *The Media Reader: Continuity and Transformation*. London: Sage Publications.

Whitley, Richard. 2000. *The Intellectual and Social Organization of the Sciences*. Oxford: Oxford University Press.

3

Alterity, Technology, and Human Nature

R. Radhakrishnan

Is there something called 'human nature?' If yes, is such a nature ontological (rooted in being) or epistemological (rooted in thought)? Where and how does the 'nature' of the human dangle in the 'therefore/*ergo*' that is positioned between the *Cogito* (thought) and the *sum* (being) in the Cartesian *Cogito ergo sum* or '*I think, therefore I am*'? What is the role of technology as 'simulacrum'[1] in the ongoing actualisation of the 'human' to itself? In the act of understanding itself through unprecedented modalities made possible by technology, does the human subject surrender its *a priori* to the unavoidable momentum of epistemology as performative?[2] If technology 'doubles' the human in ways that Michel Foucault theorised, how should a theory of the 'human as the subject of epistemology' be coordinated in response to the endless logic of 'seriality'[3] inaugurated by the process of 'doubling?' In the binary coding of reality as existence and knowledge, as living and telling, as Self and Other, what does it mean for the human subject to be interpellated by the alterity or 'otherness' of technology: a form of alterity, ironically speaking, produced by the Self of the human subject? Is technology the radical 'other' that has brought into existence the post-humanist subject? These are some of the questions that I wish to explore in an interconnected manner in this brief essay.

The Critical Excess of Technology

I begin with a few examples. I am at the USTA Tennis Centre watching an absorbing five set tussle between Rafael Nadal and Roger Federer. A harrowingly long and fiercely contested point has just ended, and here I am exclaiming from the immediacy of my excitement and involvement:

56 ► Digital Culture Unplugged

Please, can we have a replay of that entire point? Then I realise sheepishly that it is precisely because I am at the scene of reality I have to satisfy myself with less than an optimal or maximal experience of that moment. I have to deprive myself of that critical excess that has been guaranteed my human, all too human, subject by the apparatus of technology.

The second example, also drawn from the domain of sports, this time basketball: the only way I can experience the famous hang time immortalised by Michael Jordan is through the 'slow mo' camera and its immaculate virtuality. Here too, from the heart of my humanity, I want to exceed the human, and experience and relish reality 'otherwise.' There is also the other example where the brilliant phenomenological philosopher, Maurice Merleau–Ponty, analyses the impact of the 'slow mo' camera as it follows the painter Henri Matisse's hand as it is in the process of painting. This too is an unnatural perception, made entirely possible by the camera. So, where is the so-called 'primacy' of perception to be located: in the camera lens, in the human eye, and therefore in the world, or where?

The third reference is to that eloquent lyric by Paul Simon, 'The Boy in the Bubble' that is the lead song in the controversial album, *Graceland*. This song invokes the world of high tech and simulacral epistemologies and virtual realities in a tone of ambivalence. We live in a world of the 'slow mo' camera, of staccato signs of communications that crisscross the global village. We reside and function in a world where the baby carriage is connected to a bomb and the detonator—a world where self-reflexivity (we look at ourselves looking) has almost becomes *de rigueur*, if not an outright cliché. The refrain of the song 'don't cry baby, don't cry' could be read either as genuine reassurance to the baby or as an ironic evisceration of reassurance in a world presided over by indeterminacy, where opposites seem to come together in benign semantic synchrony.

Structuralist–Marxism and Its Limits

With this preamble, I approach the in/famous simulacrum as articulated initially by Roland Barthes in his essay and by the radical postmodern and post-representational turn given to this concept by Jean Baudrillard.[4] The simulacrum or representation gets instrumentalised as that necessary bridge between 'the real' and 'the intelligible.' Barthes reminds us that it is an 'interested simulacrum.' The purpose of the structuralist activity—notice it is an active and agential praxis and not an ism—is to produce the simulacrum from within the body of the real so that the real can be read as intelligible, thanks to the simulacrum.[5]

Barthesian epistemology remains mired in the complacency of a purely representational epistemology that, in its attempt to speak with fidelity on behalf of reality, puts the simulacrum back where it was, untransformed, within reality itself. The question for Structuralist–Marxism[6] in general is: Where is the alterity of 'structure?'

Alterity or 'otherness' could be ontological, or epistemological, or both. The other could be there and real, but not be available to the self as knowledge. Or, we might be aware that the other's ontology is secure in its own epistemology. Whether alterity is at the level of ontology or epistemology, there is a prior issue and that is the issue of temporality.[7]

In other words, is the temporality of ontology or the real the same as the temporality of epistemology or knowledge of the real? Are the two coeval with each other? To revisit the horizon of Structuralist–Marxism, what Louis Althusser claimed he had done by way of incorporating the micropolitical processes of structuralism into the macropolitical objectivity of Marxism was to push Marxism beyond and yet into itself, more fully, theoretically, symptomatically and diagnostically. The 'other' of Marxism is produced in symptomatic excess of Marxism, and at the same time and on another register, the very alterity of the symptom is recognised as proper to the ongoing process that Marxism is all about. Althusser would talk about 'process without subject or goal/s.' So, does process act on something, a substance, an essence, an ultimate substratum that in the ultimate analysis provides, in however an immanent manner, the process with its ethic or teleology? Or, is process a perennial de-subjectification of the real, of nature, of Being as such? Is there anything already there, as Judith Butler would ask in the context of the performativity of gender, to be acted upon; or, is ontology nothing but an effect, a stage that becomes a stage only during the aftermath of performance?[8]

Do We have Anything to Say?

I would now like to return to those issues opened up by my introductory examples. What are 'ways of knowing' and what are 'ways of being?' How are the two interconnected and on whose bidding? Does 'being' interpellate 'knowing', or is it the other way around? Also, what qualifies as a way of knowing? Clearly, not every little change in the history of ideas qualifies as a way of knowing, or as a paradigm inauguration. When is the medium the message, and if the medium is the message, what happened to the message that used to be anterior? When is form transformative of content, and when is a formal innovation merely that and no more? Ralph Waldo Emerson[9] is supposed to have responded thus, during the early days of the telephone, when he was told that Maine was calling Massachusetts: *But does Maine have anything to say*? Haughty as the question sounds as it emanates from the sage of Concord, the Emersonian question retains its pertinence, particularly during our own times when the rate of change is so fast and exponential that there is a temptation to call every change a 'revolution' or a change of the second order.

Take for example, the internal revolution within the technological domain called telephony: the cell phones and the built-in obsolescence that characterises the growth of this field. There is no question that the advent of the mobile cell phone (there is a good chance that within a generation landlines may become obsolete and irrelevant) has drastically changed the meaning of what it means to have a number and an area code. Within the field of communication, the human subject, as both receiver and addressee, has been differently located, 'locationalised' I should say, zoned, and territorialised. As we walk and talk with the phone in our hands, we are in a sense recognising ourselves differently as nodal points in a larger flow. Yet, the Emersonian question can still be raised in the face of such dazzling technological virtuosity: Has the *content* of what we are saying changed or improved or become more profound in any way as a consequence of the formal revolution? Or is it possible that what is a revolution at the micro level does not carry over as a profound effect into the level of the macro?

What has changed in this instance is the nature of the relationship between the phone and the hand holding the phone. The hand holding the phone could be moving, roving, and travelling limitlessly as the conversation happens. The fact that we can 'communicate' at any time and from wherever we are is a dazzling effect of technology. There has been a considerable enhancement of a sense of safety as a result of this. Crises, mishaps, and emergencies: there is an instantaneous way of coping with all these eventualities now, thanks to the mobile phone. But on the other hand, there is the banal spectre of people walking with phones stuck to the sides of their heads, indulging in a conversation for the one and only reason that a conversation is possible. The thematic question, 'Is there anything worth talking about?' is answered in and by the sheer immanence of 'Yes, a conversation is possible every instant.' The worth of the conversation is collapsed into the mere factual possibility of the conversation. Value is on the surface of the apparatus, and not inside the conversation, to use the register of interiority so dear to humanism. To invoke McLuhan (2001), 'the medium is indeed the message,' much like, in the words of the poet Archibald MacLeish, 'A poem should not mean/But be' (Macleish 1985).[10]

The absolute and unconditional valorisation of the medium is as much a substantive pitch on behalf of the medium and its meaning-making capacity as it is a polemical telling off a residual humanism that would rather have 'consciousness' and 'intentionality' as the drivers of the meaning and the message. At least two questions need to be answered here. 1) Can there be messages that are *hors-medium* (outside the medium), to echo the famous *hors-texte* (outside the text) from Derrida[11]? 2) What is the relationship between the self-reflexive knowledge that is about the *medium qua medium*, and what the medium is *about*? The second question could also be given the following post-modern formulation. When the medium becomes the message, are we necessarily and unavoidably pushed into the domain of 'post-representation?' What is the relationship between the representational interiority of fiction/narrative and the exterior alterity of meta-fiction/meta-narrative? Moreover, do meta-fictional and meta-narratological ways of 'knowing' augment/interrupt/problematise/deconstruct the primary fiction/narrative? In Derrida's terms, is the supplement dangerous? If Derridean deconstruction dreams up ways of playing with, dislodging, and differing/deferring the logic of binarity, Jean Baudrillard's epistemology (1991) implodes the binarity into the materiality of the machine.

In a famous and much quoted essay, Baudrillard (1991) makes a crucial distinction between the relationship that obtains between the human hand and the steering wheel of a car, and the human hand and a post-modern machine or control pad on the other. Baudrillard raises issues that are methodological and epistemological on the one hand, and ontological and 'identitarian' on the other. If in McLuhan's purely instrumentalist paradigm (2001), the machine receives its epistemological status as message, in Baudrillard's version of post-modernism, the human subject is persuaded or constrained to take a step beyond the axiology of humanism. The very possibility of human knowledge, in Baudrillard's theory, is enabled not as an obedient response to the *a priori* of human intentionality, but rather, as the function of a performative that is enacted in the 'brought into being' processes and protocols of knowing of the human interfacing with the materiality of the apparatus. Baudrillard is not questioning the reality that it was human ingenuity in the first place that brought the post-modern apparatus into being. His claim is that, in inaugurating the processes of that machine, the human subject has in fact brought into being processes and protocols of knowing that owe no ontological allegiance to the priority of the human.

These processes operate as transgressions or as excesses of the human; and as a result, the human being has to lose and re-find itself by way of processes of knowing. The duality of the Cartesian *Cogito* is now made to implode into the immanence of the materiality of the knowing process whose only accountability is to its own specific epistemic temporality. 'Ways of knowing' take the place both of 'what is to be known' and 'the knowing subject.'

All of this is a way of saying that the radical alterity of the artificial marks a major rupture in the history of human intellectuality. Even if we accept the strong Baudrillardian thesis of the post-modern as artificial, the question still remains: How and why are the 'sciences of the artificial' interpellated into being? I would now like to make a tenuous thematic connection between Baudrillard and some of the revolutionary formulations of Herbert Simon, one of the founding fathers of the domain called 'Artificial Intelligence.'

Bounded Rationality and the Constitution of the Self

One of the chief preoccupations of Simon (1996) and his colleagues was with the 'learning machine.' How can a machine be invented that in the process of accomplishing discrete tasks would also be able to take on the second order project of 'learning to learn?' The theme of course is that of heuristic recursiveness or self-reflexivity. The transformative concept that Simon formulates is that of 'bounded rationality.' How can learning be generated theoretically during a contingent act of task accomplishment or problem solving? He is attempting to bring together the richness of theoretical knowledge with the particular directedness of a specific praxis or task. What does it mean to know in the act of performing a specific task, and how can the performance of the task be realised as an opening to further learning? Bounded rationality disallows both the romanticism of idealism and the narrow certitudes of empiricism. It is precisely because rationality is bounded that it can learn from itself contingently from one task to the next.

What Simon introduces to epistemology is the notion of the artificial that poses the question of 'what it means to learn' as a moment within the continuum of practical projects and task accomplishments. Taking his cue from the thesis of human 'corrigibility' and the human ability to learn from failure, Simon thinks of the artificial machine as a thematisation of the human. The machine then would repeat what the human being does 'naturally,' and through such a repetition elaborate a theory of the artificial. When a computer beats a Bobby Fischer or a Spassky in a game of chess, it announces the possibility that simulation in fact is what constitutes the human. What Spassky does is nothing mystical or mysterious, even though his mastery of moves and his magnificent memory and recalls of earlier games and patterns definitely seem magical. Spassky is what Spassky does in the context called chess, and what he does can be replicated even better by a machine. Is Spassky a form of 'is' or a form of 'does' is the huge overhanging ontological, as well as epistemological, question here.

It will be recalled that some of the early concerns in the area of robotics had to do with the replication of the human. In a manner and modality different from DNA or cloning technology, robotics, from the point of view of task analysis that itself is based on the logic of instrumental reason, was trying to figure out if it was possible to reproduce the human non-holistically, that is, either by way of metonymy or synecdoche. Clearly, the robot could not be human, but it could be made to selectively perform the quality of the human or be part representative of the ontological range called the human. This was the context in which neurobiology, cognitive psychology, artificial intelligence, and simulation technologies came together in the interdisciplinary probe of the human. It will also be remembered that orthodox biologists had difficulty accepting the integrity of simulation technologies that seemed somehow falsely 'transempirical' when compared to work being done in the labs.

What I find most revealing in these discussions is the fact that, despite every effort to replicate the human in purely pragmatic and task related ways, at some point the question about human nature comes to haunt the debate. What is the human? Is it an aggregate of an infinite number of doable tasks? Is it a machine, a computer programme, a developing algorithm, a perennially teachable condition? When a human hand moves and swats a fly in response to a sensation, how much thinking, how much neuro-biological action takes place as prolegomenon before the hand makes its conclusive move? Could the human be assembled empirically, by examining one task at a time? Or would it be more sophisticated to understand the human in all its holistic generality, and then infer each action from the totality? Clearly, the robot was not intended as an *ersatz* human. Whether the science of robotics has developed as it had intended or not, the effect of Artificial Intelligence on the human imagination, both professional and popular, has been deep and far-reaching. In science fiction and TV shows, androids show up. The character of 'Data' in a popular science fiction series raises the question of what it means 'to be human?'

A whole range of questions arises regarding mind–body dualism. If the mind, as cognitive psychologists would have it, is nothing but the brain in action, the attempt to understand the human in functionalist terms should not constitute a violation to the integrity of the human. It could even be maintained that the human is already artificial. In other words, what we as humans think, act, and do, is not the expression of some intimate interiority that *we are*. On the contrary, it is by way of the exteriority of our actions, and performances that we are who we are. This is the cognitive or the epistemological alterity that old-fashioned humanists are afraid of, for the very simple reason that these extrinsic accounts of human reality sound so unfamiliar. The humanist would rather claim humanity as a state of intentional consciousness first before it gets recoded as a series of behavioural and somatic practices and performances. What the humanist resists is a form of knowing that operates as a process of demystification. Very few people, I would think, would like the idea of their experience of a sublime and epiphanic state of mind described as the expression of an intensified level of production of serotonin or some such chemical component. Such an explanation would seem to negate the lived verity of the experience.

Technology as Manipulation

With this little excursion, I come back to notions of agency and intentionality. Do we accept the Baudrillardian thesis that in the interface between the human and the machine, agency and intentionality are indeed re-territorialised? For my purposes here, I am assuming that the Baudrillardian reference is to information and simulation technologies that have served to unpack the human into variously assemblable databases and the configurations thereof. It is through these new and undreamt of configurations that the human is being interpellated. And there is no greater example than that terrifyingly novel field called biometrics that measures and profiles individual human life so that it can be presented as a transparently readable text to the gaze of technology that is indeed operated by state power.

Contrary to the Baudrillardian thesis, I would argue that this posthumanist strategy of disassemblage very much reinforces the traditional concept of the human person. If anything, in fulfilment of that stark Foucauldian formulation, 'visibility is a trap,' biometric technology literally hunts a person down into the juridico-disciplinary normativity of the anti-terrorist and paranoid gaze of the super state. A person is both intended and realised within the immanence of the biometric machine that in reality stands for the absolute transcendence of the super state. The model of discovery at work is that of detection whereby the ontology of the person to be detected is always already secured in a field of criminality and absolute culpability. If the Panopticon, as analysed by Foucault and the assembly line, as immortalised by Charlie Chaplin in his film *Modern Times*, drives home the thesis that the human subject can be incarcerated in the name of its knowability and the logic of instrumental reason, the biometric paradigm goes even further in the task of producing docile bodies.

The biometric probe into the 'human' brings into being a disciplinary relationship between knowability and a way of seeking knowledge called 'profiling' which in turn operates on the assumption that knowledge is a form of compliance to the gaze as surveillance. It is in the always already potential condition of criminality or culpability that a subject becomes knowable. It needs to be understood here that, under the jurisdiction of the biometric regime, each and every subject has already and *aprioristically* identified as a virtual criminal, and the physical, material, historical finding of either guilt or innocence can do nothing to undo the guilty verdict that the technology of the biometric self has already inscribed in the human subject.

It is also worth noting that even as we speak, there is talk of American passports being equipped with computer chips. Names, phone numbers, social security numbers, finger prints, and perhaps DNA readings: these and other details of an individual's ontology will be made available for instant scrutiny and adjudication. Processes are also being put in place that will ensure that no transactions will be permitted that will not allow the leaving behind of traces. The sheer alterity of technology is in fact assembling specific and vulnerable constellations of identity. The burgeoning phenomenon of 'identity theft' in turns fuels and necessitates spiralling levels of identity security, and so on and so forth.

What Baudrillardian versions of post-modern simulacra and alterity overlook is the historical reality that very often surges, with revolutions in technology being responses to heightened states of sovereign government alert. It is a well-known fact that in the USA the earliest communication networks were the result of research sponsored and funded by the Department of Defence (DOD). I am not saying that every effort sponsored by the DOD should be condemned as always already 'wrong,' or conservative. My point is deeper than that. The ideological skewing of the project is not just at the level of demonstrable teleology or objective. When the DOD sets up a specific research project, the very parameters of the project are delineated in alignment with a particular notion of 'intelligence' and information finding that rules out other possibilities and alternatives.

In the absence of other official parameters or templates of readability, the dominant profile of identity becomes the baseline against and in terms of which all other significations and representations of identity are calibrated and evaluated. Thus, if I am profiled and consequently found suspicion-worthy, based on the fact that I have a certain sounding name or that I am affiliated to a certain institution or that I sport a certain style of beard or exhibit certain dietary preferences, then it is up to me to prove that I am innocent despite and against the fact that the profiling process has already found me potentially and even pre-emptively guilty on an ontological plane. My very readable ontology has rendered me vulnerable and my performance has to dispel such an *a priori* condemnation.

   This scenario of paranoid vigilance on the part of the dominant discourse has, after 9/11, been made even more ironic and hilarious. The US government has now come to understand that now the enemy does not have to look like an Arab or a Palestinian, or sport certain 'costumes' or speak with a certain accent. Now the 'they' can look, act, speak, dress, and be educated 'just like us.' The enemy now is all pervasive, protean: s/he is now that ultimate impostor who has found a way to perform 'our' ontology as though it were his/hers. The supreme alterity of the system of detection that is supposed to work for us by smoking out forms of identity that are terror-bearing and protect our forms that are terror-receiving now has to step up its vigilance. It is not enough any more to detect dangerous ontology epidermally. It has now become imperative to 'other' the entire world of reality so that the dominant Self can revel in its infinite paranoia. And my point is that the pleasures of such paranoia would not have been possible but for the alterity of the gaze instituted in the first place by the dominant discourse and its need for complete and absolute invulnerability. In other words, the alterity of technology is indeed susceptible to ideological control and manipulation. What seems to pass off as sheer formal virtuosity or technological miracle is in fact a mode of instrumentality brought to bear on the body politic by the unilateral dominant discourse.

   I would like to conclude this article on a register of critical ambivalence: a register well employed by Paul Simon in his lyric, 'Boy in the Bubble,' where the haunting refrain goes something like this: 'These are days of miracle, and wonder. Don't cry, baby, don't cry.' The lyric is replete with images of technological razzle-dazzle, virtual instantaneity and synchronicity, immanent implosions of the world into the global village, juxtapositions of irreconcilable oppositions and antagonisms, dizzying nodal flows of communication and signification that transcend traditional understanding, and self-reflexive feats dangling in the temporality of the nanosecond. But the poet is unable to determine if these wild and exciting goings on that seem to be like a process of pure and anomic becoming are good or bad; progressive or retrogressive; comforting or terrifying. The sense of wonder invoked in the lyric is both banal and sublime: banal since the miracle is best understood as nothing more than a congeries of formal effects that are mechanically available to the apparatus of technology; sublime since the semantic consequences of technological transformations seem potentially extra-ordinary. So, which is it: banal or sublime?

Similarly, are the possibilities of infinite self-reflexivity truly transformative, or are they mere obsessive-compulsive disorders brought about by the sheer facticity of what can be done, thanks to technology. The address to the baby, the inheritor of the future from the present, borders between a real assurance and an ironic evisceration of all possibilities of comfort. This aporia cannot really be broken open unless the all-important question of the human relationship to technology and its alterity can be resolved, with some end in view. What does it mean: 'to establish a relationship?' What is the nature of the human, and what is the disposition of technology before they begin to interface with each other, seamlessly as in Baudrillard's formulation (1991)? Is this relationship optional or mandatory? Is there a human reason not to concede too much to the alterity of the apparatus? Is there a technological rationale not to concede to the ideology of the human? Does not this very alterity of the machine constitute a prosthesis of the human? Where in this play of simulation does accountability reside?

Notes

1. Increasingly, representation becomes dominant, as 'simulacra' or hyperreal representations are substituted for a reality that has little or no foundation in experience. Television images, in our present age of spectacles, are an excellent example of hyperreality—Ed.
2. According to modern philosophers like Immanuel Kant (1929), the *a priori* in philosophy is the knowledge gained or justified by reason alone, 'prior to' or 'without' experience. According to some post-modern theorists, knowledge formation or epistemology is performative, since it is defined in terms of our dynamic, shifting and temporary interaction with others. In other words, there is little certainty or permanence in our knowledge-systems, according to post-modernists like Foucault (1972)—Ed.
3. This implies fluidity, rather than fixity of identity—Ed.
4. For Barthes (1972), the simulacrum is a kind of representation of the world as seen through a selective filtering process, simply because the world cannot be represented in its sensuous entirety. For Baudrillard (1991), the simulacrum is understood in a semiotic context as a copy of a copy, which has no referent in the real world. In other words, the 'original' or the 'ideal', in the Platonic sense, does not exist—Ed.
5. Barthes (1972) makes two assumptions here: 1) the simulacrum is the structure, and 2) the structure is the ghostly 'other' that is tacit and

unexpressed within the body of the real. He was critiqued summarily by Macherey (1978), the first great Althusserian literary theorist, for Barthes' representational and representative quietism on behalf of the 'real.' Even though Barthes, a leftist if not overtly a Marxist–communist intellectual, does declare that the simulacrum is produced not disinterestedly, Macherey, the Structuralist–Marxist literary theorist, makes the claim that in Barthes' politically neutral theory, the simulacrum does not produce anything new. It does not, to use Marx's famous formulation, do knowledge with the idea of changing reality, rather than produce an acquiescent commentary that is in fact sanctioned by reality itself. Macherey, as a Marxist, is looking for a mode of production epistemology that refuses to fold back within the sovereignty of the original and the epistemology of representation that the original sanctions into existence.

6. Structuralist–Marxism is a theory developed by Louis Althusser (1998), who argued that humans have no intrinsic qualities (or essence), but socially produced attributes (accidents). These attributes are the creation of social structures or institutions. A practical result of this is that there is no essential 'human nature' which cannot be changed, and so in order to change human behaviour, it is simply necessary to alter the appropriate social structures. The problem here is that Structuralist–Marxists tend to view structures as unchanging. That is why the question regarding the 'alterity of structures' must be posed—Ed.

7. In his substantive critique of anthropology, Fabian (2002) deploys the notion of 'coevalness' to drive home the point that within the one given objective world, both the Self and the Other are nothing but coeval, and it is the denial of this coevalness by anthropology that results in the rigid and non-negotiable Self-Other form of binarity. If Fabian uses 'coevalness' in the context of inter-cultural and inter-historical understanding, what about employing the same term in the context of the production of knowledge in general? What happens when, in the context of the Cartesian Cogito, Being or Reality is to be repeated into knowledge? Is such a repetition an identical repetition or a non-identical repetition?

8. Judith Butler's (1993) thesis of gender as performance questions the conventional feminist categories of sex as biological and gender as social, by claiming that the sexed body is itself culturally constructed by what she terms the regulative discourse of disciplinary techniques. These disciplinary techniques force the subject to perform bodily in specific ways—Ed.

9. See Ralph Waldo Emerson quotation from Ted Coltman's 'See Ya at the Mall—Insights on the Evolution of Communication and Community.' http://www.mediamall.com/nowmedia/views/seeya/html/.

10. In other words, the means of representation or the representation of reality becomes more important than the reality itself—Ed.

11. Jacques Derrida (1970) claimed that neither the author nor external reality counted for much; the text was supreme and given to endless interpretation. There was really nothing outside the text—Ed.

References

Althusser, Louis and Etienne Balibar. 1998. *Reading Capital*. Trans. by Ben Brewster. London: Verso.

Barthes, Roland. 1972. 'The Structuralist Activity', in *Critical Essays*. Trans. by Richard Howard. Evanston, Ill.: Northwestern University Press.

Baudrillard, Jean. 1991. 'Two Essays', *Science Fiction Studies*. Trans. by Arthur B. Evans, 18(3).

Butler, Judith. 1993. *Bodies That Matter: On the Discursive Limits of Sex*. New York: Routledge.

Derrida, Jacques. 1970. 'Structure, Sign and Play in the Discourse of the Human Sciences', in Richard Macksey and Eugenio Donato (eds), *The Structuralist Controversy*. Baltimore: Johns Hopkins University Press.

Fabian, Johannes. 2002. *Time and the Other*. New York: Columbia University Press.

Foucault, Michel. 1972. *Archaeology of Knowledge*. Trans. by A. M. Sheridan. London: Tavistock Publications Ltd.

Kant, Immanuel. 1929. *Critique of Pure Reason*. Trans. by Norman Kemp Smith. London: Palgrave Macmillan.

Macherey, Pierre. 1978. *A Theory of Literary Production*. Trans. by G. Wall. London: Routledge and Kegan Paul.

Macleish, Archibald. 1985. *Collected Poems, 1917–1982*. Boston: Houghton Mifflin.

McLuhan, Marshall. 2001. *The Medium is the Message: An Inventory of Effects*. California: Gingko Press.

Simon, Herbert. 1996. *The Sciences of the Artificial*. Cambridge, Mass.: MIT Press.

4

What Mobile Phones Make of Us

A. Srivathsan

> *Homo Faber is inherently a creature of technology, because there*
> *could be no art without pencils and paper, paintbrushes, guitars and*
> *saxophones and word processors*
> Michael Chorost,
> *Rebuilt: How Becoming Part Computer Made Me More Human.*

In early 2006, a University in Chennai banned cell phones from its campus. The authorities went to the extent of raiding the ladies' hostels and confiscating mobile phones. Traffic Police on the streets continue to dissuade drivers from using mobile phones while driving. In West Bengal, doctors were prevented from using mobile phones in operation theatres. Religious believers squirm when priests use cell phones during rituals. Mobile phones are omnipresent and the world suddenly appears like one big chatterbox. The sign to switch off mobile phones is ubiquitous. To some, this indicates that we have gone out of control, have gone berserk, and become irresponsible. As always, we think the machines are responsible for our behaviour. This lamentation quickly leads to discipline and regulation and there is a call to regulate the cell phones, if not ban them altogether. The wishful thinking behind this is that men and women freed of machines could get back to their natural good selves. Isn't it the apple in the Garden of Eden that always takes the blame?

Equation between Humans and Tools

Do the phones make us talk more? Is it another instance of the machine taking over the human will and driving a wedge through our mortal weaknesses? Is it a familiar fear of machines manipulating mankind in their new digital avatar? Wanting to talk and share our ideas is an *uber* desire—primordial and fundamental. We have moved from small clusters of community and compact settlements to larger cities. While we had the desire to communicate and huddle, we lost the tool and believed that we got fragmented. Suddenly, cathartically, we discover no one is too far away, and we rush to huddle in company as we walk, fly and work. Old connections and urges are played through the new tool. Group messaging indicates new forms of community creatively reorganised in the address books. It is not only connecting—even bullying, stalking and all the other troubling relations continue through the phone. The desire is actualised through technology and it becomes visible. The self that had hitherto contained the urge to speak or express the fear is revealed.

I am not proposing that mobile phones are passive technological artefacts in the service of human will and desire. Neither am I suggesting that it is a prosthetic element that extends human activity and faculties. May be it is all of these, but what I wish to look at is the relation between this tool with the body and self. It makes us as much as we make of them; here the device transcends its status of being passive or prosthetic and it never isolates itself from the body and self. Whenever we discuss tools as mere tools we are not only ascertaining our authority over them but also want to inscribe that authority on them. The assertion comes in the form of erasure of traces of the tool on us. We constantly wish to assert that we could be free of them; when we are reminded to the contrary, we get concerned.

The fear and anxiety to retain the autonomy and purity of the human body has been there for long, particularly in Hinduism. A perfect body is mired in religious beliefs that are necessary to ensure a perfect rebirth. The purity of the body has to be sustained. Consequently, technological revolution and their artefacts cannot penetrate, add on and substitute bodily functions. When they do, for convenience or for other reasons, we discourage them through the rhetoric of human will over machines. Ergonomic demands on machines partly comfort us. We are reassured to know that machines have to depend on the natural body. This article is not to be constructed as a eulogy of machines, but a reminder that the tools have not been given their due in spite of their influential role in our lives.

Gordon Childe notes that human beings have improved themselves and never benefited from biological adaptations.[1] From clothes to habitat, we have always depended on the tools we have found or invented. He concludes that we improve and form ourselves in relationship to our tools. Humans have articulated self and civilisation together with their tools; they have made us as much as we have made them. The tool here is not prosthetic. The etymology of the word 'prosthetic' means 'addition to what exists'. This extension many a time is associated with or literally replaces the human organ. But tools do not always do that. Second, in the conception of the prosthetic, the relation is one way. The usefulness of the tool is understood only with reference to human purpose or interest; but what it does in return to the body or self is not registered. When the usefulness of the tool is exhibited, simultaneously, the inadequacy of the natural body is also marked. At another level, the usefulness of the tool shapes the idea of the self. The sword makes a knight as much as the knight brings the sword into being. To think of painter without a brush is impossible. Do we not often exclaim how the brush comes to life at the hands of an artist? The idea of art affects the perception of the world and brings in a sense of aesthetic that shapes the self. Imagine what notions of the body would be in circulation in the absence of the tool named cloth.

Surprisingly, archaeologists have not tried to explain human history in terms of materials and technology. Iron ages, copper ages are not just some abstract markers in time. If that was the story of the past, the story of the future will be told in terms of people's attempt to live with tools of a dematerialised world.

We could borrow Bruno Latour 's thesis (1993), to coin a new aphorism that captures the relationship between tools and humans. We could declare that 'we were never fully humans'. The idea of a human fully in control is wishful thinking rather than a reality; it is a myth a few want to preserve. When we set to understand and order the world from this viewpoint, we constantly negate the influence of many things non-human in spite of these playing a crucial role in our lives. Traditional mythologies always had animals and tools as an integral part in the defining of human beings and their gods. Contemporary interpretations of these mythologies explain animals as vehicles and tools and weapons. What they fail to see is that the idea of body, self, and image is conceived and includes non-human and inanimate entities. In fact, there are no inanimate entities. Every weapon is as animate as the person. There are instances of inanimate objects, as in the case of the *Sudharshana Chakra*, a disc-like weapon accompanying the Hindu god Vishnu, that are conceived in an iconic form. Texts and poems describe Vishnu's weapon as a person and so is it worshipped as an extension of the god. Like a *mobius* strip,[2] tool and man work one into the other.

In a few parts of the world, human life and its calendar are still imagined in the form of animals. This interaction between human and non-human in the making of the body and self seems to be lost recently. To a certain extent, environmental debates have critiqued this idea. They brought in some serious reconsideration of this inter-action. However it is limited, as nature is understood only in terms of plants, animals, land and its resources. The image of *Maximal*[3] by the Dutch architect Ben van Berkel as a source for architecture design held promise, but lost itself in the din of formal analysis and debates. Catherine Ingraham's recent work (2006) takes further the connections between the human and non-human in the making of habitat. In many of these discussions, human artefacts are not in high consideration. Environmental debates have looked at tools with suspicion. Probably, it is now, in the era of digital culture, that the tools will get recognition.

The increasing attention on cyborgs is an index of this. We can understand Donna Haraway's claims that we were never fully humans. She wraps up the issue by saying that

> a cyborg world might be about lived social and bodily realities in which people are not afraid of their joint kinship with animals and machines, not afraid of permanently partial identities and contradictory standpoints (Haraway 1990: 196).

For many years, we have allowed technological artefacts to pene-trate the human body. The idea of a healthy body is no more a given condition; it is at best an ideal. It is now agreed that human bodies require technological and chemical support. People with technological aids like pace makers, cochlear implant, pig heart, plastic surgery bring the idea of cyborgs closer to humankind. They remind us of our relation with technological artefacts. These changes to the bodies have gone well with many and they seem to have made adjustments to their identities. We have more than come to terms with this inter-action. A few now declare that they have become more 'human' ever since they became a part of a computer. As Michael Chorost would state

> I think my experience with the computer in my skull has given me an inkling of what it must be like to be Homo Faber ....The logic of the incantation has penetrated both my body and soul (2005).

What is being said of machines inside the body is not said about the machines external to it. Unlike things internal, things external are not considered interconnected or deemed influential on the body or self. External artefacts are viewed as dispensable objects, and any connection to the person is at the level of a symbol or ornament or adornment.

The Aura of Mobile Phones

A mobile phone, apart from expressing in an autonomous way that it is a phone, also brings into existence other associations like—as Andrew Ross would call it—the 'new smartness' (1994: 335). It functions as a sign—an instrument to indicate something about the person. Mobile phones are endorsed or constructed as an intelligent invention and looked at as a means to appear or get organised and efficient. To embrace it in public would be considered as a display of the user's own intelligence or smartness. In this construction also are coded other subtexts like, class, taste and so on. This argument is useful in the sense that it traces the influence of tools in the conception of the self. As mentioned earlier, this has the danger of relegating the mobile phone to the status of a symbol or an ornament. This is a one-way construction and focuses only on the external space the mobile occupies.

The concept of aura will help provide an alternative perspective to this issue. There are three concepts of aura available for consideration. First, for cultural theorists, the idea of aura is associated with the idea of originality or authenticity of an object. It is some thing that they wish to reduce objects to, as the latter multiply or proliferate. This concept would privilege the human being as the authentic reference point, and any reproduction of its function through devices like phones will only reduce his importance.

Second, the mystics look at aura as a mass of energy that surrounds the physical body. It is considered expressive of the qualities of the person. The aura is visible to the initiated and has properties such as vivid colouration that is believed to describe the character of the person. It is an external manifestation but linked organically and inextricably to the body and the self. But it still retains a one-way relation, by privileging what is within the body.

The third version of aura comes from the information technologists. Scientists at the Carnegie Mellon University have termed one of their projects as aura computing.[4] This project in its specifics is about mobile computing. It aims to produce an 'invisible halo of computing and information services that persists regardless of location'. In other words, it aims to create and make use of a large information field that surrounds the user. This information field acts on behalf of the user and works for him. This relieves him of the burden of providing details and to constantly adjust to new environments.

For example, if you are a mobile phone user, you not only exchange information through the device with another person, but also start receiving information of products or about the places you are in. You can be recognised as a foreigner in London, and the information of the place and road maps will pop up to help you navigate the new landscape. Aura is your personal information field that will interact on your behalf with others in a specific context. This aura is a two-way concept. It is externally linked as well as internally connected. Unlike the mystic aura, this aura is not unilaterally related to the user. It is not simply an expression of the inside or personal profile of the user. It is dynamic and works for and works on the context, and brings in the context to bear upon the body and the self.

The personal aura constructed through mobile devices and computing breaks the idea of a person as being anchored to a place and limited to the opportunities of that moment. It has allowed people to be anywhere anytime, and be met by others anytime anyplace. The phone does not look at a person as being fragmented or isolated from a group or a context. It seriously challenges the idea of context. The expanse of space and vastness of the community are felt as never before. It has released the idea of conversation from its immediate space and time. We have been virtually performing or creatively imagining this all along. We have always wanted to bridge the loneliness of the present, here and now, and connect with the reassuring someone at some other place.

Mobile Phones and Self-Actualisation

What mobile phones allow us is to have an intense perception of our self. To use Simmel's argument (2001), this tool has enabled the individual to positively negotiate his independence. To Simmel, the deepest problem of modern life is the attempt of the individual to maintain his identity and pace against all external powers, culture and techniques of life. The modern metropolis throws violent stimuli, unexpected fluctuations and discontinuities at the individual who is used to a different rhythm and perception of life. The individual positively negotiates these new stimuli by switching on to a familiar voice, rhythm and emotion through the mobile. To paraphrase Simmel, the individual creates a protective organ for himself against the profound disruption created by the fluctuations and discontinuities of the external stimuli. Fran Tonkiss summarises this phenomenon succinctly when she observes

> ...Mobile technology and personal stereo....these devices realize the logic of urban detachment perfectly. Immersed in a private soundscape, engaged in another interactive scene, you can set certain limits to the city as a shared perceptual or social space (2005: 117).

Shoshana Zuboff and Jim Maxmin (2002) in their study claim that people seek control over the quality of their lives, especially when they inhabit a stressful world. In their perception, individuals do not look forward to technology and artefacts, which only address their individual needs. They do not want to be passive consumers. They want the whole consuming experience to help their 'psychological self-determination'. They would not prefer to be curtailed by the technologies imposed by the inventors or the state. They are no more willing to take recourse to the safe haven of cyber space, which do not seriously help them actualise their 'selves'. Avatar and related immersive technologies are like dreams and wishful thinking. On the one hand, one has to reposition oneself in cyberspace. On the other hand, mobiles have not only seamlessly adjusted to the body, but also have opened the possibility of self-actualisation. The proliferation of the mobile comes from the experience of self-determination. It allows one to deal with people, space and time in the manner one chooses to. It has strengthened the notion of the self by positively engaging the limitations of the context. At one level, the context has become a matter of choice. One could plug into the city if one wants to or else switch on to be with someone else.

To Meyrowitz (1985), the new media convey expression with communication. He states that, 'One can stop communicating at will, but one cannot stop expressing'. He argues that what most electronic media have done is to reunite expression and communication. Mobile phones have combined this effectively and paved the way for self-actualisation. So, when people restrict the use of mobile phones in the name of rational use what they actually try to repress is its usage as an expression of the self. The prolific and incessant use of mobile phone expresses a self that has restated the urge to talk in a language as a principal means to connect with the rest of society. Short messages in the middle of the class and seminar are an act of transcending, transgressing and subverting the Establishment. If parents give mobile phones to their offspring in order to keep a tab on their daughters, the daughters switch *SIM* cards with friends to make the calls they want to make. Both fragmentation and surveillance are subverted. Fragmentation can no more be defined with confidence. The self now may not be all that alienated.

Notes

1. See Childe (1983). I thank M.S.S. Pandian for bringing to my notice this comparison.
2. A *mobius* strip is a surface with only one side and one boundary component. A model can easily be created by taking a paper strip and giving it a half-twist, and then merging the ends of the strip together to form a single strip. It is considered to be a mathematical curiosity—Ed.
3. Maximal is intended to be seamless architecture, with superimposed and blended images.
4. See *http://www.cs.cmu.edu/~aura/*.

References

Childe, V. Gordon. 1983. *Man Makes Himself*. USA: Penguin.
Chorost, Michael. 2005. *Rebuilt: How Becoming Part Computer Made Me More Human*. London: Souvenir Press.
Haraway, Donna. 1990. 'A Cyborg Manifesto: Science, Technology and Socialist–Feminism in the Late Twentieth Century', in Linda J. Nicholson (ed.), *Feminism/Postmodernism*. London: Routledge.

Ingraham, Catherine. 2006. *Architecture, Animals, Human: The Asymmetrical Condition.* New York: Routledge.

Latour, Bruno. 1993. *We Have Never Been Modern.* Trans. by Catherine Porter. England: Simon and Schuster.

Meyrowitz, Joshua. 1985. *No Sense of Place: The Impact of Electronic Media on Social Behaviour.* Oxford: Oxford University Press.

Ross, Andrew. 1994. 'The New Smartness', in Gretchen Bender and Timothy Drucker (eds), *Culture on the Brink: Ideologies of Technology.* Seattle: Bay Press.

Simmel, Georg. 2000. 'The Metropolis and Mental Life', in Neil Leach (ed.), *Rethinking Architecture*, pp. 69–79. London: Routledge.

Tonkiss, Fran. 2005. *Space, the City and Social Theory: Social Relations and Urban Forms.* Cambridge: Polity Press.

Zuboff, Shoshana and Jim Maxmin. 2002. *The Support Economy: Why Corporations are Failing Individuals and the Next Episode of Capitalism.* New York: Viking Penguin.

5

The Unplugged City and the Global Nomad[1]

André Lemos and Julio Valentim

Generalised Connection Environment

The computerisation of society, which began in the 1970s, seems to be already established in the major western cities. What is at stake at the beginning of the 21st century is the rise of a new phase of the Information Society, initiated by the Internet in the 1980s, and radicalised by wireless computation with mobile telephones, wireless internet access networks ('Wi-Fi'[2] and 'Wi-Max'[3]) and the domestic proximity networks with 'bluetooth'[4] technology. It is a question of transformations of social practices, in the experiencing of urban space and in the manner of producing and consuming information. With the emergence of the era of wireless technologies, it is the network that begins to encompass users and objects in an environment of generalised connection.

Cyberculture's development occurred with the appearance of microcomputers in the 1970s, with technological convergence and the establishment of the personal computer (PC). In the 1980s–1990s, we witnessed the popularity of the Internet and the transformation of the PC into a 'collective computer' (CC), connected to cyberspace, the PC's replacement by the CC (Lemos 2002). Here, the network is the computer and the computer is a connection machine. Now, in the 21st century, with the development of mobile computation and the new nomad technologies (laptops, palms, mobile phones), what is underway is the phase of ubiquitous, pervasive and sentient computation, emphasising mobility.[5] We are in the era of connection. Now we have 'mobile collective computers' (mCC).

With the development of mobile technologies, mCC has established itself as ubiquitous wireless computation. It is a question of forms of connection between men and men, machines and men, and machines and machines motivated by the technological nomadism of contemporary culture and by the development of ubiquitous computation (3G,[6] Wi-Fi), of sentient computation (RFID,[7] bluetooth) and pervasive computation, in addition to the natural continuation of generalised emission processes and of cooperative work from the first phase of the CC (blogs, forums, chats, free software, peer to peer, etc.). In the connection era, the network is transformed into a generalised connection 'environment', involving the user in complete mobility. As W. Mitchell shows,

> 'gradually emerging from the messy but irresistible extension of wireless coverage is the possibility of a radically reimagined, reconstructed, electronic form of nomadicity—a form that is grounded not just in the terrain that nature gives us, but in sophisticated, well-integrated wireless infrastructure, combined with other networks, and deployed on a global scale'.
>
> —(2003: 57)

Digital technologies and the new forms of wireless connection are creating flexible uses of urban space: nomadic access to the Internet, permanent connectivity with mobile telephones, sentient objects that transmit information to various devices, radio frequency tags (RFID) that permit the 'tracking' of objects, equipment with bluetooth that creates domestic networks, etc. The contemporary city is becoming a city of mobility and of permanent connection, in which mobile technologies are beginning to form part of its scenery (Furtado 2002; Horan 2000; Puglisi 1999). As Cooper *et al.* (2002) state.

> 'when we think about the empirical phenomena of mobile phone/ device use in everyday life, we find that sociology and philosophy contain a number of terms which seem apt, but have or have had somewhat different referents: for example, social mobility, the problematising of the public/private distinction, the structural transformation of public sphere, the metaphysics of presence, phonocentrism, and, of course, the immutable mobile' (2002: 288).

In this interface of contemporary cities with the new communication and information technologies, from the management of urban planning to commonplace practices of everyday life, various facets of the connection era are emerging. Mobility is seen as the main characteristic of the digital technologies. The mobile technologies,

'...are sold on the basis that they provide 'anytime, anywhere' connection, whether that connection is via voice or data connectivity. Advertising presents mobile technologies as devices to transcend the 'limitation' of geography and distance, including those posed by geographical differences in the location of work and activities' (*ibid.:* 296).

The connection era is the era of mobility. The wireless Internet, sentient objects and latest generation mobile telephony are bringing up new issues with relation to public space and private space, such as the privatisation of public space. The new forms of wireless communication are redefining the use of the space of place and the spaces of flows (Castells 1996a). In contemporary cities, the traditional spaces of place (street, squares, avenues, monuments) are, little by little, being transformed into spaces of flows, flexible communicational spaces, or 'digital places' (Horan 2000). With relation to the forms of mobile communication, we can say that,

'a reconfiguration of space and time is taking place, a reconfiguration that implies that the form and purpose of the communication is what comes to describe 'public' and 'private', rather than the space in which that communication is carried out'.
—(Cooper *et al.* 295)

'Mobile' Culture

The contemporary practices linked to the cyberculture technologies have shaped contemporary culture as a culture of mobility. Various authors have shown how contemporary societies are immersed in a process of successive territorialisations and de-territorialisations (Deleuze and Guattari 1986), of nomadic and tribal practices, both in terms of subjectivity as well as of affinities (Maffesoli 1997); of reshaping of urban spaces (Horan 2000; Meyrowitz 2004; Mitchell 2003) and of the establishment of a sociology of mobility (Cooper 2002; Urry 1999; Urry *et al.* 2000). The idea of mobility, associated with telematic connection, is essential in order to get to know the new characteristics of contemporary cities.

The social sciences, including here the communication sciences, should make an effort to understand the current transformations that take place in synergy mobility and wireless communication technologies. The new wireless digital technologies are bringing up the era of ubiquity, whose origin is in the works of Mark Weiser. His pioneering work of 1991 launched the bases for what he called 'Ubicomp', or ubiquitous computation. For Weiser, 'Ubicomp', 'takes into account the natural human environment and allows computers themselves 'to vanish into the background' (1991: 1). In Weiser's 'Ubicomp', it is the computer that disappears in the objects. As the author states at the beginning of his visionary article, 'the most profound technologies are those that disappear. They weave themselves into the fabric of everyday life until they are indistinguishable from it' (Weiser 1991).

Examples of this ubiquitous computation are becoming obvious. Projects in cities are expanding ('Amble Time', 'Sonic City', 'Tejp', 'Texting Glances', 'Urban Tapestries'), and clearly show this transition (Galloway 2003). It is really a question of hybrid practices involving physical space and electronic space. This new configuration is going to disseminate technological nomadism practices. It is in this sense that J. Meyrowitz (2004) speaks of a return to primitive nomadic culture, transforming us into 'global nomads in the digital veldt'. The central point of Meyrowitz's argument is that today's world, marked by mobile technologies and by various forms of social flexibility, is placing contemporary culture in a more fluid form of social organisation, with less rigid roles and interchangeable social places that come very close to the social form of the first human groupings. For Meyrowitz,

> 'we have returned in many ways to the overlapping experiences and role blurring of nomads. Once again, we have a hard time getting away from each other. That is, it is increasingly difficult to separate one social sphere from another, one activity from another, one set of knowledge and experience from another.
>
> —(2004: 25)

This leads us to the need for analysis of this society of mobility, having to seek the construction of what the English sociologist John Urry calls a 'mobile sociology' (2000). The various forms of contemporary mobility (of people, of objects, of information, of refuse, of products and of services) require an effort to understand them on the part of the social sciences. For Urry, we are really going from the dilemma of 'social as society' (central polemic of the sociological field) to having to think of the new paradigm of 'social as mobility'. This effort should be undertaken since the society of mobility takes the shape of an international flow of images, information, migrations, tourism, financial capital flows that places us in the midst of a society of planetary flows (Castells 1996b). These global flows had already been detected by thinkers such as Augé (1994); Castells (1996b); Deleuze and Guattari (1986); Graham and Marvin (1996); Lefebvre (1986); Sassen (2001); Wheeler, J. O. *et al.* (2002), among others, presenting the idea that thinking of society is thinking in terms of urban mobility, de-territorialisation and territorialisation, of global cities. For Urry, this contemporary society requires thinking in motion: complex, fluid and de-territorialised. Sociology and communication sciences should respond to the challenge of thinking 'new agendas for a discipline that is losing its central concept of human society. It is a discipline organised around networks, mobility and horizontal fluidities… intellectual mobilities are good for the social sciences' (2000: 200).

Based on this epistemological challenge, we can try to understand the social practices resulting from cyberculture. The new wireless technologies will give a new impulse to this society of mobility.

Mobile Phone — Remote Control of Daily Life

Today, there are more mobile telephone users than Internet users in the world, and this figure tends to grow. As we have seen, it is a question of a growing adherence to mobility, creating a new social dynamics for the city. A change in space–time perception is being established. As Licoppe and Heurtin (2002) declare,

> 'The mobile phone's use as a key resource for successful coordi-
> nation over space and time lies in part in its strong impact on
> perceptions of space. On the other hand, which is the point we will
> delve into more deeply here, the person who calls or is being called
> by the mobile phone user can no longer assign a definite location
> to the other person from either the geographical or the social
> perspective' (2002: 96).

The mobile phone is becoming a 'tele-everything', a piece of equipment that is at the same time a telephone, camera, television, movies, receiver of journalistic information, dispenser of e-mails and SMS, WAP,[8] updater of sites (moblogs), locator by means of GPS, music player (MP3 and other formats), electronic wallet. We can now talk, watch TV, pay bills, interact with other people via SMS, take photos, listen to music, pay parking fees, buy tickets for the movies, attend a party and even organise political and/or hedonistic mobilisations (the case of smart and flash mobs). The mobile phone expresses the radicalisation of digital convergence, transforming itself into a 'tele-everything' for mobile and informational management of everyday life.

The mobile phone is today in fact more than a machine for oral and individual contact. It is a true communication centre, a remote control for various forms of action in everyday life, a way of keeping in permanent contact with one's 'individual community' (Rheingold 2003). In Japan and Finland, for example, the use of SMS is a social phenomenon (Ito 2004; Katz and Aakhus 2002; Rheingold 2003), and can be used as an electronic wallet for payments, as a way of locating people, as with the 'i-mode' system of DoCoMo in Japan,[9] allowing people using mobile phones to know whether friends (registered with the system) are in the same locality, making for potential contacts. The dominant idea here is that the mobile phone enables permanent contact with the world. For the Japanese anthropologist M. Ito (2004),

> Because of this portable, virtual peer space, the city is no longer a space of urban anonymity; even when out shopping, solo youths will send photos to friends of a pair of shoes they just bought, or send fast-breaking news about a hot sale that is just opening. After meeting face to face, a trail of text messages continues the conversation as friends disperse in trains, buses and on foot, nimble thumbs touch-typing on numeric keypads.

Several studies point out the various characteristics of the use of mobile phones in various countries (Cooper *et al.* 2002; Katz and Aakhus 2002). Despite the cultural peculiarities that determine ways of using mobile phones, the expansion of their use seems to be unanimous, in the number of users and in forms of utilisation (voice, SMS, purchases, contacts, etc.). According to Katz, since the invention of the telephone in 1876, this equipment's use has placed in discussion the social role of this invention and the forms of relation between public and private space. The need for permanent mobility and contact appear to be the major propelling aspects of mobile telephony consumption today. The emphasis is on the possibility for control and coordination of everyday actions, as an indispensable instrument for the working world, as an instrument for mobility and speed in the exchange of information, as a way of maintaining a circle of friends in 'perpetual contact' (Katz and Aakhus 2002); and as a way of increasing security and contact with relatives. As Katz declares,

> 'The telephone has dramatically changed how people live their lives and see their world. Another change of perhaps similar magnitude is in the offing with the mobilisation not only of speech but also of a novel array of compute-support communication and social interaction'.
> —(2002: 1)

The 'thumb tribe' phenomenon in Finland and Japan, for example, shows a growing use of the mobile phone as a dispenser of rapid, inter-personal and massive messages. The speed of the messages and of the contacts permits questioning as to whether what is at stake is a true process of communication, or whether this type of contact would only be for rapid exchanges of information, not characterising a true communicational activity. In a study on telephony in Italy, research shows that,

> 'the word "communication" is rarely associated with the mobile (3 per cent of cases); more people associate the telephone with the word "communication" (11 per cent). Evidently the mobile is considered an instrument that is not very suitable for communication, but is perhaps more suitable for a rapid exchange of information'.
> —(Fortunati 2002: 44)

According to Myerson (2001), the mobile telephone companies' strategy (and that of their advertising and marketing agencies) is to sell these instruments as a 'personal and mobile communication centre'. There is no differentiation between information and communication, and the emphasis on the image of a communication device seems to be filled with an ideology that seeks to show the 'communicational' revolution underway. We can say that what is at stake are processes for exchanges of information that are not necessarily characterised as complex communicational forms.

In developing countries like Brazil, the use of mobile phones is a constant aspect of everyday life. There is not a great use yet of SMS or of the smart phones' other possibilities, but the growth is exponential.

In Brazil, mobile telephony possesses two types of mobile tele-communication service: Cell Mobile Service (CMS) and Personal Mobile Service (PMS). CMS is the terrestrial mobile telecommuni-cation service, interconnected with the public telecommunications network, and accessed by means of portable terminals for individual use. PMS is the terrestrial mobile telecommunication service with collective interest that enables communication between mobile stations and from mobile stations to other stations. PMS is charac-terised by making possible communication between stations in the same Registration Area or access to telecommunications networks with collective interest. Starting in 2002, the Brazilian operators had to begin migrating from CMS to PMS. The Personal Mobile Service (PMS) is available to 86 per cent of the population and 48 per cent of the municipalities in Brazil. Eighty-seven per cent of the population is concentrated in municipalities with more than 15,000 inhabitants (38 per cent of the municipalities), and 13.8 per cent of the munici-palities in Brazil are still served by only one operator.[10]

If we compare the technologies and the services existing for mobile phones in Brazil with the Wi-Fi technologies and services available in the hotspots, we will notice that the Internet access velocities attained by the Wi-Fi technology are much higher than those obtained through connection by means of mobile phones. However, the area of coverage of the Internet via mobile phone is wider and the connec-tion is more stable. This leads some specialists to conjecture the replacement of mobile phones by Wi-Fi technology, including for telephone calls, by means of VoIP—Voice Technology using Internet Protocol. Other specialists believe that the Wi-Fi network will not compete, but rather will ally itself and integrate itself in a much more compatible way with the CDMA and GSM technologies which today dominate the mobile telephony world. The user, depending on his or her location, and on the type of connection he or she is establishing, one moment would be using the mobile phone infrastructure and the next moment the Wi-Fi, without even realising this. In this way, if the close relationship between Wi-Fi and mobile phones is well developed, we will be able to obtain great benefits in wide band diffusion.[11]

Although there are not yet any advanced uses of mobile telephony with the 3G pattern, we can say that the use of mobile phones in Brazil is growing. Since the population's access to mobile phones is greater than to computers and the Internet, mobile telephony can be a way to diminish the digital inclusion problem in Brazil, and could be associated here with new services such as 'm-gov' (electronic government with access based on mobile technologies), public utility services in general, access to the Internet, among other services.

Unplugged City and Wireless Internet

Contemporary cities are witnessing the growth of wireless access to the Internet (Wi-Fi). For access, a computer equipped with a wireless modem suffices. New practices and new uses of urban space will, little by little, constitute the main places of the connection era. The user will no longer go to the network point. The network is ubiquitous, surrounding the user in an environment of access. Several cities in the world are offering Wi-Fi to their citizens, making for a true 'unplugged city'.[12] Cities in France, Sweden, Switzerland, England, Estonia, Canada, Italy and several American cities are putting Wi-Fi networks in subways, buses, ships, in rural areas, in the cities' downtown sections. In Brazil, experiments are beginning to appear in small cities in the States of Rio de Janeiro[13] and São Paulo, in addition to airports, coffee shops, hotels and restaurants in several capital cities, as we will see below. The era of connection and of the mobile collective computer is changing the practical and imaginary relation of space. As Steven Levy states, 'when digital geography teams up with wireless technology and the web, the world takes some new dimensions' (2004: 56).

Since the beginning of 2000, a new Temporary Autonomous Zone—T.A.Z. (Bey 2001) is being created with wireless communities, known as Wi-Fi movement. Activists did the propagation, and today several companies and institutions are adopting the pattern. A mixture of clandestine radio and Web, the movement had the aim of releasing idle bandwidth (of users and companies) and the radio spectrum. These zones are called wireless local area networks (WLAN). The NYC Wireless group[14] is one of those responsible for the dissemination of free connection zones, small wireless 'WLANS' in New York. Other experiments are underway around the globe in which several cities are offering this alternative access, sometimes in a gratuitous way, to their citizens.[15]

The movement for release of wide band through radio waves is not so new and goes back to the pioneers of the Ethernet, such as

Brewster Kahle, founder of SFLan. Today, activists are seeking to build wireless networks in various points of the cities in a cooperative, distributive spirit. The defenders of free wireless are convoking all those who possess a high-speed connection (cable, DSL, TI) to 'lend', gratuitously, their bandwidth to the public. The sharing of information, 'information wants to be free', the slogan of the digital counterculture, is now enriched by the sharing of bandwidth, seeking to democratise access to cyberspace. For Adam Shand of Portland's Personal Telco Project, in Portland,

> 'we are trying to bring the Internet back to the old times, before the commercial interests dominated it (...). We also hope to create point–to–point networks linking homes, schools, and cafeterias. As James Stevens, of London's Consumer in London states, "the question should be, how should we distribute these resources to people who do not have them? If you possess a 2 *megabits/s* DSL line in your work and everyone closes the doors at five o'clock, this line is available. It can be adjusted for public use."'
>
> —(Krane 2001)

The challenge is worldwide and we can even think of geometric growth if every personal computer becomes a hot spot. An open source Wi-Fi system can be created, a Wi-Fi Linux, or LI-FI, as Michael Schrage (2003) of *Technology Review* prefers: 'the concept is to create a Wi-Fi cooperative that turns individual laptops into potential nodes, routers, and hub of a global network...' (2003: 20). The connection era is in fact a wireless one. As an activist states, 'you cannot stock bandwidth. If you do not use it, it is wasted' (Krane 2001). The freedom of cyberspace may be blowing up.

Amidst growing debates on digital exclusion, democratisation and access to the new technologies, the activists of the wireless communities are building simple, creative solutions. The question of the spectrum is becoming essential for the development of wireless Internet systems (Albernaz 2003). For Weinberger (2003), the liberalisation of the spectrum is central to the connection era[16] since 'current spectrum policy is based on bad science enshrined in obsolete ways of thinking. The basic metaphors we've used are just plain wrong' (Weinberger 2003). Authors such as Larry Press are showing that the Wi-Fi forms of connection can be solutions for developing countries (Press 2003). What matters is putting on the agenda the democratisation of access through the spirit of sharing that made the Internet a social phenomenon. For Anthony Townsend, responsible for the NYWireless project, the emergence of this 'untethered city' is due to the development of the mobile technologies. For Townsend,

> '... the implications of the new infrastructure model were only just beginning to be understood as the first decade of the 21st century unfolded. Instead of being isolated within offices and homes, connectivity was spreading to streets, parks, coffee shops, and other newly digitally mediated urban public spaces. Instead of bringing the user to the network, for the first time the network was being brought to the user'.
>
> —(2003)

The practice of putting antennas made at home in order to increase the range or to locate points of access on the street (practices known as warchalking and wardriving) are expanding.[17] Unusual practices such as bicycles and knapsacks that create temporary wireless access zones are appearing in the USA and in Europe. Regarding the 'magic bicycle', the author states: 'mixing public art with techno-activism, Magic bikes are perfect for setting up ad hoc Internet connectivity for art and culture events, emergency access, public demonstrations, and communities on the struggling end of the digital divide'. The same thing occurs with the Bedouin project,[18] a knapsack that furnishes wireless access and can be used in political and/or artistic demonstrations.

But there is resistance. Several access providers prohibit retransmission, vetoing, by contract, making their connection available (they consider it as subleasing) to third parties (Thompson 2001). Others declare that the lack of security limits the idea. Specialists are showing that the network is not secure, since cybernetic vandals (crackers) could take advantage of the free connection to disseminate viruses or steal credit cards. Crackers and hackers, who have available access to the public areas of these networks, can easily invade systems by means of the creation of a false disconnection message.

Since 2001 companies have placed hotspots in coffee shops and stores following the new trend to mobile internet. One of the current problems lies in the companies' difficulty in setting up a network that is operational in a specific urban space. For this, some thousands of hotspots would be necessary, since the range of hundreds of metres is much less than the coverage of mobile telephony networks. The idea is to merge GPRS networks, mobile phones, and Wi-Fi, enabling the user to change networks when necessary. If you are in a coffee shop, you can access the Wi-Fi network and if you are in the square or garden, the GPRS network, for example. For this constant change of IP (Internet protocol, an address on the network), the 'Mobile IP' was developed, which prevents the connection from falling or going from one network to another. Another problem involves the several existing networks that prevent the subscriber from having access to all the hotspots (for example, in the airport but not in the corner luncheonette). One foreseen solution is the 'aggregators', companies that give access to several Wi-Fi and mobile telephony providers. In this way the user can change networks without even paying attention. Another problem arises here: how to charge for the use of several networks at the same time. Solutions are underway.

Smart and Flash Mobs

Contemporary practices of social aggregation are using mobile technologies for actions that bring together many people, sometimes crowds, who perform an action jointly and disperse rapidly. These practices can have artistic purposes, such as a performance, or have a more committed objective, of a political activist nature. This group of practices has been called smart mobs. It is simply a question of the use of mobile technologies to form social aggregations with the objective of action in the cities' public space. The first type, hedonistic, are the flash mobs, instantaneous mobilisations with the objective of swarming to a place and rapidly dispersing, creating a stupefying effect on the public. The second type, activist, have the objective of mobilising crowds for the purpose of political protest in public places. Both are forms of social aggregation based on the utilisation of mobile technologies such as mobile phones, Wi-Fi networks, blogs...

Smart mobs is the term created by H. Rheingold (2003) to describe the 'new' forms of swarming using mobile technologies such as mobile phones, with voice and SMS, pages, wireless internet, blogs, etc. The objectives are quite varied. For Rheingold, the smart mobs 'consist of people who are able to act in concert even if they don't know each other. The people who make up smart mobs cooperate in ways never before possible because they carry devices that possess both communication and computing capabilities' (*ibid*: xii).

Cases of smart mobs have already occurred and are occurring around the world. Those with the greatest impact were the demonstrations that brought people together by means of SMS in the political protests in the Philippines and in Madrid, after the terrorist attack on the trains in 2004. In these cases, the exchanges of SMS messages caused the movement of a crowd in order to protest, resulting in the deposition of President Estrada in Philippines and the defeat of the party in power in Spain. Although we cannot attribute the political consequences just to the mobilisation by means of mobile technologies, it seems clear that the latter represent important tools for mobilisation. The use is growing and worldwide. The utilisation of mobile technologies is basic to the organisation of the events. In Africa, for example, SMS were used for a petition supporting women's rights.[19] In the last election campaign in the USA, SMS (TXT mobs) were used as a form of protest. A *New York Times* article showed that:

> 'As thousands of protesters marched through Manhattan during the Republican National Convention last week, some were equipped with a wireless tactical communications device connected to a distributed information service that provided detailed and nearly instantaneous updates about route changes, street closures and police actions. The communication device was a common cell phone. The information service, a collection of open-source, Web-based programming scripts running on a Linux server in someone's closet, is called TXTMob'.[20]

Smart mobs fit in with Elias Canetti's definitions of mass and with Jose Ortega Y Gasset's view of the revolution of the masses. We should quickly show this connection so as not to fall into the naïve view of the phenomenon's originality. The novelty is instrumental: the use of mobile digital technologies in large contemporary metropolises. The question of the crowd interests the author as an urban and industrial society phenomenon. The following sentence could very well express what is happening today, in the connection era:

> 'the crowd, suddenly, becomes visible, and establishes itself in the places preferred by society. Before, if it existed, it passed unnoticed, occupying the background of the social scenario; now it has advanced up to the stage lights, it is the main character. There are no more leading actors: there is only the chorus'.
> —(Gasset 1962: 62)

And further,

> 'I believe that the political innovations of the most recent years do not signify anything but the political empire of the masses (...). Today we witness the triumph of a hyper-democracy in which the mass acts directly outside the law, by means of material pressures, imposing aspirations and its inclinations' (*ibid.:* 66). 'We are living in the brutal empire of the masses' (*ibid.:* 69).

Elias Canetti, in a seminal work published in Hamburg in 1966, traced an x-ray of the masses that can help us understand the concept of 'intelligent masses' proposed by Rheingold. For Canetti, it is by means of the mass that man frees himself from the phobia of contact and through it can be integrated as a whole. In the mass man feels '*a l'interieur d'un même corps*' (1966: 12). Canetti will show that masses are made up basically of the 'closed' (limited, circumscribed, formalist, institutional) and 'open' (that aggregates and does not stop growing, the mass, strictly speaking) types, in which their formation is accomplished by '*décharge*' (form of discharge that aggregates). It is through '*éclatement*' (explosion) that a mass of the closed type can be shaped as a mass of the open type. Canetti describes the four properties of the mass. They are: 1. It always tends to grow; 2. In the mass, equality reigns; 3. The mass loves density; and 4. The mass has need of a direction. These characteristics lead to a classification of masses as: 1. closed and open (referring to properties 1 and 2, growth and equality); 2. rhythmical and stagnant (referring to properties 3 and 4, density and direction); 3. slow and fast (refers to the objectives).

We do not have room here for going more deeply into these characteristics, but for what interests us at the moment, we can see that the phenomenon of the 'smart mobs' fits in perfectly with the dynamics of the masses as analysed by Canetti. We can say that 'smart mobs' are mass phenomena. They are characterised by being: 1. open, that tend to grow and where equality reigns (the mass formed is open *a priori*, made up of individuals who do not belong to the same group and who are going to exercise the feeling of equality by getting together); 2. they are rhythmical (they go according to the movement of the convocation, by SMS, e-mails, blogs), and 3. they are fast.

Although the phenomenon is characteristic of all masses, according to Canetti (1966: 29), the current development of new wireless technologies leads us to believe that the use of these technologies for the formation of masses is going to increase. The use of digital technologies helps to create this profile and create the '*décharge*' necessary for its formation as an open mass.

The 'smart' concept is questionable, revealing a certain exaggeration and ideological character. The novelty lies in the new technologies that permit coordination in the flow of time, adjusting places and times in a flexible way. What characterises 'smart mobs' and differentiates them from other mass or crowd formations is the use of the new mobile wireless technologies for social aggregation in public places. The technologies are thus instruments of '*décharge*', of mobilisation in contemporary cities. The term is associated with the adjective 'smart', of the 'smart' technologies, such as cards and other equipment that utilise 'intelligent' devices. In this connection, youths utilise SMS as a form of social aggregation for various purposes. Several other forms of mobilisation using the technologies of the connection era have arisen since then, such as the practice of toothing[21] in England, the anti-globalisation protests, as well as flash mobs.

The flash mob practices can be considered forms of smart mobs. The flash mobs became a fever in 2003 and diminished in 2004 and 2005, but they are not dead. Even serious institutions are utilising this practice as a form of promotion of events in public places. Flash mobs are lightning demonstrations, apolitical, in which people who do not know each other choose, via networks (blogs, mobile phones using voice and SMS), public places for gathering together and then dispersing, causing astonishment and perplexity to passers-by. Flash mobs began in New York and have spread throughout the world. Cities like Amsterdam, Berlin, Boston, Budapest, Chicago, London, Melbourne, Oslo, Rome, San Francisco and Zurich have already experienced this new practice. In Brazil, flash mobs have been organised in São Paulo, Rio de Janeiro, Salvador and other capital cities.

It is a question here of a movement closer to performances and happenings than to traditional political mobilisation. As all smart mobs, flash mobs put in synergy the virtual space of telematic networks and the concrete spaces of the city, in the same way as a new practice of games, the 'wireless games', that utilise mobile technologies for games in the physical space of cities such as 'Pacman NY', 'Noderunner', among others.[22] The network is the organisation space and the street, the meeting space of the game.

The connection era seems to be putting in synergy virtual space, urban space and mobility. After centuries of emptying of political debate in the public space, this phenomenon shows the wearing out of classical political activities and the emergence of new micro-political forms of action. The mobs being meetings of people in a performance without any political nature, or with explicit political nature, reveal, so to speak, their most radical social dimension. Global activism, hedonism, micro-politics and nonsense, marks of post-modernity, are obvious here. The social vitality of the mobs shows this desire for connection beyond an institutionalised political life. In the case of the flash mobs, the movement is apolitical and an appeal to astonishment at the suspension of the space–time of every-day life. In the case of political mobs, the objective is to use swarming (thronging, aggregation and rapid dispersion) and netwar (network war practices) (Arquila and Ronfeldt 1993; Bateman III 1999) for socio-political changes in the cities.

Smart mobs reveal two interesting dimensions: political and hedonist. Flash mobs, being apolitical, hedonist, tribal and ephemeral are another example of the various contemporary forms of sociability typical of cyberculture such as chats, personal diaries, games, and discussion groups. The political dimension points to rapid mobili-sations with the use of mobile technologies for aggregation used for the purpose of escaping from police control and vigilance. In both actions, it is a question of the logic of the use (Perriault 1989) of these technologies that presupposes appropriation and social use for the action.

Smart mobs are located at the centre of the debate, very current, of the reconfigurations of urban space based on various practices born from the new mobile technologies of communication and information. Mobile phones, pages, notebooks, palms—all these tools establish an electronic nomadism in the midst of steel and concrete urban space. Amid individualism and forms of privatisation of the public space and publicising of the private spaces of modernity, the collective spaces of the cities are disappearing as the locus of sociability. Ubiquity, reconfiguration of the public space and of its practices, forms of access to the network by means of environments of presence instead of points of presence, the examples are countless. Mobile telephony networks, wireless internet—Wi-Fi, bluetooth household networks, radio frequency tags, RFID, are transforming our cities, and developing countries like Brazil are entering this 'connection era'.

Conclusion

The Internet today is a gigantic machine for contact and exchange of information. We are indeed entering the mobile connection era. After the isolated PC (personal computer) of the 1960s–1970s, the popularisation of the fixed Internet with the CC (collective computers) in the 1980s–1990s, we are seeing, at the beginning of the 21st century, the emergence of the mCC (mobile collective computers) era. New practices and uses of Information Technology have arisen, as we have seen, with the change of paradigm. The fixed internet showed the communication technologies' potential for aggregation. Now the mobile Internet is bringing man closer to the desire for ubiquity, making a new telematic culture emerge, with new forms of consumption of information and with new practices of sociability. As Townsend states,

> 'Wireless communications are quickly defining the very nature of 21st century urban streetscapes. The global cellular network has combined with the surface and air transportation system to provide unprecedented levels of mobility. The rigid system of commutes and work schedules introduced during the industrial age is breaking down into a constantly renegotiated swarm of communications and movement.'
>
> —(2003)

The worldwide practices for utilisation of mobile phones such as SMS, the access to databanks, acting as a remote control of everyday life, both for political as well as hedonist purposes, are showing the potential for digital inclusion and social participation in the cyberculture. The revolution of wireless access to the Internet, the Wi-Fi, shows how social relations and the forms of Internet usage can change when the network moves from an 'access point' to an 'access environment' that places the user at its centre. If the user used to go to the network in a fixed way, in the era of connection and smart mobs, it is the network that goes to the user.

In the connection era, an environment of access and exchange of information is created, involving the users. The current phase of ubiquitous computation, of sentient objects, of pervasive computers and of wireless access shows the emergence of the connection era and of the ever more intrinsic relation between the cities' physical spaces and the virtual space of the telematic networks. The challenge facing the informational, communicational and urban management of the cities requires recognition of this era of connection and mobility.

Notes

1. This article is part of the 'Cibercidade' (Cybercity) research done with the support of the National Research Council (CNPq), Universal announcement. For this research, see *http://www.facom.ufba.br/ciberpesquisa/cibercidades/*.
2. Wi-Fi stands for wireless fidelity. Typically, any Wi-Fi product, using the same radio frequency, will work with any other. A person with a Wi-Fi enabled device, such as a computer or a cell phone, can connect to the Internet when in proximity of a wireless access point.
3. Wi-Max is short for 'Worldwide Interoperability for Microwave Access'. Just as cell phones have replaced 'land lines', Wi-Max could replace cable services, providing almost universal Internet access anywhere one goes. In practical terms, Wi-Max could operate similar to Wi-Fi, but at higher speeds, over greater distances, and for a greater number of users.
4. Bluetooth is the connection standard for wireless networks with a range of 10 metres in general. For more details, see *http://www.grouper.ieee.org/groups/802* and *http://www.bluetooth.org/*.
5. Pervasive computation is directly linked to the idea of ubiquity, and is characterised by the introduction of chips in equipment and objects that begin to exchange information. For more information, see the 'Center for Pervasive Computing, Concepts and Technology for the Future', in *http://www.pervasive.dk/*. 'Sentient computation' refers to the possibility of interconnection of computers and objects by means of sensors that begin to recognise each other in an autonomous way and exchange information. For more information, see *http://en.wikipedia.org/wiki/Sentient_computing/*.
6. 3G is short for 'third-generation technology', and is used in the context of mobile phone standards. The services associated with 3G provide both voice data (a telephone call) and non-voice data (such as downloading information from the Internet, exchanging email, and instant messaging).
7. RFID is the acronym for 'radio frequency identification' and is characterised by tags that emit radio waves that can inform us regarding the location and properties of various products. For more information, see *http://www.rfidjournal.com/*.
8. SMS is the acronym for 'short messages', sent via mobile phone to a person or group of persons. WAP is the acronym for 'Wireless Application Protocol', a protocol that enables mobile phones to have access to the Internet.
9. Regarding the 'i-mode', see Rheingold (2003) and the site *http://www.nttdocomo.com/corebiz/imode/index.html/*.

10. Cf. in *http://www.teleco.com.br/comentario/com86.asp/*.
11. The major problem faced by this integration between Wi-Fi and mobile phones still lies in the enormous quantity of available technological patterns. Devices that possess compatibility with all the patterns, or with the patterns universally accepted, are needed.
12. In order to follow up the various daily initiatives for placing Wi-Fi access in cities (recently Amsterdam, Los Angeles, New York, Philadelphia have projects underway), see the cybercities research site, *http:// www.facom.ufba.br/ciberpesquisa/cibercidades/disciplinas/*.
13. For more information, see *http://www.pirai.rj.gov.br/*.
14. See NYWireless in *http://www.nycwireless.net/*.
15. In the USA, Asia and Europe there are several projects in progress, ranging from the creation of a Wi-Fi network in all of Paris based on the subway stations, to hot spots in luncheonettes, hotels, airports, squares and coffee shops, downtown areas of the cities. The movement is expanding.
16. See the sites 'Greater Democracy', in *http://www.greaterdomocracy.org/ OpenSpectrumFAQ.html* and the 'Reeds Locus', in *http://www.reed.com/ dprframeweb/dprframe.asp?section=openspec/*.
17. Wardriving is a practice involving the seeking of points of wireless access to the Internet, hot spots, inside a car with antenna and laptops. Regarding wardriving see *http://www.worldwidewardrive.org/*. Warchalking is the same process, only on foot, marking open connection points with chalk.
18. See Magic Bike in *http://p2pnet.net/p2p.rss/*. Regarding the knapsack with Wi-Fi connection, see Bedouin Wi-Fi in *http://www.techkwondo.com/ projects/bedouin/index.html/*.
19. See 'Mobile Phone Users in Africa Are Being Encouraged To Send Text Messages In Support of a Women's Rights Petition', in BBC, in *http:// news.bbc,co.uk/2/hi/Africa/3937715.stm*. 30/7/2004/.
20. See article in *http://www.nytimes.com/2004/09/09/technology/circuits/ 09mobb.html/*.
21. Toothing is a practice of contact in subways and buses in which the users, without knowing each other, establish connection via bluetooth in their mobile phones and from there can start a chat or carry out a meeting for rapid sex. See *http://www.wired.com/news/wireless/0,1382,62687,00.htm/*.
22. See 'Noderunner' in *http://uncommonprojects.com/noderunner/index.php* and 'Pacman NY', *http://stage.itp.nyu.edu/~w1364/biggames/final/, http:/ /www.wifiplanet.com/news/article.php/1445341/*.

References

Albernaz, J.C.F. 2003. 'Spectrum Management for Mobile Technologies of the Future'. *http://www.anatel.gov.br/Tools/frame.asp?link=/ acontece_anatel/palestras/tecnicas/palestra_wcnc03_20_03_2003.pdf/*.
Arquila, J. and D. Ronfeldt. 1993. 'Cyberwar is Coming!', *Comparative Strategy*, 12(2): 141–65.

Augé, M. 1994. *Não-lugares: Introdução a uma antropologia da supermodernidade*, (ed.) Bertrand Editora, Campinas, São Paolo: Papirus.

Bateman III, R.L. 1999. *Digital War*. New York: ibooks.

Bauman, Z. 2001. *Modernidade Líquida*. Rio de Janeiro: Jorge Zahar.

Bey, Hakim. 2001 (2004). *T.A.Z. Zona Temporalmente Autonoma*. São Paolo: Conrad Livros. Trans. into English, *T.A.Z.: The Temporary Autonomous Zone, Ontological Anarchy, Poetic Terrorism*. 2nd edn with a new Preface. Brooklyn, NY: Autonomedia.

Canetti, E. 1966. *Masse et puissance*. Paris: Éditions Gallimard.

Castells, Manuel. 1996a. *The Rise of the Network Society*. Oxford: Blackwell Publishers.

——————— 1996b. *The Information Age: Economy, Society and Culture*. Cambridge, Mass.: Blackwell Publishers.

Cave, D. 2001. 'Unchaining the Net'. *http://www.salon.com/tech/feature/2000/12/01/wireless_ethernet/index.html/*.

Cooper, G., N. Green, G.M. Murtagh and R. Harper. 2002. 'Mobile Society? Technology, Distance, and Presence', in Steve Woolgar (ed.), *Virtual Society?: Technology, Cyberbole, Reality*, pp. 286–301. Oxford: Oxford University Press.

Deleuze, G. and F. Guattari. 1986. *Nomadology*. New York: Semiotext(e).

Fortunati, L. 2002. 'Italy: Stereotypes, True and False', in James E. Katz and Mark Aakhus (eds), *Perpetual Contact: Mobile Communication, Private Talk, Public Performance*. Cambridge, Mass.: Cambridge University Press.

Furtado, B. 2002. *Imagens eletrônicas e paisagem urbana. Intervenções espaço-temporais no mundo da vida cotidiana. Comunicação e cidade*. Rio de Janeiro: Relume Dumará.

Galloway, A. 2003. 'Resonances and Everyday Life: Ubiquitous computing and the City'. *http://www.purselipsquarejaw.org/mobile/cult_studies_draft.pdf/*.

Gasset, Jose Ortega Y. 1962. *A rebelião das massas*. Rio de Janeiro: Livro Ibero-Americano.

Graham, S. and S. Marvin. 1996. *Telecommunications and the City*. London: Routledge.

Habermas, J. 1978. *L'espace public*. Paris: Payot.

Heidegger, M. 1964. *Être et Temps*. Paris: Éditions Gallimard.

Horan, Thomas A. 2000. *Digital Places: Building Our City of Bits*. Washington, D. C.: Urban Land Institute.

Ito, M. 2004. 'A New Set of Social Rules for a Newly Wireless Society'. *http://www.ojr.org/japan/wireless/1043770650.php/*.

Jacomy, B. 2004. *A era do controle remoto. Crônicas da inovação técnica*. Rio de Janeiro: Jorge Zahar.

Katz, James E. and Mark A. Aakhus. 2002. *Perpetual Contact: Mobile Communication, Private Talk, Public Performance*. Cambridge, Mass.: Cambridge University Press.

Krane, J. 2001. 'Digital activists Want to Share the Internet's Wealth — er, Bandwidth'. *http://www.nycwireless.net/press/apwire20010804. html/*.

Lefebvre, H. 1970. *La Révolution Urbaine*. Paris: Éditions Gallimard.

——————. 1986. *La production de l'espace*. Paris: Anthropos.

Lemos, A. 2000. *Cibercidades*, in Andre Lemos and M. Palacios (eds), *Janelas do Ciberespaço. Comunicação e Cibercultura*. Porto Alegre: Sulina.

——————.2002. *Cibercultura. Tecnologia e Vida Social na Cultura Contemporânea*. Porto Alegre: Sulina.

——————.2004. 'Cidade Ciborgue'. unpublished.

Levy, S. 2004. 'Making the Ultimate Map', *Newsweek*.

Licoppe, C. and J. P. Heurtin. 2002. 'France: Preserving the Image', in James E. Katz and Mark A. Aakhus (eds), *Perpetual Contact: Mobile Communication, Private Talk, Public Performance*, pp. 94–109. Cambridge, Mass.: Cambridge University Press.

Luhmann, N. 2001. *A improbabilidade da Comunicação*. Lisboa: Passagens, Vega.

Machrone, B. 2001. 'The People's Wireless Web'. *http://www. nycwireless.net/press/pcmag20011127.html/*.

Maffesoli, M. 1997. *Du Nomadisme. Vagabondages initiatiques*. Paris: Livres de Poche.

Martino, L. 2001. 'De qual comunicação estamos falando', in A. Hohlfedt, L. Martino and V. França (eds), *Teorias da Comunicação. Conceitos, escolas e tendências*, pp. 11–25. Petrópolis: Ed. Vozes.

McCaughey, Martha and Michael D. Ayers. 2003. *Cyberactivism. Online Activism in Theory and Practice*. New York: Routledge.

Megna, M. 2001. 'In the Zone: Wireless Areas Around the City Let You Access the Internet for Free'. *http://www.nycwireless.net/press/ nydailynews20011023.html/*.

Meyers, P. 2001. 'Motley Crew Beams No-Cost Broadband to New York High Speed Freed, Village Voice'. *http://www.nycwireless.net/press/ villagevoice20010815.html/*.

Meyrowitz, J., 2004. 'Global Nomads in the Digital Veldt', *Revista Famecos*, July, pp. 23–30. Porto Alegre: PUC-RS.

Mitchell, William J. 2003. *Me++: The Cyborg Self and the Networked City*. Cambridge, Mass.: MIT Press.

Myerson, George. 2001. *Heidegger, Habermas and the Mobile Phone*. Duxford: Icon Books.

Negroponte, N. 1995. *Vida Digital*. São Paolo: Cia. das Letras.

Perriault, J. 1989. *La logique des usages. Essais sur les machines à communiquer*. Paris: Éditions Flammarion.

Press, L. 2003. 'Wireless Internet Connectivity for Developing Nations'. *http://www.firstmonday.org/issues/issues8_9/*.

Puglisi, L.P. 1999. *Hyperarchitecture: Spaces in the Electronic Age*. Birkhäuser: Basel.

Rheingold, Howard. 2003. *Smart Mobs: The Next Social Revolution*. Cambridge, Mass.: Perseus Publishing.

Sassen, Saskia. 2001. *The Global City: New York, London, Tokyo. 2nd edn*. Princeton, N J: Princeton University Press.

Schrage, M. 2003. 'Wi-Fi, Li-Fi and Mi-Fi.', *Technology Review*, 106 (6).

Thompson, C. 2001. 'Geeks Worldwide Unite to Wire Up Their Communities'. *http://www.nycwireless.net/press/newsday20011014.html/*.

Townsend, A. 2003. 'Wired / Unwired: The Urban Geography of Digital Networks', unpublished PhD diss., Massachusetts Institute of Technology.

——————. 2004. 'Digitally Mediated Urban Space: New Lessons for Design'. *http://urban.blogs.com/research/townsend.pdf/*.

Urry, J. 1999. 'Mobile Cultures'. *http://www.comp.lancs.ac.uk/sociology/papers/Urry-Mobile-Cultures.pdf/*.

——————.2000. 'Mobile Sociology', *British Journal of Sociology*, 51(1): 185–203.

Westwood, S. and J. Williams. 1997. *Imagining Cities: Scripts, Signs, Memory*. London: Routledge.

Wheeler, James O., Yuko Aoyama and Barney Warf. 2000. *Cities in the Telecommunications Age: The Fracturing of Geographies*. New York: Routledge.

Weinberger, D. 2003. "Why Open Spectrum Matters: The End of the Broadcast Nation'. *http://www.evident.com/*.

Weiser, M. 1991. 'The Computer for the 21st century', *Scientific American*, 265(3): 66–75.

6

Internet, Mobiles, and the New Digital Lifestyle

A. Vishnu

Towards the fag end of the 20th century, Andrew S. Grove[1], the co-founder and long-time Chief Executive of the world's biggest computer chip maker, Intel, made an observation that was to be rather controversial: 'The more interesting we make the content on a personal computer ….., the more progress we are going to make stealing of eyeballs from the television to the personal computer.' When he said this in the mid-1990s, the number of personal computers sold in the US had exceeded the sales of television sets, an inflection point that had not yet occurred in most other countries. Grove was right in anticipating the central role that Information Systems would play in the new millennium, a trend that was to be sharply driven by the galloping usage of that massive global network of information sharing known as the Internet.

But even a technocrat like Grove could not, in the fading months of the last century, have anticipated that the PC itself would soon be threatened by another compelling personal appliance—the mobile phone. And while all of computer technology—of which the PC was only one fast-growing sector—was essentially driven by the needs of the corporate world, the mobile phone was very much a device for the rest of us. And interestingly, while the more developed economies of the West were fairly slow and hesitant in embracing the un-tethered joys of the cellular phone, it was in India, China and rest of the Asia Pacific rim, that millions of the young'n restless gleefully embraced all that mobile telephony offered.

Indeed, some of the numbers that emerged from countries like India, which swiftly and systematically deregulated its telecom appara-tus, and opened the arena to private enterprise, astonished demo-graphers and sociologists alike. At the turn of the century when the national penetration of telephones was less than one in twenty, a small hilly town in Kerala created an amazing statistic. The residents of Malappuram town owned between them, 22,000 landline phones and 44,000 mobile phones. For the 59,000 residents of the town, this gave them a mite more than one phone per person.

Malappuram was the main town and marketplace for the hill produce of a district, which was such a logistical challenge that the government-owned landline phone agency had a waiting list going back more than a decade. When the telecom revolution came, bringing with it the instant connectivity of a mobile phone, Malappuram embraced it with enthusiasm, buying two, sometimes three phones in a family. Today, thanks to the sane initiatives of what is India's first 100 per cent literate state, Malappuram is also the town and the district which boasts of 100 per cent e-literacy, with a wireless-linked 'Akshaya' e-centre[2] for every 1,000 families.

The compelling 'combo' of a virtually free messaging system, and a slate of made–for–dummies productivity tools, is what has 'sold' the PC to millions of lay and non-technical users worldwide. Sabeer Bhatia,[3] who 'invented' the concept of a free e-mail service—*Hotmail*—sold it to Microsoft and went on to incubate a number of other compelling Internet-age companies with the $400 million he received. But, *Hotmail* and its clones—*AOL, Yahoo Mail* and more recently, *Gmail*, have made it virtually impossible for lay users to be ever charged money for exchanging mail in whatever form—words, pictures, sound or video.

The impatience of youth with any system that was not instantaneous, gave rise to instant messaging. The ability to be constantly in touch with dozens of like-minded friends throughout the wakeful hours, created a whole new sub-culture, which made the upwardly mobile teens' and the twenties' age group the biggest fans of the Internet. And when a young American college dropout, Shawn Fanning, built upon this system, to create an Internet-driven file–sharing and music swapping system named *Napster*, he had created the mother of all killer 'apps'. Fanning's *Napster* service, as it turned out, suffered from one technical flaw. It routed the millions of shared files through a central clearinghouse. It was to prove *Napster's* 'Achilles' heel', and well-entrenched corporate entities like the Recording Industry Association of America (RIAA), seized on this to convince American courts that *Napster* was constructively responsible, every time two anonymous users exchanged a music track, which at least one may not have paid for. *Napster* was swiftly driven to bankruptcy and allowed to rise again only when it adopted the much less popular 'pay' mode.

But, one of the biggest realities of the new Internet Age was that you cannot keep a good idea down, and *Napster* soon gave rise to other file sharing technologies, under a new model called Peer–to–peer (P2P). By taking away the central clearinghouse and allowing individual file swappers to connect with each other directly from computer to computer, P2P offered a virtually undetectable way of exchanging files over the Internet. The fact that P2P was also central to the newly-emerging concept of grid computing, where the un-utilised number-crunching power of millions of PCs, was harnessed to crack global problems like genome mapping or cancer cures, gave it a certain legitimacy.

In mid-2005, the U.K.-based Net traffic management player *CacheLogic*, carried out the first definitive study of the P2P phenomenon and found that the favoured technology for file-swapping came from *BitTorrent*: For a time, it accounted for half of all file sharing traffic on the Net. *CacheLogic* also discovered that when music and movie companies made things too hot for one P2P tool, users merely moved away to another less high-profile service. When the British *BitTorrent's* zippy download speeds over broadband made it the video traffic leader, the Hollywood studios breathed fire—which saw millions of users quietly migrate to a New York-based service, known colourfully as *eDonkey*. Meanwhile, other file swapping tools like *Kazaa* and *Gnutella*, continue to make money with their legitimate business even while facilitating the free exchange of Internet files. *Kazaa*, for example, made history when it offered the first-ever download of a full-length feature film for $2.99, a B-grade Hindi film named *Supari*.

The ability to buy and sell over the Internet was another compelling application whose time had clearly come. The US-based e-*Bay* soon became, by far, the biggest player in this niche. Sites like *eBay*, racked up phenomenal business—70 million users, nearly 200 million items listed; revenues of nearly $2 billion. And clones like the Indian *Baazee.com* soon ended up being acquired by the dominant player. Interestingly, the e-Bay success soon spawned some other inspired business opportunities. Manjul Shah, a Stanford University computer science major in his twenties, came together in 1999, with three other Indian friends, to start a California-based company, Andale, the first-ever provider of auction management tools and services for sellers and auction-related research for buyers. Their products were priced very low: typically $ 7.99—but Andale soon accounted for $5 billion in sales on *eBay* alone, and become a major catalyst for the auction major. The company, whose creative workforce is based in Bangalore, now receives privileged access to *eBay's* data base which it leverages for its own customers. Sites like *eBay* and *Amazon*, the world's largest book and music shop, represent one face of what is generally called e-Biz or e-Commerce. The other, more evolved side is what is loosely called *B2B* or Business to Business, where the world has become one huge electronic marketplace. What is still holding back the full potential of the Internet as bazaar and auction-house is the public's scepticism about the robustness of its payment mechanisms. *PayPal* is one fix for the problem; but lack of a secure payment mechanism has held back the growth of e-Business in developing countries, where a credit card is still a minority possession.

While the Internet was refining its act—bigger and better e-mail, faster instant messaging, faster video-enhanced messaging, seamless file sharing and secure buying and selling—it was challenged on two simultaneous fronts. One was the speed (or rather the lack of it) that came with the telephone-based dial-up access technology, which could not cross the modem's limitation of 56 kilobits per second. The broadband option, which potentially offered download speeds, which were between 5 and 10 times faster than the previous option, required costly infrastructure, much of it in the form of optical fibre cabling. While a few nations like Japan and South Korea soon led the world in broadband networking, speed still remained a major constraint in otherwise well-connected nations.

The other challenge to the combination of the PC and the Internet was something no technological crystal gazer could predict till it actually happened: the mobile phone.

The untethered portable telephone has been around since a Motorola engineer Martin Cooper, made the world's first cellular phone connection in 1973 to a friend at rival telecom company, AT&T, on the streets of New York. Yet, the technology ramped up only in the late 1990s when European and Asian providers ditched the existing analogue technology and moved to a new era of digital cellular services, harnessing the two alternative technologies of Global Services Mobile (GSM) and Code Division Multiple Access (CDMA).[4] Since then, mobile phone usage, particularly in Asia has outstripped almost all projections and by end 2005, 1 billion mobile phones were reported to be in use worldwide. There were two reasons for the galloping popularity of mobile phones. One of course, was all about affordability. Fierce competition among multiple mobile service providers, wherever this was encouraged, saw the cost of talk-time tumble to the equivalent of 2–4 cents a minute. The change was particularly dramatic in growing economies like India and China, which saw mobile phone usage shoot up dramatically, as the cost of connectivity came within reach for the first time, of a new young, more upwardly mobile middle-class. Even in islands of relatively rich connectivity like Singapore, the Government nudged well-entrenched fixed line phone providers into a competitive marketplace where they would have to compete with new and compelling technologies like Voice over Internet Protocol (VoIP), or fall by the wayside. Its quest was to constantly increase the installed base of mobile phones on which to build lucrative value-added services like Short Message Services (SMS), Multimedia Messaging Services (MMS), Net access via GPRS (General Packet Radio Services) and Wireless Applications Protocol (WAP).

The GSM association, a loose network of the world's GSM players, launched an emerging markets initiative daring its members to produce a handset for a hitherto unattainable price of below $40. Motorola became the first handset maker to rise to the challenge and chose India as the first market in the world to launch a phone for Rs. 1800 (roughly, $40). The canny calculation in all this was that, having tasted the freedom of untethered communication, customers would soon ramp up and pay for a slat of additional services. Here, as in the case of e-mail and Internet, some opportunities emerged: ring tones, polyphonic or otherwise, became one of the most lucrative sidelines for mobile operators, second only to SMS. Indeed, the young embraced SMS in a way no one ever foresaw, and a whole new vocabulary and sub-culture of abbreviated communication has taken such a grip that educationists are already decrying the threat it poses to conventional (and grammatically correct) usage, take for instance, *D uth of 2day talk thru msg, nt thru wrds.* The language of the young continues to be a closed book to the older generation.

By 2004, mobile phones felt the heat of another trend. The name of the game was convergence, the coming together of multiple compelling applications on a single platform. The handheld computer or Personal Digital Assistance (PDA), exemplified by the Palm, was soon under threat and had to reinvent itself hastily by adding a communication umbilical to its computing power. Today, pocket PCs are communicators by default and middle–to–high end mobile phones, almost always, include the basic functionality of a PC. The Nokia Communicator was the iconic product of this category, but its bulky full-function keyboard was soon shrunk by nimble cloners in Korea and Taiwan, into a more compact form factor.

The seamless merging of a mobile phone with a digital camera was yet another milestone on the mobile phone's roadmap to convergence, and manufacturers like Samsung quickly upped the stakes by putting the equivalent of a semi-professional digital camera on their phones, providing picture resolutions of 5 mega pixels or more. One message that the mobile phone industry was never allowed to ignore was the primacy of the young at every technology cross-road. If 2004 was generally reckoned to be the year of the camera phone, 2005 soon emerged as the year when the mobile phone met the portable music player. This was in part triggered by the runaway success of Apple's iPod player, which soon became the standard against which all portable players were judged. Sony, inventors of that other iconic product, the Walkman, were happily already in lucrative partnership with Swedish handset makers, Ericsson. This allowed them to mate Walkman and phone to create the 800i Sony Ericsson Walkman phone. This was a game at which more than one could play and within weeks, Apple has successfully grafted the iPod with a Motorola phone, to create its own phone-music player 'combo'. Apple had the added advantage of already having put in place a very successful music download service called iTunes where individual tracts of popular music could be legally downloaded at 99 cents a go. The ease and ubiquity of online music had already achieved something that the macho noises of the music industry could not, weaning away the young from Napster-like illegal downloading, to a cheap and legitimate paid service.

The beefing up of mobile phones to serve as small computers or music players depended on two crucial technologies that emerged at the right time. One was Flash memory, which squeezed enormous storage—upto 5 gigabytes—on hardware that was smaller than a thumb nail. The other was Wi-Fi or wireless internet, which complemented the primary networks used by the mobile phone with a public and unlicensed frequency spectrum that was literally free-for-all. Wi-fi or to give it its technical name, 802.11 a/b/g, was excellent for wirelessly connecting mobile phones to PCs, laptops and other information appliances as long as they were within line of sight and not more than a couple of hundred meters away. Wi-Fi led to the creation of thousands of 'wireless hotspots' in public places like coffee shops, airport lounges and shopping malls where laptop or mobile phone users with the right equipment, could access the Internet for free as long as someone was paying for the network. Yet, the limitation of Wi-Fi is already seeing a new challenger, Wi-Max, which could theoretically provide four or five times faster access and increase the range to a few kilometres. Wireless technologies like Wi-Fi and Wi-Max are already seen not so much as yet another 'cool app.' for the already connected, but as a vital component to enlarge the access of information across the so-called 'digital divide' to the world's underprivileged. Nations like India, where the magnitude of the digital divide problem is matched by the emergence of a new and technically savvy professional class, have seen dozens of innovative products bubble to the surface.

In an annual summary of technology breakthroughs, the *New York Times* wrote: 'The most significant innovation in computer technology in 2001 was not Apple's gleaming titanium PowerBook G4 or Microsoft's Windows XP. It was the Simputer, a Net-linked, radically simple portable computer, intended to bring the computer revolution to the third world' (Sterling 2001). The Simputer, was the brainchild of a small group of motivated students and teachers at the Indian Institute of Science in Bangalore. This handheld computer, which uses a free and open version of Linux and comes with a voice recognition interface, has been brought to market by two different commercial entities. Sadly, the Indian Government failed to recognise the potential of this path-breaking device and denied it any form of fiscal encouragement or subsidy. Hamstrung by the high cost of imported components, the Simputer was never to be priced in a way that could compete with the products of multinationals, and it is yet to attain its full potential.

In *The Road Ahead*, Bill Gates (1996), founder and chief mentor of Microsoft, the world's most successful software company, spelled out the possible directions that technologies would take in the emerging Information Age. More than a decade after the book was published, it is instructive to see how many of his predictions have become true. He accurately foresaw what he called 'friction-free capitalism'. Web-based services like *MSN*, *Yahoo* and *Google*, all have profitable tie-ups with thousands of corporate organisations and sellers, and make their money by the number of 'eyeballs' they deliver. The links that bubble to the top of any *Google* search are the ones that are paid for. The free and non-commercial sites are relegated to the bottom. That is the price one pays for the so-called 'free' Internet.

Gates has been proved less prescient when it comes to information appliances. The prototype he suggested, of a wallet PC, a small credit card-sized device that would serve as cheque book, address book, notebook, calculator, compass and identity card, all rolled into one, has not happened, possibly because the primary technology—a secure and robust Internet payment mechanism—has not happened. But, in one crucial respect, the road ahead is exactly what Gates suggested. The book includes a famous cartoon from *New Yorker* magazine, dating back to the early days of the Internet. It shows a dog seated in front of a computer terminal, when the human members of the family are away. The 'he' dog tapping away at the keyboard tells the 'she' dog: 'In the Internet, nobody knows you are a dog.' For millions of lay users, the Internet is the most democratic thing that has come into their lives, and as attempts to choke off the channels of communications in nations as disparate as Bosnia and Burma, Nepal and Iraq, have shown, the Internet knows no boundaries and respects no restrictions. Together, Internet and mobile communications are transforming the lives of billions, worldwide in a manner that no affirmative action on the part of government can ever hope to achieve.

Long before the network of DARPA—the (US) Defence Advanced Research Projects Agency 'morphed' into what is today the Internet, the British science fiction writer, William Gibson, had coined the word 'cyberspace', in his novel *Neuromancer* (1984). A decade after its publication, an interviewer asked Gibson what he thought of the reality of cyberspace and how it measured up to his fictional vision. What he replied could well serve as the central reality of the 21st century as the world's people harness computers and communications in their ceaseless quest for a better life: 'I'm not a user (of Internet), but I'm a big fan. I like the idea that it's extra-national, and no one particularly owns it (Rosenberg 1994).

Notes

1. See *The PC is Where the Fun is*, Intel Keynote Transcript, June 20, 1997. *http://www.intel.com/pressroom/archive/speeches/asg62097.htm/*.

2. Akshaya e-centre is located in Kerala and headed by A.M. Hameedkutty. The organisation interfaces with government agencies and focuses on the creation of ICT access points up to the village level through public participation.
3. For information on Sabeer Bhatia, see *http://en.wikipedia.org/wiki/Sabeer Bhatia*.
4. For information on GSM association and Motorola, see *http://www.gsmworld.com/emh/*.

References

Gates, Bill. 1996. *The Road Ahead*. USA: Penguin.

Gibson, William. 1984. *Neuromancer*. New York: Ace Books.

Rosenberg, Scott. 1994. 'The Man Who Named Cyberspace: An Interview with William Gibson', *Digital Culture*, 4 August.

Sterling, Bruce. 2001. 'The Year in Ideas: A to Z.; Simputer', *The New York Times Magazine*, 9 December.

7

Digitising the Sociological Imagination

Rahul Srivastava

Introduction

This article is based on my experiences as a teacher of sociology and anthropology at Wilson College, Mumbai, between 1995–2001.

It is also about my own discovery and exploration of new digital technologies that had become recently accessible to Indian middle-classes, mostly in urban areas, around that time.

These explorations eventually became an integral part of my classroom practices and helped formulate new assumptions about the learning process. However, almost immediately, these assumptions were supplanted by strong qualifications that ultimately convinced me that the best way to work with these new technologies was to connect them organically to the faculty of the imagination and the creative process. I became intensely aware that these had been seriously damaged by cultures of pedagogic practices that dominated much of the 20th century. Ultimately, the process helped transform my understanding of the disciplines of sociology and anthropology as well.

It became apparent that my attraction to digital technology and its paraphernalia could be traced to my own oppression—both as a teacher and a student—by pedagogic practices that gave creativity and imagination a marginal status. Such a marginalisation is, of course, a more universal phenomenon and emerged whenever educational practices prioritised institutional and bureaucratic concerns over that of learning. In terms of the disciplines of sociology and anthropology, the impact was particularly felt in terms of methodology and a suspicious attitude to the space of subjectivity. An attitude that was critiqued in the 1960s by sociologist C.Wright Mills who first coined the term 'the sociological imagination'

(1959) and brought in a dignity to subjectivity in the form of attention to ideology and the biographical context. Very simply, the sociological imagination refers to the bringing together of historical and biographical experiences within the context of social structure and fortifying the analyses with ideological concerns.

What my engagement with digital technology did was to build on this vision and stretch the concept to engage more strongly with the processes of creativity as well—that is, to pay greater attention to the 'imagination' component of the concept. This tempered my relationship with these technologies and helped to sharpen my pedagogic concerns. It helped me develop the sociological imagination through a special engagement with the ideas of context and biography through the 'Neighbourhood Project'—an attempt at getting students to engage with their locality and their families and develop narratives about the city through this process. Digital cameras—both still and moving—and the Internet facilitated this entire exercise. At the end of the experience I emerged wiser about many things, including the irreversible role that digital technology has come to occupy within the educational context as well as about the way in which this is connected to deeper questions about creativity and imagination within the pedagogic context.

The article outlines the process through which I came to this realisation and also provides some theoretical justifications for the same.

The Assumptions

The assumptions about the learning process, referred to above, can be listed as follows:

1. The image has become consciously integral to the learning process with a greater force. It is, of course, the teacher more than anybody else who has become acutely aware of this. Besides, in no way does this imply that words have lost their potency. After all, as Umberto Eco (1996) reminds us, the importance of words has only escalated with the widespread use of computer technology. What has in fact happened is that there are more honest attempts taking place today at reclaiming the powerful dialectic between the image and the word. This is being reclaimed from modernist pedagogic practices, which used to have a strong bias *against* the image.

2. Digital technology allows you to engage with the act of writing using both—words and images—and this helps us to actively adopt the above-mentioned dialectic more effectively. Digital cameras and appropriate software allow an approach where one can cut and paste words and images, images within images and create all kinds of new texts.

3. The *moving* image, that has had a particularly strong enchantment on the public mind all through the 20th century, has recently become accessible as a tool for learning as well. The digitisation of the moving image is a particularly potent initiative that complicates the world of education. The idea and practice of literacy that has dominated the cultures of educational practices has been strongly subverted with this move. Thus, people are able to connect with knowledge through oral traditions mutated by movies and television even without direct access to a world of active literacy. This becomes particularly evident when teachers are regularly confronted by a bunch of students who are theoretically literate but haven't read a book in a decade and have in fact received much of the basic stock of their knowledge through TV and Film.

4. The interactive world of cyberspace and video games is the backdrop against which all these transformations take place. The related mythologies enshrined by Hollywood movies like the *Matrix Trilogy* are subliminal reference points that cut across class, linguistic and ethnic backgrounds in most urban spaces. Cyber-cafes have made a world of interactivity accessible to a wide section of the middle-class population in cities. The use of chat-forums and easy access to the Internet has developed skills in most urban, middle-class citizens that can be harnessed by new learning practices.

However, as hinted earlier, my equation with these assumptions has been complex and contradictory.

When I purchased a digital video camera for the students and embarked on living out these assumptions in the classroom and attempted to integrate the world of cyberspace and the image into learning practices, I constantly encountered peculiar responses. The students had to confront their engagement with the word and the image in an unfamiliar context—that of their own imagination. This was unfamiliar, because, for most of the time, they had been encouraged to dissociate much of the learning process from creativity and imagination within the formal structures of education. Thus for most of them, knowledge was about information, distilled as much as possible from contexts, and the use of imagination was synonymous with leisure and mediated entertainment. This resulted in a kind of split in their work. Thus, while they excelled in the use of digital technology there were strong limitations to their full expression as a knowledge-based activity. They could compose beautiful pictures but could provide little commentary. They shot excellent footage but could not produce a coherent film. As a result, I found myself spending more and more time working on skills that did not seem to be obviously connected to the new technologies.

For example, I started relying more on an editor's skill; both in a literary sense and the cinematic one. It became increasingly evident that use of these technologies could be honed as much by the techniques of writing poetry as with learning the tools of the appropriate software. Guest resource-persons invited to share skills on editing spent as much time with workshops on poems as they did with Adobe premier.

Similarly, while continuing to firmly believe that knowledge had to be framed, the framing device needed the student to be acutely aware of the practice of screenplay writing—the emphasis being on the aspect of writing. It became increasingly aware that these convictions were coming to the fore because—ironically—the most evolved use of these very technologies demanded it. Ultimately, it was the faculty of the 'imagination' and the process of 'creativity' that was being restored to its rightful place in the learning process. It became increasingly clear that the textual bias in modernist education practices had not just been anti-image, but anti-imagination and creativity as well. The tendency of quantifying learning and auditing knowledge had became the dominant culture of pedagogy, and this inevitably meant that measurable ideas and a positivist bias always tended to dominate the proceedings. This was of course rooted in a very complex socio-historical moment. Historians of knowledge point out how the secularisation of knowledge was accompanied by a heavy reliance on certain methodologies that created a huge rift between the humanities and the sciences. Ironically, the discipline of philosophy, at one time a powerful whole that included literary, mythological, religious, scientific and artistic impulses, and had been so central to the development of the Enlightenment process, was ultimately its biggest casualty. Subjects like sociology and anthropology too, over the 20th century, found themselves torn between their acknowledgement of subjectivity as an essential feature of human life and the institutional demand towards rationalising their theoretical foundations.

Ultimately, intellectual traditions that acknowledged subjectivity and were based on a more complex philosophy of knowledge had to make way for the stronger waves of rationalised and quantifiable traditions.

How damaging this is in the world of mass education in general, became evident in my conversations with some colleagues who taught science and mathematics in college. Quite a few of them felt that their students' lack of communication vocabulary and linguistic skills was the most significant reason why they were not performing well in their subjects. After all, even mathematical equations and scientific propositions need a certain leap of thought—a leap that could only come from a confident use of words aided by a fertile imagination. In the absence of these, most students looked at learning of science and mathematics as yet another space for rote learning.

On making inquiries with the Department allocated with the responsibility of teaching these students 'communication skills', I came across disgruntled teachers of English Literature who were themselves fed up of reducing language and communication to the bare act of stringing together grammatically arranged words—that was all they were supposed to do—nothing more, nothing less. They were as much a casualty of the university enforced practice of teaching their discipline in a manner devoid of imagination, as were the science and mathematics teachers. The alienation of both sets of teachers constantly reinforced each other and the process of learning continued to be as dry as the desert.

In such a barren world, the entry of new digital technologies and the seductions of cyber space inevitably have a heady effect. They give you the impression that all problems will be instantly solved once you are at ease with these new technologies.

Of course, it cannot be denied that they do admittedly help in bypassing many decades of fossilised teaching practices. However, I learnt from my own experience, that one needed a particular vision of learning that placed the faculty of the imagination and the creative process at the centre of learning to make a real breakthrough.

The section below outlines the process that ultimately convinced me of the same in the context of my own discipline. A listing of some theoretical arguments that endorse the propositions that are made follows this.

The Context

Wilson College caters to a mixed group of students, mainly from middle and low middle-income groups. It is a privately-run but state-funded institution and reflects the typical schizophrenic existence of such pedagogic spaces; tightly monitored syllabi and exams, strict auditing of knowledge and a bunch of rebellious and opinionated teachers ready to make guinea pigs of bored and intelligent students.

During the years I taught there, I found many of these students to be well aware that such educational spaces were slowly vanishing. Their city had recently come to terms with the idea that education must become more quality conscious and therefore more expensive. This of course meant that a large chunk of the students would soon not be able to afford a general liberal education at all.

In fact the college had itself, under university directions, started a new course on mass media that was entirely funded by student's fees. Relatively rich students who formed their own sub-culture, something that inevitably led to subtle, class fuelled tensions within the campus, patronised this course.

These tensions were often discussed in class.

It soon became apparent that my students were deeply resentful of the fact that they were not part of these new learning environments, primarily the course on mass media. They saw them as distinctly more exciting and relevant than the fare being dished out in my sociology and anthropology classroom. Their resentment was also underlined by the uncomfortable awareness of their class backgrounds and its role in this divide.

As a bored teacher myself—bored by the insipid syllabi and by the fact that I had to deal with students completely uninterested in the nuances of my disciplines but who were otherwise very intelligent and perceptive—I saw this bubbling resentment as a useful opportunity to experiment.

Coincidentally—around the same time I came across Janet H. Murray's book, *Hamlet on the Holodeck: The Future of Narrative in Cyberspace* (1997). These were reflections on the teaching of literature in a world where narrative devices were being stretched through technological advances in the world of cyber-space.

While the book focuses on video games, its basic premise is that the relationship of technology, historical context and narrative structures, has an older history and it is vital for every one involved in the practice of literature to explore this relationship carefully.

The book helped me to re-connect with many other works closer to my discipline that dealt with the relationship of new digital technologies and cultural practices. This was like opening up a Pandora's box. Very soon I was convinced my classroom needed a touch of hi-tech and a dollop of the digital imagination.

Of course, one could only consider this option at all because a certain technology had become publicly accessible. My students, in spite of their economic backgrounds were already familiar with the shadowy world of cyber-cafes and the creative uses of borrowed digital cameras. The only thing was that they did not see this as being relevant to the classroom.

A bridge needed to be built.

I realised that this had to be made of the scattered pieces of deadwood floating all around me: deadwood of the old and tired practices of learning and teaching that had dominated much of our life in educational institutions.

The digital camera became the magic wand. It made a bunch of the brightest minds gravitate towards me and take on the most challenging of assignments. Theories of visual anthropology were discussed with interest, abstract ideas were concretised through the frame of the camera—there was an instant transformation of the 'class-room' atmosphere.

A short twenty-minute film on Irani cafes owned by Wilson College students, as part of the Neighbourhood Project, another pedagogic initiative, became the crowning glory of the process. It was shown at a prestigious Arts festival in the city, at the National Centre for the Performing Arts and continues to be shown in film festivals quite regularly.

Since then, the project itself has grown outside the context of the college and under the aegis of PUKAR (Partners for Urban Knowledge Action and Research) has entered into a more public and non-pedagogic realm. At all points, the use of digital technologies, especially those linked to producing visual narratives, continues to be an organic extension of the methodology of the project.

The Neighbourhood Project is rooted in the concept of the sociological imagination, which encourages an engagement with biography and history within the context of social structure. Its formation was further instigated by an essay by Arjun Appadurai (1996) that helped root it within the fabric of Mumbai's socio-historical context. The article looks at the complex ways in which locality is a process that manifests itself in the form of neighbourhoods with inhabitants being the most active agency in this production. The production of locality becomes a factor that is vital to the creation of identities and contexts, which, in the final order of things are the ultimate frontiers of social analysis and political engagement.

The Wilson Neighbourhood Project

This invited students and other citizens to write ethnographies and histories of their own localities and neighbourhoods. Using the lens of biography and family history, the project documented visual (using photographs and videos) as well as textual data (in the form of essays and stories), valuing the special ability of such knowledge to provide an unusual, interior perspective on the sociology and history of the city.

The idea was to explore the historical links between the college and the dense neighbourhoods around it where most of the college students reside, which mostly emerged in the 19th and early 20th century. These neighbourhoods represent a vital aspect of Mumbai's urban history and complicate its self-definition as a global modern city. The college too plays a role in the process through which its students negotiate their citizenship in different ways. Most of the students involved in the project were first generation graduates, with some even being first generation learners, for whom English is a second language.

The project yielded a 23-minute film entitled 'Aur Irani Chai' about Irani Cafes in Mumbai owned by Wilson students and ex-students; a photo exhibition on 'Habitats and Homes' in the vicinity of Wilson College; a neighbourhood website; twelve diaries written by students over a year and about a hundred essays on family histories and narratives on specific localities.

It considered the very act of recording personal histories and biographies, located within the diverse localities of Mumbai, as a means of transforming one's position within urban public life. It provided a platform for students to reflect on their relationship to the city and then share their narratives and images with each other through exhibitions, film shows, publications or websites.

The project is based on the belief that local spaces are intensely political and thinking and writing about them or imaging them is an act of political involvement. It privileges the knowledge which students and citizens have of themselves, their familiar worlds and makes that the entry point to engage with the equally complex politics of nationalism and globalisation.

Digitising the Sociological Imagination

It became clear through the process that the project managed to capture the student's interest because of two factors. One was the privileging of local knowledge and the accompanying act of making students produce texts, rather than simply consuming them. It built on the well-known dictum that the familiar and the local are ideal starting points to the learning process. Second, it also paid attention to the counter-argument, that one should allow the realm of fantasy and the imagination to reverse the familiar to unknown argument. John Wilson's book, *Fantasy and Common Sense in Education* (1979) has/had a strong impact on me. In it, he makes a strong plea for balancing the learning equation by encouraging the imaginative and creative quotient through the act of story telling.

Even though the project was about urban sociology and the act of producing texts, it was rooted in a methodology that privileged subjectivity and made the act of story-telling and empathetic exchange of stories its main exercise. The story telling was, of course, very obviously mediated by the world of images since most students in class were part of a celebrated oral tradition through the act of engaging with films and television alone. It was not surprising therefore to note that they took to digital video and still cameras to tell their story with remarkable ease. Even though many of them had never directly used these technologies before, affordable access through my own intervention allowed them to bring to surface their creative desires rather quickly.

Even their textual work, essays about their neighbourhoods, had been obviously influenced by the image rich world that they inhabited. They were written in the idiom of the movies that they watched. Grandparents became heroes, localities became settings for all kinds of dramatic events and the essays were structured using narrative devices they were used to through the act of watching films.

My own pressures on them were not in the direction of sharpening their skills on gathering authentic data and facts about local history but on getting them to sharpen their story-telling abilities. I firmly believed that by doing this, their sensitivities to facts and history would become heightened on their own.

This rather slippery proposition on my part was rooted in a conviction of late 19th–early 20th century sociologist Max Weber's work, *The Methodology of the Social Sciences* (1949)—in which he rejects any move within sociological inquiry that is suspicious of subjectivity and an empathetic understanding of the social process. In it he also asserts that, rather than trying to achieve an objective understanding (which is virtually impossible given that sociologists themselves are social actors caught in the web of social life) it becomes vital to tackle prejudice as an obstacle to scientific understanding of social and cultural 'lifeworlds'.

This made it easier for me to convince the students that they should concentrate on producing narratives that were honestly trying to dispel all kinds of prejudices that they could be susceptible to—communal, gender, caste, urban or class based, and that they should attempt at producing a good story. It is this challenging dialectic that would help them produce valuable sociological knowledge. My own discussions in the classroom became the basis for exercises dealing with prejudice and a caravan of resource-persons looked after the question of producing a good story.

The photo-essays and screenplays the students wrote (only one became a film due to financial limitations) were buttressed by the skills of photographers, filmmakers and screenwriters rather than by academics. Marianne Pearl, Paromita Vohra, Hansa Thapliyal and Gauri Patwardhan were some of the resource-persons who helped hone their skills. Coming from the world of practice, their approach was far from being dazzled by the medium. Instead they came from the point of view that privileged the process of writing and training students in the craft of image-making in a more traditional sense. They stressed the need for creating a realistic and plausible story that had to ultimately rely on high-quality research and a quest for reliable facts—but not in the self-sufficient and insular way of the positivist.

These were really vital inputs that helped enrich the student's digital imaginations from an unexpected entry point. It became quickly apparent to them that taking good photographs and composing digital moving images was only a tiny step. Using the Internet and exploring cyber space were moments that needed to be built up by sharpening their imaginations and creative skills. Otherwise connections couldn't be made, convincing stories could not be told and their neighbour-hoods could not come to life the way they wanted to. A website needed good stories and a community of individuals eager to share them, a film had to engage the history of the locality in a forceful and imagi-native manner, one that matched the relatively high visual grammar of the people who watched passionately engaged with moving images all the time.

Conversations with resource-persons pushed me to look closely at the film-editor's job very carefully. When we started the process of making the digital film for example, our initial emphasis was on the camera-person and the energy of making moving images. At the end we realised that the cinematic imagination is as much rooted in the ability to connect images and for which the students had to engage in exercises that had little direct interaction with digital technologies.

Working with a poet became particularly rewarding and the distinction between the projected image and the way images are used in a literary sense helped anchor this process. What is interesting is that this exercise had an influence far beyond the world of digital filmmaking alone. It explored a deeper equation between the image and the word, an equation that had gotten skewed by biases within modernist educational practices as well as by the reactions against it. A situation best expressed in the differences between the theoretical orientations of media theorists Marshall McLuhan and Umberto Eco. For the former, the image is the projected, cinematic and televised image that came into its own in the 20th century and has a future, however twisted, that builds from this moment. For the latter, the image has an older history and a life much larger than its projected 20th century avatar. My own tilt is towards Eco, and it certainly had the desired effect on the exercises done by the students.

It allowed for an easier negotiation between different skills and creative processes. Thus, the poet and the editor could come together to look at the way images work and the connections that can be made using them. This process made it possible to unearth stories about the city that would otherwise have remained hidden—in the memories of older citizens, in the silent history of families. A process that may well have been possible without the digital touch, but would have then lost out on the enthusiasm of an enjoyable and democratic learning environment. It would also not have allowed the aesthetic of a younger generation of learners to be freely expressed. On the other hand, the special effort this particular set of exercises demanded, also made it evident to them that this new technology and its accompanying aesthetic is not a break from the past at all, but inherits so many of ancient skills that make the endeavour equally rewarding.

Vice Versa: In Conclusion

Much of my own theoretical framework that guided the above-described process has been shaped by the writings of Marilyn Strathern (1991), Umberto Eco (1986) and Arjun Appadurai (1996).

Strathern's writings on new reproductive technologies first alerted me to the way in which human thought is organically connected with technological innovations and how technological transformations reproduce familiar concepts and ideas in unexpected ways. She also made it clear that it could well be an image more than a concept or an explanation that tends to influence the way in which we think about technology. Her own analysis of the influence of the image of the 'cyborg' is a very illuminating one, since it evokes irrational fears on one hand and one-dimensional fantasies on the other in contemporary societies.

Eco's writings are unafraid by the world of new knowledge technologies. They reveal a genuinely inquisitive mind—one that is rooted in a deep scholarly frame of reference and is confident enough to be irreverent (without being rude) to traditional ways of learning. He immediately introduces us to a world at least as old as European medievalism in which the word and the image have always been a victim to all kinds of historical and political factors. He looks at contemporary society and all its technological paraphernalia as one more episode. However, this does not make him cynical. He insists that computers, cyberspace and multi-media are potentially liberating and more importantly, irreversible. What we need to do are find the right handles so that our relationship with knowledge continues to be genuinely challenging and satisfying.

Appadurai provides a rich and complex canvas for a scholar to work from. He points out that the contemporary scholar is part of a shifting, moving and fluid landscape that has only recently acknowledged this theoretically. New technologies help us express these further and connect to the 'scapes' that make up our social imagination in more ways than one. This 'social imagination' continues to be rooted in a complex, ever-changing context, one that is inevitably local, because locality is always being produced. However, at the same time, it is acutely aware that national boundaries, like many others are being challenged by new constantly mutating technologies. The globalised world is, for him, not Marshall McLuhan's mediated global village, but one that is about movement of people, greater awareness of the history of the interconnected world, and the way in which media and new technologies become a means of coming to terms with these shifts.

These frameworks helped me come to terms with the challenges faced within the classroom as a teacher of sociology and anthropology. Eventually the focus was on methods and new technologies became a sophisticated version of these methods, but not as external attachments, but accompanied by deep conceptual shifts. However, these shifts did not mean a sacrifice of well-known learning processes but a re-alignment of forces to tackle the real villain—an educational context devoid of subjectivity, imagination and creativity.

One image that kept coming to my mind during this entire process was constructed by a literary work by Ray Bradbury called *The Illustrated Man* (2001), first published in 1951.

This collection of short stories, about a dystopic future in which the media literally comes alive, is extremely layered. The stories are embodied on a man in the form of moving images, tattooed by some enchanted artist from a local fair. The man himself could be from any point from the past or future. The stories his body 'reveals' ultimately end with one that reflect the life of the person presently 'watching' them. They are futuristic stories about a world where a giant screen absorbs human beings into its digital folds, about human impulses emerging through the ruins of a nuclear devastated world and about the intricacies of faith. But what is striking is that it places at its centre the figure of the storyteller itself, weaving images and worlds about the past, present and the future. It is ultimately about the triumph of her imagination that cuts through the varied contexts in which one finds her telling her story—performing around a fire, thundering in an auditorium, whispering through cyber-space, crackling through television or hitting back at the player in a video game.

It is this vision that ultimately helped me connect with my own discipline and the experiences described in the classroom.

References

Appadurai, Arjun. 1996. 'The Production of Locality', in Arjun Appadurai (ed.), *Modernity at Large: Cultural Dimensions of Globalization*. Minneapolis: University of Minnesota Press.

Bradbury, Ray. 2001. *The Illustrated Man.* New York: William Morrow.

Eco, Umberto. 1986. *Travels in Hyperreality: Essays.* San Diego: Harcourt Brace Jovanovich.

————. 1996. 'Afterword', in Geoffrey Nunberg (ed.), *The Future of the Book*. Berkeley: University of California Press.

Mills, C Wright. 1959. *The Sociological Imagination*. Oxford: Oxford University Press.

Murray, Janet H. 1997. *Hamlet on the Holodeck: The Future of Narrative in Cyberspace.* New York: Free Press.

Nunberg, Geoffrey. 1996. *The Future of the Book.* Berkeley: University of California Press.

Strathern, Marilyn. 1991. *Partial Connections*. Savage, MD.: Rowman & Littlefield.

Weber, Max. 1949. *Max Weber on the Methodology of the Social Sciences.* Trans. by Edward A. Shils and Henry A. Finch (eds). Glencoe, Ill.: Free Press.

Wilson, John. 1979. *Fantasy and Common Sense in Education.* New York: Wiley.

8

The 'Real' Story of Children's Publishing

Sandhya Rao

'The story does not make a world view. A world view gradually
emerges through the accumulation of many sources from a
community—its myths and legends, its accounts of traditions and
practices, and a vast amount of cultural knowledge...'
—David Crystal, *Language Death*
(Cambridge University Press, London, 2000)

Why do we create anything for children? Like books, toys, films, a
school and a curriculum? To keep them busy while they're growing
up? To build something useful for children, along the way? To help
them acquire a world view by drawing from their environment, give
them a sense of history, and the capabilities to savour and experience?

Whatever the answer, unless we have the vocabulary, we do not
have the language to express and to understand stories, and languages
lie at the heart of cultures. From naming things in the immediate
environment to articulating ideas and abstractions, to creating a
network in cyberspace, these stories create the language of different
cultures. Actually, stories don't need paper or printing ink, internet
or websites, celluloid or silver screen: they simply exist, and manifest
in engagement, like fire and flint. And because they exist, they are
real. When they are pressed to the outer edge of an ever-expanding
reality, we think they are imagined. But maybe they are not. If some
stories exist in our imagination, and if we agree that imagination is
real, wouldn't all stories then exist in reality?

Yet, it seems to me, that very often, our books and things for
children ignore many children's lived ways of seeing and imagining,
they ignore their engagement with real and 'imagined' worlds, and
they ignore their natural bonding with and inarguable need for stories
that gather in their consciousness in response to their individual and

collective cultural spaces. In this essay, I try to represent the idea of the story being at the heart of culture—no matter the medium—by attempting a physical interaction between a real story and the concerns of children's publishing in India, issues that powerfully impact the lives of the mostly forgotten majority.

In order to understand what these are, we need reference points: they have to do with the fact that it is mostly adults who write children's books; that the maximum number of books written for children are textbooks; that the maximum number of books published for children in India that are not textbooks and that are in the retail trade are in English—the language accessible to barely 2 per cent of the population; that, curiously, it's the books in English that register the biggest sales and possibly the largest readership (not counting textbooks); that there is a huge gap between the literary written and the comfortable spoken and by insisting on the one, especially in some languages, there is a very real possibility of losing those languages due to discomfort and alienation; that languages live in being used; that films often use language in the most dynamic and creative ways; that although the literature–literacy debate exists in children's literature across the world, it operates only in the case of children's books, and is much more invasive in children's publishing in the developing world.

Attempting a discussion around these questions begs two more: the first, to ask ourselves, is which children are we talking about? The second, asked by children, whether in a city bookstore or municipal school or small village, is this a real story? This is why I have told a real story about children in a tiny Bengal village. Ideally, it should be told with pictures—and there are pictures—because we are surrounded by pictures whether in the mind, on paper, on computer monitors, on television screens, or in 70 mm, sound and all. Read the story as you read about the story, look at the pictures you make in your head, and I hope some lines will connect and cross over.

* * *

I really went on a bus to see a tiger. I left Kolkata early in the morning. The bus stopped at Ghotokpukur for breakfast—the usual kochuri and daal and roshogollas. The roshogollas were only one rupee each. They were delicious and I ate about five or six.

On the bus again, I slept for a while, then looked out of the window.
The land was mostly flat. There were more trees closer to the villages,
but there were plenty of ponds with lilies and lotuses shining pink
and white. A Buddha story says we must be like the lotus which is
beautiful even though it grows in a dirty pond.

What chance does the lotus in the pond have in a world of instant
foods and constant entertainment? Do readers have a chance in a
milieu in which publishing for children is dominated by the textbook
industry which is highly competitive and extremely financially viable?
Because of and despite this, the market for other children's books is
booming. Today, many small and big private print enterprises produce
well-packaged and smart-selling products, mostly in the English
language. Parents are beginning to buy because they feel they must
offer some resistance to the pull of moving pictures on computer
monitors and television screens. Many parents support the philosophy
of many publishers that their children need books with messages,
books that teach: moral stories. Or at least, that they need to 'study'
their textbooks instead of wasting time on storybooks, wildlife
channels and outdoor games.

Yet, a child I know who, as an infant, was so traumatised by the
sound of temple bells in Thiruvananthapuram that he froze everytime
he heard chimes, and who, therefore, viewed all religious symbols
with fear for many years, was so taken up with the animation film
'Hanuman' that he 'became' the superhero. It helped, of course, that
the hero was a monkey. The child began to read everything that he
could lay his hands on that would tell him more about Hanuman and
all the others who interfaced with his hero. His process of healing
had begun. But he also asked, at regular intervals: Is Hanuman real?

When the bus stopped again, we were in a place called Baasanti
where we got off and went through a busy bazaar selling slippers and
clothes and coconut and moori (that's puffed rice, great with
chopped boiled potato, roasted peanuts, onions, coriander, salt and
lime, laced with mustard oil). The narrow street wound on and on
until it seemed as though the sky had come to touch my feet and I
would topple over the edge. I stopped. My heart beat fast.

It was the river, wide and rolling like the sky. Grey and billowing. I
had never seen such a grey and rolling river.

Far below, the jetty was crowded with boats. Passenger boats, fishing
boats, tourist boats, motorboats. It was crowded with people too,

mostly waiting to cross the river. They stood pressed against each
other in long, wooden country boats.

It is unlikely any of their children has ever stepped into a bookstore.
Or even a library. Perhaps they find themselves in their textbooks, if
they go to school, if there is a school in their village. It is unlikely
they or their worlds get written about in children's books. Perhaps
they get a glimpse of the world outside through cinema and television,
if they have access to these. Maybe their villages have community
television sets—but do they have electricity? If they are lucky, they
may even have a computer kiosk in their village which may also stock
some books in the language of their choice, thanks to the grassroot
work of NGOs to promote reading and literacy in innovative ways
across the country, in places unknown and unreached. Cinema and
television, however, have made the greatest inroads. At one time, it
was the radio. Then, it was farmer's programmes and song-based
sequences on the national television channel. Today, it is a babel of
languages and a riot of images. What do children make of this?

I was in Sundarban, home of the Royal Bengal Tiger. 'Sundarban'
means beautiful jungle. Or maybe it is sundarban because this
mangrove forest is full of sundari trees (Heritiera fomes). What I
think is, if this is where the tiger lives, it has to be beautiful. Because
the tiger is beautiful. The tiger is like a golden sun in the jungle.

Sundarban is spread over several small and big islands and mudflats
crisscrossed by creeks and streams and estuaries and canals and
waterways where the Ganga, Brahmaputra and Meghna rivers meet
and lead into the Bay of Bengal. That is why the water here is
salty—because of the sea—even river water is usually sweet.
Sundarban covers an area of about 10,000 square kilometres (by
one estimation) and is a little bit in India and a lot in Bangladesh.

The Bangla language boasts a longstanding literary tradition. Not
all other parts of the country can, however, claim the same, and in
the absence of deep enough roots, the vicarious appeal of the cut-
and-paste visual overwhelms the relevance or otherwise of the
message, and the unknown, the alien, even the uncomfortable quickly
begins to govern life.

Have you been in a boat on a river? Sat in the front, nearly at the
edge, and felt the wind in your hair? With warm spray wetting your

face? It was a hot day, I remember. But I didn't feel the sun, lying stretched out, eyes shut, face up. A small boy joined me. His mother came too but she sat on the steps near the deck – to keep an eye, I suppose.

A fishing boat drifted lazily past. We passed some villages, but most of the time it was only water and sky. The riverbank had dark and light bands on its side, and the boats pulled up on shore looked like they had been painted on to make a border of river, bank, boat and sky, and sometimes a tree. I was fascinated by the pattern this made and as I gazed I thought – suppose, suppose a tiger suddenly appears on the horizon?

When the boat reached our destination, we couldn't get off. The steps at the entrance were at least twenty feet away, with neither water nor platform in between. There was only black silty clay, squelchy and slippery. We made the crossing on wooden planks.

Writer C. S. Lakshmi speaks of visiting a home in a small village in Nagaland that sheltered some 50 children orphaned by insurgency. They had no milk, no fruits, and when she asked them what they wanted, they said, 'Books. Give us books.'

That evening, I went on a motorboat to see the tiger. There are deer and monkeys and wild boar and lizards and pythons and many different kinds of birds in Sundarban. And crocodiles. Everything on these islands happens on or with or by or from the river. We searched for the tiger among the trees as we passed the islands. The sun began to set slowly beyond the mangroves which grow thick and low on the forest floor. The islands filled with shadows and even though the engine droned, we heard the birds fall silent. On that first ride, we didn't see even the tip of the tail of a tiger, but I'm not so sure the tigers didn't see us. There were staring eyes in the jungle that night.

Getting off the boat this time, there was another surprise. We didn't need wooden planks to cross—the water came right up to the steps. Where did the twenty feet of squelch go?

While we were at dinner, a man appeared beating a drum, followed by two women singing, and two girls dancing. After a while I joined in. It was cold, I didn't know anybody, and it helped me get warm. That night I couldn't sleep because a bunch of silly geese kept chattering and honking worse than a traffic jam until it was nearly dawn. In the morning they were all fast asleep, one leg tucked beneath a wing! Since I was awake, I decided to go for a walk. It was misty, so misty that the sun in the sky looked like a reflection of the sun in a stream.

The gap between the spoken and the written, especially in some languages, is a major issue in children's books. Too high-flown and literary alienates the children, many of whom are first-generation readers. Too simple and colloquial alienates those who choose the books, either at home or at school. Children pick up advertisement jingles and film songs and dialogues—some of it quite challenging—without difficulty. The popular film song-based programme, *Chitrahaar*, has, since 1997, been scrolling the lyrics while the song sequence plays. Called Same Language Subtitling (SLS), this ingenious system has, apparently, helped to up the reading capabilities of the partially literate.

Later in the morning, I set out for the village. From nowhere at all a small group of children gathered, curious and shy. I was shy and curious too. They began to follow me and when I stopped to look at things I had not seen before, the gang stopped too.

A man was winnowing paddy, and a woman in another house was spreading it out to dry. I saw two women at the pump, collecting potable water. Surrounded by water—sea, river, and ponds with lotuses—the people in Sundarban did not have water fit to drink.

The gang tugged at my kurta and dragged me off to their special tourist attraction—the bank. It looked quite proud—the little bank—sitting among the trees. 'There's Shona,' said one of the kids. 'Shona! Shona! Esho! Ekhaane esho! Come here!' the others shouted and flitted like delicate butterflies towards her.

She was the one who had danced last night. She recognized me too. She turned to the gang and shooed them way: 'Go, now go!' Without a murmur, the gang disappeared. 'Come,' Shona said, now that I belonged only to her. She took me past the LIC agent's house to another house under a neem tree. 'Look,' she said, pointing to a solar panel fixed on the roof. 'It catches the sun.' I was more fascinated by the cowdung cakes drying below. She told me about her older sister Rupa, her mother and aunt who sang, her father the drummer who was a farmer. Then, as suddenly as she had appeared, she said, 'Now I have to go,' and ran away.

India lives in her villages, said Gandhiji long before Independence. That hasn't changed 60 years later, and even if there is caste discrimination and no water, the national television channel, *Doordarshan*, lives in a box. While families gather beneath the single weak light bulb for the night's entertainment, some children in some villages run to the 'hole in the wall' to press on buttons and make things happen on computer screens; some others go to tuition centres to learn what was not taught at school. The lucky ones borrow books. Some of them read.

> *My feet found their way to a temple with Goddess Durga and some garlanded gods. There was a figure of a man in a blue lungi who, we were told, had bravely fought man-eaters. Since people and tigers live so close to each other, sometimes tigers attack humans when their land is taken away, and when they have gone without food for a while. A hungry tiger is a very hungry tiger.*

> *Sundarban is famous for its honey-gatherers who collect bee-hives from the jungle. Sometimes, when humans go into the jungle they wear tiger masks on the back of their heads so that tigers will think they are one of them. I don't know if the trick works, but maybe that's one way of being brave! But, what happens to the jungle inhabitants that depend upon honey and bees for their nourishment?*

'Are you okay with showing death in a book for children?' a young city mother asked. It's a loaded question, and calls for another discussion. What do children make of the killing and bloodshed and violence they see on television, in films, and around them in their daily lives? How do they come to terms with things they have no knowledge of, yet seem to understand from deep within? They don't always all live happily ever after at the end of a 'fairytale', less so at the end of a folktale. As for stories with morals...

> *On the last ride of my visit to Sundarban, I noticed a boat on which the men looked as if they had been on the river for a long time. Lungis and shirts lay strewn about, cooking pots and pans rattled. The boat was from Bangladesh, I discovered. Boats from Bangladesh came into India quite often. Sometimes they were apprehended by the river police.*

> *Do they come to fish, or in search of work, or to trade? What happens if they get caught? Are they beaten up? Are they put in prison? What about their families? What if they can never return*

home? What will their children do? Do Indian boats stray into
Bangladesh? What happens to the people on these boats? How do
they know where they are? Can you draw a line in the water?

Without language, without words, without a rich and
compassionate vocabulary, how can we enable children to absorb
and recharge, understand and express, traverse worlds, articulate
and hand on history? If, some will argue, there is earth and air and
water enough to bear that history along. Why not, others will argue,
when there are technologies available?

'Engine off! Engine off!' a voice crashed into my reverie. 'Closer!
Closer! Look! Tiger!' Everybody rushed to one side of the boat,
nearly tipping it over. 'Look!'

There were deep impressions on the soft, wet ground. Footprints.
Tiger footprints? The prints looked fresh. Had we missed the tiger by
a whisker? Was it a tiger? I don't know. But the water was low
again, so low that the roots of the trees were completely exposed.
The bottom part was sickly grey, the upper green. Grey because of
being submerged in water, exposed when the water level went down.
Tide rising, tide falling. Ebbing and flowing. At night the tide is up
and water from the sea rushes into the streams and inlets and canals;
by day water drains out, drawing away from the sides of the islands
and mudflats. That's what makes the pattern—river, bank, boat
and sky, and sometimes a tree. That's what makes the 20 feet of
slush. If we didn't know about tidal activity, it would be like magic.

Maybe it is magic, with a name.

As I got ready to make the crossing one last time, 'Didi!' I heard
someone call. It was one of my village gang with three older boys.
'For you!' he said, and thrust into my hand a coconut-leaf lotus.
'Don't forget us!' That's why I have written this real story. Because I
want to remember everything. Because, as Mamadou Kouyate, a
West African oral performer is quoted by Crystal as saying, 'we are
the memory of mankind'.

Sometimes I think of the men on the boat. Did they find their way
home? Or did they stumble over a line in the water?

Reference

Crystal, David. 2000. *Language Death*. Cambridge: Cambridge University
Press.

9

The Digital Phenomenon:
Panacea or Faustian Bargain

Ashok Panikkar

Gone are the days of half empty shelves and material scarcity that was the bane of the upwardly aspiring Indian through much of the past century. Gone too are, for most urban educated folk, the days of living frugally and skimping on anything but the absolute necessities. We, the newly liberated citizens of Emerging India, the next global economic powerhouse (China's current pre-eminence notwithstanding), are now in the process of integrating with the rest of the world. What this means is that we now have access to the seemingly inexhaustible supply of new products, gadgets, contraptions and devices that are as good as any that one can buy in the malls of Middle America, the markets of Hong Kong or the *souks* of Dubai.

Where once even middle class Indians had to wait for years to get a phone connection, now we have instant access to mobile technology and practically every person you meet on the street—from the IT business man, his thirteen-year-old daughter and the auto-rickshaw driver have spanking new cell phones that can pretty much do anything but heat your lunch for you (though I believe the smart folks at Caltech and MIT are working on that even as we go to press!). A confession: after resisting to get a cell phone for years. I finally caved in and bought one three years ago when a new job required me to travel frequently out of town on business.

All these wonderful products are now freely available for our comfort, convenience and consumption. They help us move faster, talk cheaper and accomplish so much more during a normal working day or, for that matter, even while we are on vacation. As some 'globalists' are wont to say with much glee, these products maybe conceived at MIT in Cambridge, Massachusetts, coded in the Electronic City, Bangalore and produced in an industrial estate in Shanghai. This, indeed, is the magic of globalisation at work and we are all its benign beneficiaries.

Or are we? If, as many say today, technology is the answer to deprivation, poverty, slavery and inequity, then what are the questions that we should pose to it and to ourselves? For that matter, why would we need to even ask these questions? When there is so much that promises liberation from the drudgery of grunge and the banality of routine work, would it be foolish for us to even question whether we need to pay any attention at all to what this proliferation of digital technology means for us as a people and a society?

Lest I be branded as an incorrigible cynic, a sorry technophobe, or even an out of touch Luddite, my intentions are not to bash progress or technology but to pose a few questions that all of us—creators and consumers of these technologies—need to ask ourselves. Media/ technology watcher extraordinaire and iconoclast, Marshall McLuhan's main theme (1994) was the extension of our senses and limbs through the use of technological media. He was particularly curious about, what he termed, the extension of the nervous system through the use of 'electric' technologies' ['McLuhanese' for digital and electronic technology] and what he saw as the complete break with 5,000 years of mechanical technology. He did not say whether this was a good or bad thing, thinking that to do so would be meaningless and arrogant. Instead he thought it would be vital that we ask—What's Going On? In other words, what are the processes at work when new technologies appear and how do they affect the human being and life as we know it?

Hence, rather than leap to judgment about whether digital technology is good or bad I would like to explore the question *'What's going on?'* as a framework, for which I will use Neil Postman's 'Ten Principles of Technology' (1996)—a useful instrument to analyse the impact of technology on the political, economic, social and cultural life of a society.

Technology and Media—A Definition

Technology, according to Neil Postman (1985), is a physical apparatus, in other words, a machine. When technologies employ their own unique symbolic codes they become media. These media then, in turn, through popular use and acceptance get integrated into the social, economic and political context. A medium therefore, for Postman, becomes the social and intellectual environment that a machine creates.

At the broadest level then, technology may be defined as any process or system that serves either an economic, manufacturing, social, governmental or artistic function. These include communication and entertainment media (television, the Internet, headphones); transportation systems (planes, trains and automobiles); instruments of measurement and evaluation (clocks, thermometers, academic and intelligence testing); financial instruments, markets and banking institutions. Taken a step further governments and bureaucracies can be seen as machinery for creating and facilitating social and political order.

A medium may be any interface (system, device or technology) that human beings use to communicate with each other, such as the radio, telephone, the Internet, the printing press or language. Machines such as phones, televisions and radios become media because they employ unique symbolic codes that help create their own social and intellectual environments. Similarly, the symbolic and, to the uninitiated, mystical codes and processes (paperwork, rules and regulation) that bureaucracies employ can create a medium that can either facilitate or come in the way of communication and social engagement.

The Ten Principles of Technology

Neil Postman designed this instrument as a tool to analyse the intellectual, social, political and economic effects of a given technology (1996: 192–93). While the worry that questions, coming from these ten principles, maybe inherently slanted against technology is a legitimate concern, I have found them to be a neutral tool that is invaluable in bringing to light (the often less obvious) effects of a technology or process upon society. My standard for ensuring that these or any other questions are not leading or inherently loaded questions is fourfold.

1. That the questioner, in asking the question, does not already completely 'know' the answers.
2. That the questions are asked in a genuine spirit of curiosity and there is the real possibility of discovery and uncovering new knowledge and understanding.
3. That the framing of the question is not inherently skewed against the subject of the questioning.

4. That the questions are intended to aid learning rather than to manipulate the conversation.

Using the Ten Principles of Technology to examine the processes and effects of, say, the automobile, the printing press, the radio or the Internet is educative and can, often, be a revelation. I will use this instrument to explore, both, the advantages and what I call the Faustian Trade Offs of digital technologies. However, I am going to mostly limit myself to digital communication technologies in order to keep things relatively simple.

1. All technological change is a Faustian bargain. For every advantage a new technology offers, there is always a corresponding disadvantage.

The Advantages

These are considerable and, seemingly self evident:

1. Given the fast paced lives we lead, these gadgets have made modern urban life so much more convenient and easier. We can cook while on the run, change meetings and plans from any place on the earth and entertain ourselves with a flick of a remote button.
2. It has allowed the development of products and systems that help us move vast amounts of information at incredible speeds. This means that we can now send data from one end of the earth to another in less time than it would have taken a tribal chief to send a runner to the next village with news of an upcoming feast.
3. It allows an amateur astronomer in Ludhiana, India, to correspond with a fellow enthusiast in Bremen, Germany, and share thoughts about the stars and perhaps even swap recipes for barbecued chicken.
4. It has allowed, under certain conditions, for people who might share a common political, philosophic or religious ideal to create a virtual mass movement that can sometimes turn into a real one on the streets.
5. It has allowed folks, who may never have otherwise met, to connect via the Internet, collaborate, start businesses and perhaps even start families.
6. It is harder now for governments and corporations to hide gross injustices and misconducts that may otherwise not have easily come to light, thereby increasing the possibility of redressal through public exposure and scandal.

7. It has sometimes allowed both citizens and consumers to complete and file applications online, thereby avoiding both long lines and the harassment of touts and middle-men who have long profited from the cumbersome bureaucratic procedures of governments and corporations.

8. It has allowed people to be constantly in touch with each other, regardless of where they might be at a given point in time.

9. This technology has greatly enabled us to communicate in times of crisis. A cell phone when your car breaks down, or if you need to reach a doctor in an emergency, is an unmitigated blessing.

10. The introduction of this technology has helped create millions of well paying jobs, especially in hitherto economically depressed countries that have an educated labour force. Some countries such as India and China may potentially transform themselves into economic powerhouses through the exploitation of these technologies.

The Faustian Trade Off

1. The amount of information that is available now to the average person on the street or at a computer is so vast that it has resulted in an information glut. Moreover, the information is largely unregulated and is not filtered for veracity or appropriateness, and comes to the individual randomly and in an unstructured manner. This has created a situation where most people have difficulty discriminating between reliable and unreliable information.

2. The larger problem being when individuals in a society are unable to distinguish between fact and fiction and truth and falsehood, over a period of time they lose the capacity to distinguish between what is good for them and what is not. It may even seem anachronistic to talk about good and bad or truth and falsehood in an age where relativism and post modernism have decreed that these notions are subjective and unknowable, ergo all attempts at understanding them being futile. However societies, unlike some highly independent individuals (such as artists, some academics with tenure and eccentrics), cannot sustain themselves through purely subjective and idiosyncratic exercising of choice. Societies, in order to survive and thrive, require commonly accepted norms and ideals that every member can live with. An

environment that either overtly or covertly militates against the recognition and institutionalisation of common norms and values will find itself unable to develop the ties and networks that bind: at best, the needs of a healthy and unified community is compromised; and at worst civil society fragments into self-serving units that tend to be focussed on their own subjective special interests without a commitment to larger and unifying societal goals. Fragmented and highly partisan units such as these are likely to see no reason to make the critical accommodations necessary for the continued survival of the larger group.

3. The sheer quantities of information available and the multiple media that are used as conduits for dissemination make it very difficult to control it for appropriateness. Young people, for instance, are subject to information that may not always be either age appropriate or safe. Given the ubiquitous nature of this information it is well nigh impossible to keep this out of the reach of populations that may be vulnerable to its effects.

4. The larger consequences of this are many and include the following: Children are today exposed to adult information at an age when they neither have the emotional maturity nor the worldly experience to understand it or put it in perspective. This 'pre-mature ripening' leads them to either accept age inappropriate behaviours as normal or they develop an all too early cynicism about the world and how it works. Mimicking the observed norms and proclivities of adults that would otherwise remain mysterious and hidden until they are much older, children also run the risk of getting sexualised at an early stage. This in turn leads to them developing a blasé attitude to issues that they do not, really, understand. It also leads to the possibility of increased commercial and social exploitation of children by the fashion, entertainment and consumer goods industry and puts them at risk at the hands of older children and adults who might either not respect or, indeed, even recognise their vulnerability.

5. The very capacity to interact virtually with people 10,000 miles away can sometimes prevent us from developing skills needed to connect and sustain relationships with family or people who live in the neighbourhood. Creating a community requires that we develop not merely a common purpose, but a healthy interdependence, which is invested in the growth and well-being of other members of the community. This commitment is not an

abstract or theoretical one (despite the fact that many of us may slip up often and fall short of our own high standards); requires that complex human and people skills be available to make good on it. Moreover, creating real as opposed to virtual community requires from the members seemingly extraordinary patience and tolerance, given that the connections are not remote and members have to interact on a daily basis. This level of social intimacy brings to the surface many of the member's own foibles and idiosyncrasies that need to be either accepted or negotiated.

2. The advantages and disadvantages of new technologies are never distributed evenly among the population. This means that every new technology benefits some and harms others.

The Advantages

1. Since new technologies are sometimes expensive and complex to use or understand, the groups that have access to them will usually be from the affluent and highly educated elite. There is always the *theoretical* possibility that when these technologies are the preserve of the 'best and brightest' in a society there is the likelihood of high moral and cultural standards being maintained.
2. A case may be made that the educated and the cognoscenti use these technologies for constructive and productive purposes. For instance, some may argue that professors and social leaders use the Internet for research, and intellectual networking to promote social change, unlike a large section of the population that supports the enormous pornographic industry on the net.

The Faustian Trade Off

1. There are few advantages to an uneven access to these technologies. The affluent and those who have access to new technologies are more likely to feel the direct effects of the technology on their social and cultural lives. Technologies, that help mediate experiences between these individuals, and between individuals and the environment, will succeed in increasing the fragmentation of society and the feeling of alienation that many people in a highly mobile technological society feel.

2. Those who have less access may be affected less directly. However, the actions of those who embrace the new technologies *on those without access* will be considerable. For instance, when the economic, cultural and political elite of society lose emotional and social connection with each other and the lives of those that they affect, their decisions, economic, social, cultural or political, will adversely affect the entire society. In other words, they will neither be sufficiently cognisant of the needs of those who don't have access to the technology nor will they be empathetic to those who may lack the voice to protest against it.

3. There will continue to be a difference between those who know what the advantages are and those that don't, the ones who know being able to (somewhat) protect themselves from the more egregious effects of these technologies.

4. Yes, the differences in access will also contribute to the growing chasm between the lives of the haves and have-nots (regardless of the advantages or disadvantages of the technologies).

3. Embedded in every technology there is a powerful idea, sometimes two or three powerful ideas. Like language itself, a technology predisposes us to favour and value certain perspectives and accomplishments and to subordinate others. Every technology has a philosophy, which is given expression in how the technology makes people use their minds, in what it makes us do with our bodies, in how it codifies the world, in which of our senses it amplifies, in which of our emotional and intellectual tendencies it disregards.

The Advantages

1. Digital technology with its emphasis on random browsing, hyper links and the ubiquitous mouse click changes our thinking process in dramatic ways. The linear and sequential thinking process of printed technology is now replaced, in the younger and techno savvy generation, with a more organic and flexible thinking structure that is not as constrained by the logical patterns of an earlier age.

2. Email has increased the use of writing amongst large sections of society that would otherwise not have written letters.

3. Word processing has made writing so much faster, and this has radically transformed the publishing industry.

4. Today, every man or woman with an idea, a computer and access to the internet can potentially have a voice on cyber space. A soapbox in every bedroom and a blog to boot.

The Faustian Trade Off

1. With Gutenberg and the arrival of the first printed book, oral society gave way to a more symbolic and visually oriented society (story telling moved from the community sitting around the kitchen table or the campfire to the privacy of the printed page). The stories that we tell about our lives and the ways in which we seek to give meaning to it often determines the ways in which we perceive the world and the way our mind, in turn, works. What used to be a non-linear and organic story telling style in the oral tradition became linear and sequential on the printed page, giving rise, for instance, to the structure of the essay and the kind of analytical thinking that is the hallmark of what we, today, call reasoned argument and logical exposition. Much of the scientific progress in the past several centuries came out of this kind of logical reasoning. This is in danger of being lost through a shift in the culture of thinking.

2. Digital technology with its emphasis on random browsing, hyper links and the ubiquitous mouse click changes our thinking process in dramatic ways. The linear and sequential thinking process developed through hundreds of centuries of printed technology now runs the risk of changing into a non-sequential, non-linear, therefore possibly a 'non-rational' process. This process can, in time, become part of our cultural and political thinking and our social landscape, further fragmenting the often tenuous social fabric.

3. SMS or 'Texting', with its brusque and fragmented style, its terseness, abbreviations and truncated use of language puts a premium on continuous communication and keeping in touch, not so much on the quality or the meaningfulness of the communication. This has the potential for seriously affecting the more arduously cultivated discipline of forming linear, sequential arguments through fully formed sentences and complete, well reasoned thoughts. The results are now being seen by school teachers in societies where kids have learned to 'text' before they can learn to write (and by extension 'think') in logical and sequential ways.

4. Human beings do not merely 'use' machines; they immerse themselves in the 'system' that the machine brings with it. Most people remain unaware of the underlying system or medium that govern these machines. Societies, sub-cultures or communities

that embrace such digital technologies without, either, under-standing or being aware of the big ideas that are embedded in them put themselves at risk of having their own traditional pers-pectives and values altered unbeknownst to them. The new ideas chip away at the old ones incrementally, until one day they and the values that they brought with them are made obsolete and redundant. This happens covertly hence people become aware of the change only after it has, in a sense, already taken place.

5. When Internet communication, which often seems to prize speed over clarity, attitude over depth and easy opinion over rigorously formed ideas, takes over as the prime medium of communication, the skills of reflection and critical thinking are likely to be subordinated to the kind of 'thinking' that allows for quick and often facile reactions to complex issues.

4. A new technology usually makes war against an old technology. It competes with it for time, attention, money, prestige and a 'worldview'.

The Advantages

1. Who can quarrel with the fact that digital technologies and new generation diagnostic tools now allow doctors to identify micro-scopic changes and tumours in the body that can help us in the battle against diseases? The conveniences and advantages are both tangible and have helped millions, especially those who can afford these services.

2. It is now possible through Internet and digital technology to do research and study while sitting at home. Those without access to world class libraries and/or universities can still keep abreast of the best think tanks on a subject.

3. Digital technology makes it possible to create safer and 'smarter' automobiles, aircraft, machines and homes, again, for those who can afford them. Older technologies get relegated to museums or poorer economies that cannot afford the new devices.

4. The cell phone and the personal computer allow individuals to work and communicate from anyplace, even from the privacy of one's kitchen or, with wireless technology, the great outdoors. In a global economy the new employee is able to plug in and sign on anywhere and at anytime. This renders the 'old' work ethic that was regulated by pre-determined schedules and limited roles obsolete.

The Faustian Trade Off

1. In an earlier era television displaced radio as the primary mode of communication. Today the cell phone and the Internet displace newspapers and books as the primary source for information. Television and the Internet with their multiple programming choices and, in the case of the Internet, with its seemingly infinite options and opinions, also bring about a change in the social habits of people, who now (especially in the industrialised world) increasingly prefer the high stimulation and individualised offerings of these media to the company of family, friends and neighbours. Your neighbour cannot be as consistently witty or exciting as a stand up comic on a sitcom or a 'reality' show. Community and face–to–face social networking become less relevant.

2. Even when newspapers are read today they tend to mimic the high stimulation, graphic and visual style of the digital media. Under these circumstances even when social engagement occurs there is a tendency for people to be drawn to high stimulation (as in watching movies or your favourite TV shows together, walking in the malls, etc, bungee jumping.) and low conversation activities.

3. As the Walkman changed the act of listening to music from a communitarian to an individualised activity, similarly the laptop and the personal computer, like the cell phone, makes it possible to 'liberate' the individual from the shackles of designated space to one where he or she is always on call and at work. So much for not taking work home and for any pretence at achieving a credible work/life balance—the new employee is always at work.

5. Technological change is not merely additive; it is ecological. A new technology does not merely add something; it changes everything.

The Advantages

1. Word processors and desk top publishing did not merely make it possible for writers to write more efficiently. It turned everybody into a potential writer and a 'published' one at that.

2. When individuating technologies such as automobiles, cell phones and personal computers are introduced into the society they change the relationships between the individuals and groups. Previously defined roles and power structures are challenged,

and people are liberated from the constraints of age, gender, caste or ethnicity. Entire social systems are shaken to the core. Sometimes traditionally oppressed classes are liberated.

3. Where once political movements were slow and unwieldy affairs that took many weeks, months and even years to mobilise, today, with the Internet, groups can be mobilised within days, if not hours (even if they are likely to be just as unwieldy).

4. These technologies are also changing the ways in which social events are organised and daily activities are coordinated, leading to greater awareness and participation.

The Faustian Trade Off

1. The cell phone does not merely make it easier to call people when you are on the move, it also completely erases spatial boundaries and changes notions of public and private space. This is not always an advantage as anyone who is travelling in a train or sitting on a park bench knows when confronted with intimate details of their co-passengers lives as they bellow them into their phones.

2. The WalkMan or the iPod does not merely allow you to listen to your choice of music anywhere and at anytime. It effectively individualises the activity of listening to music so that what was once a shared community experience no longer brings people together. It is now more than ever a solitary activity that further separates members of a family and community by taste, mood, access and choice.

3. A technologically mediated, digitised and (for some) an increasingly virtual experience of the world makes for an emotional disconnect from the lives of people who are closest to us. When our relational energies are focused on intense and continuous communication with people who do not inhabit our physical world, there is less attention left for us to give to those like our family and neighbours—that is people we see everyday.

4. The greater the use of these (simultaneously engaging and distancing) technologies, the less we are able to communicate or relate to those who inhabit our physical space. The less we have to do with friends and neighbours, the more we lose our skills of intimacy and relationships. Relational skills and skills of intimacy are learned, nurtured and developed by consistent practice. The

less opportunity we have to use them, the less adept we become, hence the less willing we are to engage in them.

   6. *Because of the symbolic forms in which information is encoded, different technologies have different intellectual and emotional biases.*

The Advantages

1. These different biases help create diversity of thinking and the differing perceptions militate against a uni-dimensional understanding of society. This can help create a far more textured appreciation of the complexities of human experiences.
2. This increased diversity can also, potentially, result in greater creativity.

The Faustian Trade Off

1. The specific intellectual and emotional biases created through the use of certain technologies affect the cultural and intellectual environment in ways that are not always apparent or desirable.
2. The symbolic forms in which information is coded in the new technologies have the capacity to alter intellectual and emotional biases and their use brings about a change in the thinking and feeling processes of the individuals and groups who use them. For instance, the special effects, visual treatment and editing techniques now possible because of digital technology that are used liberally in TV shows, films, music videos and video games have a distinct intellectual bias: they tend towards montage like, fragmentary and non-linear narratives: this non-linear approach militates against the logical and sequential thinking that contributed to the development of what we call critical thinking. The thinking processes of those who use this technology consistently or those who grow up with it, is unbeknownst to them, changed.
3. Video games, for instance, also have a distinct emotional bias: They contribute to the participants getting used to a high stimulation and high engagement relationship with virtual characters that are at many levels easier to 'deal with' through physical manipulation of keypads and joysticks. Children who grow up with these games discover soon enough that the 'real' people they have to deal with—peers, siblings, parents and teachers—do not respond to this kind of manipulation. To their young

minds these 'real' people, while made of flesh and blood, are not as likely to be responsive as the more accommodating 'virtual' folk. It becomes so much more difficult to, hence, build emotional bonds with them.

4. Highly graphic and illustrated media with explicit descriptions and depictions are also 'hotter' in that they give maximum information to the viewer or player, this obviates the necessity to interpret or read between the lines, since there is nothing really to read except what is spelt out in a zillion pixels of colour. When children or adults are bred on a diet of explicit narratives, they lose the ability to develop their own nuanced interpretations of situations. Emotionally speaking, the effect of this is akin to the critique that is levelled against pornography, in that, it desensitises and numbs the viewer/user to the emotional lives of the subjects. In other words it objectifies and commodifies.

   7. Because of the accessibility and speed in which information is encoded, different technologies have different political biases.

The Advantages

1. With the lightening speeds at which data is communicated world wide, information can now reach citizens and consumers almost in real time and this can help them make better educated decisions.
2. These speeds send sensitive information all over the world and help mobilise groups that are widely scattered into taking unified political action. The furious pace at which information is coded and transmitted has the virtue of making information generation and communication far more democratic. This can help hitherto powerless groups level the playing field as far as their capacity to reach and influence broader audiences.

The Faustian Trade Off

1. With the lightening speeds at which information is communicated world wide, receivers and audiences are forced to react to complex situations on the basis of short bursts of data or 'breaking news'. This kind of information delivery does not allow for the creation of nuanced and analytical information. It leads, instead, to sound bites and highly charged posturing on the parts of, both news persons and newsmakers. This also leads to every

position being articulated as extreme and highly polarised, all parties turned into adversaries and all discussions into debates.

2. Conflict provides drama. This technology favours the communication of points of view which benefit political ideologies that perceive the world and issues in blacks and whites.

3. Mobile technology media, while useful in spontaneously mobilising self-organised demonstrations and group events, are biased towards decentralisation. These demonstrations and events often have no stable core and can thus easily go out of control.

4. Because of the speed with which the problems are identified and communicated, the pressure is on for quick solutions that can satisfy the need of the group or the audience for fast action and quick results.

8. Because of their physical form, different technologies have different sensory biases.

The Advantages

1. Pre-digital technological media such as print tended to favour the visual sense. Digital technologies on the other hand, being multi-sensory, tend to simultaneously stimulate the aural as well as the visual and the total emotional stimulation is high.

2. This technology utilises all the senses (synaesthesia), and the user experiences things both intensely and intimately in a way earlier technologies don't allow.

3. These multi-sensory technologies stimulate the creativity and innovation of engineers and designers by, amongst other things, creating opportunities for new content development and opening up the possibilities of interesting interfaces between humans and machines.

The Faustian Trade Off

1. These multi-sensory media create very intense 'all-factory' experiences that do not allow the viewer to step back from the experience and see what is *really* happening. This creates a veritable Disneyland experience where everything is happening all at once and little needs be deliberated or even understood.

9. Because of the conditions in which we attend them, different technologies have different social biases.

The Advantages

1. These technologies allow us to escape our constraints of space and time, enabling us to work, contact and play regardless of time and place.
2. Digital technologies help shift the prevailing social biases and help erase social boundaries, uniting groups that once were kept separate because of wholly distinct values, norms and experiences.

The Faustian Trade Off

1. These technologies by allowing us to escape our constraints of space and time and thereby enabling us to work, contact and play, regardless of time and place, blur the boundaries that separate work, play and rest. This blurs the definition of, what once was, the private and the public and often ends up diminishing both.
2. This blurring changes the ways in which people socialise. Even when people meet socially today, there is the ever present possibility that one of the parties may interrupt their visit to talk to a caller on the cell phone. Meetings today are often punctuated by such digital interruptions that make social engagement a far more fragmented and less attentive affair. Mindfullness as a state of being is as much a cultural quality as it is an individual virtue. It is hard to cultivate, as anybody who has ever practiced meditation knows and a traffic intersection is not the best place to develop it.
3. Public spaces are also not solely 'public' today, given that this technology helps us impose our personal space onto whatever space we are in. Whether we are in parks, streets, trains or at concerts, we are privy to the conversations of our fellow citizens who talk with loud voices into their cell phones, or 'tune' off from the rest of the world by tuning into their iPods and MP3 players.
4. The private becomes public too, with us sharing our personal thoughts and concerns in the full view (or hearing) of strangers. Once we have breached this wall, moving onto Jerry Springer like talk shows, reality shows and internet voyeurism is but a small step.

   10. *Because of their technical and economic structure, different technologies have different content biases.*

The Advantages

1. Perhaps these differing content biases may create a rich marketplace of ideas, enriching us with the virtues of diversity.

The Faustian Trade Off

1. Digital technologies are developed by large corporations that can recoup their investments only by having as wide an application as possible. This requires the content developers to gear much of their materials to the lowest common denominator.
2. Digital media with visual or photo capability tends to have a bias towards visually stimulating stories. This can and has the unfortunate effect of relegating to the shadows stories that are important and nuanced, but without visual appeal. Rising interest rates because of IMF and World Bank strictures or the psychological challenges of rural youth have limited visual appeal.
3. Remember the tabloids and their motto: 'If it bleeds, it leads'?
4. Smaller screens such as cell phones will attract visuals that can be easily seen and enjoyed at that scale. This will again influence the selection of content that finds its way into these devices.

So What?

What is the difference between a whole family watching a TV show together, night after night and all members of a family sitting in separate rooms, watching different shows? What is the difference between sharing a meal and conversation with your neighbours and the whole bunch of you watching a TV serial or show instead? What is the sound of a man thinking alone or, again, what is the sound of a group deliberating together? What is the difference between learning from your bedroom in front of a computer and from a teacher in front of a black board? What is the difference between going for a community music festival and the sheer freedom and convenience of using an iPod or an MP3 player? What is the difference between serial monogamy (having one temporary relationship after another) and having one committed relationship that you try and make work despite all the challenges and misgivings? These are some questions that we need to address if we are not to follow blindly into whatever ocean the Pied Pipers of Change Inc. lead us with the haunting strains of their seductive and stimulating music.

It may be argued that such questions have been asked at the introduction of every new technology as, indeed, they are being asked now. The disadvantages of digital technologies may be common knowledge for many, after all they are being talked about in seminars, academic papers and even in the feature sections of newspapers. However, many of these discussions are at the micro level and refer to specific 'ills' or concerns such as, say, the explicit nature of shows on television or the fact that working families don't spend time eating dinner together anymore. At many levels, like the proverbial fish in the pond that is unaware that its primary environmental characteristic is water, we are awash in so much technology that we have become numbed to its ubiquitous presence in every facet of our lives. While some of us may, sporadically, recognise that all is not well with the corporate advertiser's picture of technological bliss, in the main we are accepting of their larger story of a life of unceasing and unquestioned technological progress. This essay is an attempt to start a conversation by bringing many of these questions to the table. In the process perhaps we can have a deeper and more comprehensive critique as well as engage in a public dialogue about these issues.

At the turn of the century we are poised at the edge of an information and technological revolution with major implications in the way all human activities such as trade, transportation, communication, social and personal relationships are ordered. Amidst the euphoria that is generated by the new vocabulary of the age, giga-bytes, e-commerce, internet, and virtual reality, it might be prudent to ask ourselves what the human and social costs of embracing these technologies might be. How much of this 'progress' is really inevitable and how much is indeed acceptable?

It is worth remembering that when, at other moments in history, major technological change such as the wheel, agriculture or the printed word forever changed older modes of thinking and living, the changes happened relatively slowly and over centuries. Increasing mobility, the global reach of markets and never ending growth of research and development have presented us with a wholly different set of conditions. Today, we are faced with a pace of change that has compressed the gestation time for society to that of less than a generation and in some cases to even within a span of five years or less. In other words, earlier societies could assimilate new technologies and over a period of time absorb or adapt themselves by altering their social structures to the new media. Today, however, we are thrust into the deep end of our new environments and forced to adapt to changing conditions, often within spans of less than a couple of years or even months.

The Cost of Change

Living with constant change is akin to being on a treadmill or, even worse, a roller coaster without any option to get off. We are constantly compelled to change the ways in which we communicate with each other; the ways in which we store and access information; create learning environments; order time; build communities and invest in neighbourhoods. And we change all this—including the notion of what is meaningful or of value to us as people and indeed our notions of what is moral or ethical by allowing technologists, designers, inventors and marketing wunderkinds, and the gadgets that they have begotten to decide how we will use them or whether we, indeed, should. This brings to mind what sceptics of the unbridled 'progress' of technology have always warned us about. Henry David Thoreau (1854) said that we must be wary of railroads lest the rails ride upon us rather than we ride upon them. He also wondered what kind of news could ever be so important that we would have to send it instantly across the country by telegraph. What was so important that he could not have waited for a few weeks to get it by horse and rider? From Thoreau's fear of the railroad riding upon us to McLuhan's infamous notion of the medium becoming the message it is a small, but very ominous step.

Change is the NEW Status Quo. Or, as an old adage goes, 'the only thing that is permanent is change'. This bears some thinking about. There is a tendency for most folks to accept the larger social, cultural, political and economic forces and its actions as a *fait accompli*. In critical thinking terms, this is a classic case of confusing 'what is' with 'what should be'. By not questioning these macro changes we run the risk of accepting the changes thrust upon us as a given and presuming that we have no option but to accept them. We allow ourselves to be co-opted without a dialogue or having a voice in the matter.

Hidden Processes, Persuaders and Pacifiers

There are many reasons why recognition and understanding of the macro-processes that govern the ways in which our society, culture, economics and society operate do not become part of the public consciousness or conversations. *One reason is that these processes are usually hidden.* They are inherent in the form of the system, medium or technology rather than being apparent in the content. As Marshall McLuhan says, it is not surprising that we hear indignant criticism of the increase in sex and violence in television programmes. It is less likely that there will be serious concern on the effects of the medium itself on the cultural and relational mores of a society. Even social conservatives who are much exercised about crumbling values and norms adapt and use these technologies. They do so oblivious of the fact that rigorous scrutiny and control of the content is not protection against radical, social and moral change wrought by the media that they embrace, albeit tactically. Interestingly, the most dramatic effects of a medium or technology on people have little or nothing to do with the educational or inspirational value, such as it may be, of the content. When modes of communication change, while it is indeed true that what people have to say to each other changes, more importantly the ways in which people relate to each other changes. Similarly, prurient and abusive lyrics garner much attention and debate, but the not entirely healthy change in the role that music plays in the cultural life of the community, with the advent of individualised technologies for its delivery, such as 'Walkman' or 'Discman', attract little comment or criticism. On the contrary, individualised technologies (gadgets that allow for personal rather than collective enjoyment of experiences) are celebrated as liberating and democratising.

The other reason is that the economic compulsions of the market which are usually determined by the producers, inventors, marketing people and the financiers do not encourage a close inspection of the processes of production or consumption. In an otherwise information rich society, it is difficult to find much information about the social, cultural or moral costs of the public's own fascination with media, technologies or gadgets. Protective of their access to (continued) profits, the manufacturers and the advertisers are, for good reason, unlikely to either fund or otherwise encourage much study of these processes.

...and the Fish Disagreed with Something that Ate It

To use an old example, if you put a goldfish in a tank and very gradually increase the temperature of the water, it will keep swimming unaware that it is being slowly cooked to death. In much the same fashion, human beings that live under adverse conditions learn to adapt to their situation unaware of the often life or soul threatening effects of the changes that are happening in their own environment. It is usual for those under immediate threat of physical danger such as mugging or bomb raid to feel threatened and fight back or at least react by running or moving to a shelter or to safer areas. However, when the systemic changes are slow and ubiquitous, one feels quite silly trying to fight them or run away. If everybody is in the same situation, it is tempting to believe that 'oh well, this is normal and must be what life is all about, I should get REAL'. It is also true that we are often least able to understand our own predicament when we are surrounded by the stress and strains of coping with them.

Digital media, in the form of mobile telephones, Internet and photography have profoundly altered our social, economic, cultural and political life. To avoid the fate of the slow cooking fish we need to develop the kind of skills that are necessary for us to, both, recognise and understand the radical changes that beset us.

Talking Cheap or Cheapening Talk?

As a wit was heard to ask upon hearing constant talk about the telecommunication revolution, *Great, now that we have a world wide communication system, I have a question—Do we, indeed, have anything to say?* We might add to that the question. 'And in any case, what does it cost us, as a people, to be able to say it?'

As digital technologies makes talking cheap, is it simultaneously cheapening talk?

Note

My thinking on this subject has been influenced by many thinkers and writers on media, technology and society, particularly Marshall McLuhan and Neil Postman. Those interested in exploring these ideas further would greatly benefit from perusing the following books. I have borrowed liberally from both.

References

McLuhan, Marshall. 1971. *The Gutenberg Galaxy: The Making of Typographic Man*. London: Routledge & Kegan Paul.

McLuhan, Marshall. 1994. *Understanding Media: The Extensions of Man.* Cambridge, Mass.: MIT Press.

Postman, Neil. 1985. *Amusing Ourselves to Death: Public Discourse in the Age of Show Business.* New York: Viking.

——————. 1993. *Technopoly: The Surrender of Culture to Technology.* New York: Vintage Books.

——————.1996. *The End of Education: Redefining the Value of School.* New York: Vintage Books.

Putnam, Robert. 1995. 'Bowling Alone: America's Declining Social Capital', *Journal of Democracy*, 6 (1): 65–78.

Thoreau, Henry David.1854. *Walden. http://thoreau.eserver.org/ walden02.html/.*

10

Blog In, Blog Out

Dilip D'Souza

Had dinner with a blogger once, at a time when I was still new to the experience. He, on the other hand, was steeped in blogging, so caught up in its potential and allure that he could barely speak about anything else. I learned a lot from him, but the greatest lesson was one I didn't quite catch at the time. The greatest, in the sense that it told me something about one of the prime motivations for blogging.

After dinner, a late night blogging session, and then this conversation:

Him: You know, the sad thing about India is that no really good writer here also blogs.

Me: You think so?

Him: Yes. No good writers at all. Of course, except you and me.

Me: Oh.

A few minutes later, he repeated this, if with a small variation.

There's no good writing on Indian blogs, he said, 'except for yours and mine.'

It should have been something of a warning to me. After all, one thing we all learn, sometimes the hard way, is that bombast is always a cover for mediocrity. I remember it from the fellow graduate student in my Computer Science days who, with every homework assignment turned in, invariably spoke in terms of 'discovering' new theorems. This was a claim I always marvelled at, and thus held him in awe. Because it is no small thing to prove new theorems. (I was managing no such thing; I was just trying to get done with the homework). But yes, it is no small thing, and that should have quickly told me the truth that we all realised in time. The man's grades didn't quite measure up to his claims. He was just bluffing away his incompetence.

And that's the way I should have understood my dinner companion. More important, I should have understood right then what I know well now: blogging has much to do with the ego.

Let me expand on that. Any public writing, almost by definition, is an exercise in self-indulgence. You write to express your thoughts, to clarify them, and then offer them for public consumption. Every writer feeds off the responses to her writing, whether critical or appreciative. That's the way it should be. Nothing wrong with stroking the ego.

But until now, if you've wanted to get published, you've had to deal with a beast they call an editor. The editor critiques your writing, asks you to check your facts, fixes mistakes, suggests changes—All necessary things, for any writer. But perhaps most necessary of all is that the editor pricks balloons. With his critiques, he shows you where you've gone wrong, where you're not quite as good as you thought you were, where you can and must improve. He/She is the filter that every writer needs to fine-tune his/her craft.

And with a good editor, the ego stroking comes to mean more. Because you know you have put your writing through a hard-nosed filter that can only make it better. I don't know a single serious writer who doesn't appreciate this; who doesn't, in fact, crave what a good editor says.

But now there's blogging. Suddenly, there's no filter. You write something and in seconds, it's out there for the world to read. And yes, people do read, and they react, sometimes also in seconds. You get the ego-boost and it feels great. You may even come to believe you're an excellent writer, even that you and your dinner companion—whom you have to include only because he would think a statement like 'I'm the only good writer in India' is mildly bizarre—are the only such.

In place of such delusion, give me the filter, please. Every time.

This post-dinner conversation may be something of a funny story, but somewhere in there is the essence of blogging, at least as I have experienced it. There's great power in blogging, enormous potential, it can be a wonderful outlet for creative expression. Yet there are also enormous egos. They often produce a deal of viciousness.

I'll return to that. Until then, three vignettes from my time in the blogosphere, to fill in the picture I'm trying to paint here.

I mentioned egos. Just by going about what they do, bloggers develop a certain impression of themselves. Out of the blue once, one decided to explain to me what blogging meant to him: 'The world is changing, and its not just the *jhola*[1]-carrying, chain-smoking, black-rimmed-spectacle wearing, *kurta*–and–jeans crowd that can pass off as intellectuals. Now, everyone can!'

Well, yeah! Congratulations! Here's someone who wants to 'pass off' as an intellectual. What else is there to say but wish him the best? Never mind what his outburst says about blogging. Or about this person himself.

Another intriguing feature of blogging is that bloggers appear to assume that they are less responsible for what they say than other writers are. That therefore they can say anything. And they do, and often it is snide, vitriolic stuff. I brought this up once in an argument I got into with one of the best known Indian bloggers out there. As the man in this exchange from the always-suspect mainstream media, I got firmly put in my place with this: 'A blog is supposed to be a lot more personal than a professional column is. You are being paid to express your opinions, so we expect a lot more work and restraint in your tone in your columns than in [what we bloggers write].'

The hardly-subtle implication: if you're not paid, thus if you blog, you can be both abusive and lazy about what you write. If you blog, you're not subject to the standards the media must uphold, the very standards you complain that they do not uphold.

And this final vignette, which persuaded me that some bloggers manage to develop blinkers about the outside world. A third well-known blogger wrote to me to suggest that if I wanted my arguments to persuade anyone, they would have to contain 'facts and superbly argued logic', and that these were features I would find in the writings of... three other popular Indian bloggers.

Leave aside any possible differing opinions about just how 'superbly argued' that logic is. No, the world does contain non-bloggers too, but that is something that bloggers too often forget. They quote, and read, and draw inspiration from other bloggers. Period.

Before this turns into an entirely pessimistic polemic, let's look at some of the promise of blogging.

There is great potential in blogging, and it comes from the imme-diacy of the technology and the medium. Never before have we had this immediacy: consider that even television is, at a minimum, hours behind the news. But when the tsunami happened in December 2004, blogs fired up overnight, acting as a clearing house of news and information about fast-breaking events. *Tsunami Help*, which later became the *South-East Asian Earth Quake and Tsunami* (thus sporting the unfortunate acronym SEA-EAT), was the best known of these. Within hours, it was being used widely; within days, it was known all over the world.

Tsunami Help carried everything from offers of help to requests for specific material to on–the–spot reports by SMS. Its story is well known enough that I don't need to recount it here, and its success stimulated the creation of similar blogs after Mumbai's July flood, and Katrina, and the October earthquake in the subcontinent.

With *Tsunami Help*, people suddenly had a one-stop place to get up–to–the–minute tsunami information. Its great attraction was that it was run by motivated, energetic and enthusiastic people. No media outlet could match that edge, and that itself tells the story of the power of blogs. And it went beyond that as well. Bloggers travelled through the tsunami-hit areas—a companion and I were two— reporting first-hand. Unbound by deadlines, yet able to publish imme- diately, not restricted by word-lengths, these travelling writers painted the picture of the terrible devastation in ways that, again, newspapers and magazines would find hard to match.

And besides reporting on disasters like the tsunami, blogs seem to be ideally suited to a watchdog role, a new trend of journalism by and for citizens. In the best traditions of journalism, these are people who take nothing at face value, retain a healthy scepticism, and dig away. In some ways, it's almost as if blogging, by its very nature, attracts such people.

And more often than not, they come up with the goods: The unravelling of Dan Rather[2] and various exposes of plagiarism are well-known. Bloggers have also delved deep into declared assets of politicians running for election; into census figures; into intricate webs of links between sites on the net, showing they are all phoney; and much more. It's not that more traditional media cannot do these things; it is that some bloggers have made it their business, using the power of instant exposure, to follow these trails.

And that is, truly, the power of blogging.

But of course, with power must come responsibility. As I touched on above, sometimes it seems bloggers don't fully understand that. The lack of an editor is one reason, but it goes beyond that. There have been some truly depressing episodes among Indian bloggers that, to my shame, I have been part of. These were collective, deter- mined efforts to crucify people and ruin their reputations using every web trick in the book.

In January 2005, a well-known Indian blogger stumbled on a blog that consisted of nothing more than posts stolen from others' blogs. Reprehensible, and the plagiarist needed to be punished. But anything more than a cursory glance at his blog, at what he had done, showed the obvious truth. This guy was copying stuff so widely, so openly, so utterly without guile, that he could not be anything other than simple-minded. He didn't change a single word. He even copied comments from others' blogs.

This was no malicious Macchiavelli, this was a dope.

Yet a band of Indian bloggers, led by the well-known one, joined hands and went after this man with everything they had, digging diligently into his life. They issued him ultimatums, demanded apologies in language they would dictate, posted widely about him so that any web search about him would show he was a plagiariser.

So far, OK. The man did wrong, after all. Dope or not, you can't steal other people's writing. He had to pay for doing so. And he did.

But the blogger band went further, I believe inexcusably further. On shaky grounds, they decided that he was also a credit-card fraudster. They decided to report him to the FBI. They went about looking for ways to file suit against him. They wrote about him in just these terms, explicitly using the phrase 'credit-card fraud', so that any web search for him would throw that up as well.

The well-known blogger even approached a legal help site to ask what the options were in connection with the accusation of credit card fraud. Here's how that site responded:

If he were to be charged with a crime unrelated to website copying, [we] would be concerned that he not be convicted in the court of the blogosphere, as appears to be happening now. Unsubstantiated allegations about [the plagiarist] are potentially libellous and will be removed from this thread.

'Unsubstantiated allegations.'

Nobody but this band, intent as they were on blood, saw any evidence for credit-card fraud. They had not a shred of evidence, yet they damned their man by conjecture.

And that returns me to a number of simple questions that I'm sure others have grappled with before, questions to do with the impact and implications of blogging. What happens when bloggers post lies, knowingly or not? What happens when they post rumours, knowingly or not? What happens when they post unsubstantiated assumptions, knowingly or not? What happens when they call others names? (Those, in what I see as a descending order of severity).

All those things happen, in plenty. In some cases, they get pointed out to the blogger concerned. In enough of those cases, the blogger concerned has done nothing.

Yet, champion bloggers will tell you faithfully that the blogosphere is famously self-correcting, that it has its own checks and balances. That when bloggers post lies and insinuations, their readership will naturally crumble away, and that's the best form of correction. No need for editors or regulations or anything.

Only, in the face of stuff like the episode I've written about here, what is this famously self-correcting, checked-and-balanced blogosphere to do?

After all, those who told lies and spread rumours at the time remain popular and respected bloggers nevertheless. Clearly, they didn't give much of a damn for being correct, being corrected, or making corrections. Obviously that self-correcting mechanism isn't doing all that it must.

And when I look at it this way, I am reminded of Harshad Mehta, whose underhanded doings in the Mumbai stock market scam eventually mattered very little. Partly because he never paid for his misdeeds, but mostly because he became a greatly respected newspaper columnist on the economy and the stock market. I am also reminded of the Lalus and Modis,[3] who frequently point to their electoral triumphs as proof that they are innocent of charges against them.

And I am reminded most of all of Pavan Varma, who in his book writes of the 'moral relativism' of us Indians. He thinks our 'understanding of right and wrong is far more related to efficacy than to absolutist notions of morality' (2004: 76).

In other words, if I've got where I want to get, or am getting there, to hell with the ethics. Nobody really gives a damn anyway, and people are still flocking to listen to me, so why should I correct myself?

It saddens me, yet perhaps it should not, that this is the attitude I sense in the blog world. It should not sadden me because the mistake is to presume that bloggers are in any way different from the milieu, the society, they inhabit.

Finally, ideological wars and some fun.

A friend called one day: Join me and a few blogger pals for coffee?

Sure, I said. I like the guy, I can use an hour just chilling. So I met these guys at the nearby Barista, talked cricket, tsunami, travel, this and that. Good time, tasty coffee concoction or two, headed home.

Only ... well, these were bloggers after all, and everything has to be blogged. So the morning after, one already had his impressions of the meet up. So I followed my modem's blinking lights to his blog, to find this: 'I'm sure you are all wondering what happens when a bunch of free-market cheerleaders face-off against one leftist.'

'Face-off.'

I was the 'leftist' he meant, see, and the rest were free-market types. Hey, you might have thought this was just shooting the breeze, downing the brown stuff. Silly! It really was a 'face-off', and an ideological one too.

Now 'leftist' hardly mattered to me, but I was stunned by that 'face-off'. I mean, plenty of my friends think along diverging ideological lines. Yet we meet, chat, argue, play tennis, swap notes on girls. (Well, that last in the past tense). The things that friends do. Never has anyone called this a 'face-off.'

But then those friends are not bloggers. And somewhere in there is some more essence of a modern phenomenon. The freewheeling world of the Web attracts people looking for the last great frontier of individualism. They like that Wild West quality, the lack of rules. They think of themselves as 'very bright' (yes, someone actually used that phrase about himself) and forthright. They are fiercely combative, always ready for battle. My coffee companion sees the world in disparate camps, itching for those face-offs. Fine, but must everyone else see it that way too?

With blogging, after a while of reading carefully crafted opinion on screen, comes the urge to put faces to opinions. Even denizens of the Web want to meet other denizens, after all. So bloggers meet, usually at a coffee joint. (Like my face-off, though in greater numbers).

And with the charms I've described, these blog meets must be unbearably dreary affairs. Right?

Wrong. The next time I met some bloggers like this, one told me:

'Nobody reads what you write! Nobody wants to read what you write! How do you earn a living if nobody reads you?'

Who said that about 'dreary'?

But seriously: many bloggers—those to whom 'ego' means nothing—are normal, charming people. They talk, bake delicious puddings, like to travel. Some are outstanding photographers. I know one who won a poetry–by–SMS contest. Another combines technology, politics and sharp–but–never–cutting humour in a delight of a blog. A third writes about her adopted city with such knowledge and passion that you'd swear she was born and bred there.

People I enjoy meeting and chatting with. People much like any other friends.

Though not many friends have this cherry on top: a truly endearing tendency to refer to people by blog monikers. Really, how can you not like a guy who says, twinkle firmly in place: 'Went to Delhi last week, I met Ball Toad, Black Pad and Minorly Orbiting Fun Days! We had fun!'

Notes

1. Sling bag.
2. On September 8, 2004, Dan Rather of CBS News aired a report about documents that had come to light critical of George Bush's service in the US National Guard in the early 1970s. While he claimed they had been authenticated by CBS, within hours, bloggers were raising questions about these documents. They centred on the typeface used in the documents, which were quite clearly what you'd find in a modern Microsoft Word document, not in a 1970s-era typewritten one. For two weeks, Rather continued to claim they were authentic. But on September 20, he and CBS publicity repudiated the documents. After an investigation, several CBS news executives resigned. Rather also stepped down as anchorman of the news on CBS, though it was not made clear whether this had to do with the controversy over the documents. This whole episode has come to be known as 'Rathergate'. For more information, see *http://en.wikipedia.org/wiki/Rathergater*)
3. Lalu Prasad Yadav, ex-chief minister of Bihar state, was ousted from office for alleged corrupt practices. Narendra Modi is the chief minister of Gujarat state, charged by human rights activists with masterminding the communal carnage of Muslims in 2002—Ed.

Reference

Varma, Pavan. 2004. *Being Indian: The Truth About Why the 21st Century Will be India's.* New Delhi: Viking.

11

The New Technologies and the Constitution of 'Theft'

Nalini Rajan

The objective of this article[1] is to rework the ways in which the new technologies erode the notion of private property. While it is true that the new digital technologies envisage a 'public' realm as never before, it is equally true that they emphasise the integrity and purity of the 'private'. I discuss the manner in which computer systems, for example, are viewed as pristine, self-contained bodies that must be protected from the invasion of viruses and other such undesirable aliens. As more and more corporations, banks, governments, military and academic personnel start moving into the world of networked computing, more and more viruses line up for the attack, and the security of digital systems is increasingly under threat. New protocols of computer language now integrate language pertaining to 'theft' and 'private property'. The article also attempts to demonstrate that the theory of property, even in the best of contexts involving land or movable property, is poorly grounded in philosophical or logical terms. Using an example of digital audio sampling, I analyse how and why the new technologies completely render meaningless the notion of private property. This article also notes the ill-advised and logically untenable move of traditional communities to copyright their cultures.

IPR Law and the Real World of Computer Viruses

In the developing world, a new class of 'digitally homeless' is emerging. The rich in these high-growth emerging markets—especially in countries like China, Brazil and India—are using digital technologies to maintain their class locations, while the poor are becoming poorer with additional information poverty. According to UNDP's 'Human Development Report 2001', among India's 1.4 million Internet connections, more than 1.3 million are in the five states of Delhi, Karnataka, Maharashtra, Tamil Nadu and Mumbai (2001: 40). Given the large illiterate or semi-literate populations in many third world countries, some more complications occur. The new information technologies offer new management technologies of control, with the parallel increase of part-time and casual labour.

However, it is not only the new labour practices that require a new protocol. The new technologies themselves are being subjected to rules and regulations, and intellectual property rights are being tightened all over the world. As signatories to the World Trade Organisation's TRIPS (trade-related aspects of intellectual property rights) agreement, a handful of developing countries are now implementing national systems of intellectual property rights, following an agreed set of minimum standards, such as 20 years of patent protection. The Indian Copyright Act, 1957, was amended in June 1994 in order to include the definition of Computer Programming. Under these amendments, civil or criminal action may be instituted for duplicating, selling, or hiring copyrighted software. The Copyright law makes no distinction between duplicating software for sales or for free distribution.[2]

Since the 1980s, when computer systems started gaining popularity, viruses erupted and proliferated in such a manner that their existence was soon perceived as being analogous to biological viruses, like the AIDS virus.[3] One notorious virus writer or 'hacker', identified as the Dark Avenger in Bulgaria, alone created over 75 viruses! In line with the science fiction tone of the emerging computer security language, early books on the subject had titles that suggested a low and dirty status for the virus on the biological totem-pole, like Lance Hoffman's *Rogue Programs: Viruses, Worms and Trojan Horses* (1990) and Alan Lundell's *Virus! The Secret World of Computer Invaders that Breed and Destroy* (1989). The past decade has witnessed tens of thousands of viruses going under a series of colourful and semantically loaded names like 'Festering Hater' or 'Blaster' or 'Sasser'. The use of organic metaphors suggests a kind of timelessness or a-historicity to the actions of this kind of hacker. The end of the 1990s also saw the emergence of a small industry dedicated to antivirus protection software to create a kind of immunology system, as it were. In other words, the networked computer user was variously imagined as a high-status Brahmin, or alternatively, metropolitan heterosexual white male, who needed to protect himself from invading armies of lower castes or Black gay migrants, respectively.

The point, of course, is that these viruses are not mere accidents or faults in a complicated technological process; they are created by real people with real motives. Furthermore, they are selective about who they attack—usually Microsoft Windows Operating Systems, hardly ever Linux or Apple-Mac. The stereotypical vision of a virus creator is that of a disgruntled, unbalanced, frustrated former employee or adult or teenage—often non-white—psychopath. To look for psychological motives for the virus writer is also to obfuscate the political nature of this kind of hacker. The truth is that today's creator of viruses is often a highly educated individual who belongs to the mainstream, and who is making a political statement in favour of the obverse of copyright, namely, copyleft, or the need to regard the Internet as a public domain of sharing of knowledge and other resources. In that sense, then, the Indian Copyright Law, in its modified 1994 version, is held to be invalid for political reasons by those who endorse the idea of copyleft or open source.

The Right to Property

So what is the fight really about? It is about the erosion of the notion of ownership in intellectual property involving the new digital technologies. As digitised information challenges the nature of property and ownership, it has the capacity to subvert a market economy. By the same token, the illusion of the individual creator of knowledge dissipates and the social processes of control, monitoring, management, and evaluation of signals and data are exposed. These democratic dimensions of information technology give rise to what is called 'textualised' work process, by which the distinction between manual and mental labour is blurred.

The question, however, is whether or not property rights are defendable in the context of Information Technology. The truth is that these notions of property and ownership have proved to be philosophically and logically problematic even with respect to the older mechanical technologies of production, or to immobile natural resources like land.

Theories defending private property—a central institution of state power—go as far back in history as ancient Greece (circa 600 B.C.). Nevertheless these have been written down in the form of treatises only in the modern era. According to John Locke (1690), in the 17th century: 'every man has a property in his own person. This nobody has any right to but himself. The labour of his body and the work of his hands, we may say are properly his. Whatsoever then he removes out of the state that nature has provided and left it in, he has mixed his labour with it and joined it to something that is his own, and thereby makes it his property.'[4]

This may be rephrased thus:

(a) Human beings are inviolable.
(b) Inviolable persons own their bodies and their labour.
(c) Person A mixes his labour, which he owns with X, which is not owned by anybody, and is an external resource.
(d) A has a property right in X.

Assuming that there is a clear argument from (a) to (c), how do we get from (c) to (d)? Except in the case of hunter-gatherers who eat wild fruit and forest animals and thereby literally incorporate them into their bodies—and presumably have property rights to them—there is no reason to believe that the analogy holds in the case of other tangible resources like land or machinery.

In order to surmount this difficulty, libertarians like Robert Nozick (1974), following John Locke, uphold the inalienable right of individuals to exploit natural resources, provided those adversely affected by this appropriation are compensated on the basis of what their welfare would have been in the state of nature. This stipulation, of course, poses several problems: in order to estimate what one's level of welfare would have been in the state of nature, one should know the exact number of competitors (for natural resources) involved; one cannot take population size in the state of nature to be what it is now, since that would ignore the tremendous demographic impact of private land ownership. Most importantly, this theory applies to face–to–face peasant proprietors—how would it apply to societies in which other kinds of people inhabit?

Apart from this brand of theory inspired by Locke, which sees private property as a right in terms of 'just acquisition' that someone may have in a contractual or promissory note form, there is another philosophical perspective, inspired by Jean–Jacques Rousseau (1762) and G.W.F. Hegel (1821), that sees private property as a human right—say, like the right to free speech or to an elementary education—which will enhance the freedom and autonomy of agents in a polity. The point to keep in mind is that these two theories—the Lockean and the Hegelian—are mutually incompatible.

The clearly libertarian Lockean theory is riddled with internal contradictions and theological overtones, and seems to suggest that property is a malleable institution. The main moral basis of this argument is that private property protects individual liberty against state power. There is no need, as followers of David Hume would say, to seek a moral justification for the original acquisition of private property. After all, the early historical periods are marked by far too much strife and conquest for any legitimate acquisition of immovable property like land. Given this background, it is perhaps more judicious to concentrate on the present day demands of justice and redistribution. It may also be necessary to consider the inter-generational interests of ecological balance in any discussion of private or individual economic interests.

The Hegelian view is more complex. It has its basis in the fact that private property is really not 'private', but must be universalised, since viewing it as a human right necessarily means recognising its universalistic implications. By asserting that common property in the means of production is necessary to eliminate exploitation, we find ourselves at the anti-private property camp. In other words, the Hegelian theory provides no coherent defence of private property. It would seem that the notion of property *tout court* does not represent an independent value, whether in its Lockean or Hegelian avatar, but embodies other value commitments involving negative and positive freedoms.[5]

What is interesting about the Hegelian conception of property is that it could provide a limited defence for the notion that property rights need not be vested in the individual, but in the local community, the tribe, or the indigenous nation. The conflict between recognising collective ownership and following the private property regime, that focuses on individual rights, has arisen in the context of multicultural theory. This suggests that recognising the rights of diverse groups within a polity is likely to strengthen, rather than weaken the nation state. Indigenous people have strong spiritual and cultural connections to their traditionally collectively-owned land. This is the reason why many of them oppose development efforts like extractive industries within their territories. In this context, it would seem that there is a greater basis for defending a theory of collective property in the Hegelian than in the Lockean version.

The Strange Case of Digital Sampling

If it is hard enough to establish the legitimacy of private property as material mobile or immobile resources, it is even more difficult—if not impossible—to prove the legitimacy of intellectual property rights.

In an essay written in 1936, the famous art and culture critic, Walter Benjamin, maintained that the concept of intellectual or artistic originality was already in trouble in the age of mechanical reproduction. What Benjamin claimed as being true for the photograph or the cinematic object is easily applicable to the artefacts in this age of information technology: '(T)hat which withers in the age of mechanical reproduction is the aura of the work of art. This is a symptomatic process whose significance points beyond the realm of art. One might generalise by saying: the technique of reproduction detaches the reproduced object from the domain of tradition. By making many reproductions it substitutes a plurality of copies for a unique existence. And in permitting the reproduction to meet the beholder or listener in his own particular situation, it reactivates the object reproduced. These two processes lead to a tremendous shattering of tradition' (1936).

The mimetic capabilities of the new information technologies lead to an even more resounding shattering of tradition. Consider the case of digital audio-sampling, whereby it is possible to encode a fragment of sound, comprising a few seconds in duration, in a digitised binary form and then store in computer memory. This stored sound fragment may either be accurately reproduced or digitally manipulated, and then taken from one context and placed in another. These possibilities of sampling have forced members of the music industry and the legal profession to ask the question as to whether it is possible to ascribe ownership to a sound.[6]

The issue of sound ownership in the context of digital sampling seems to have originated in the dispute in the 1980s surrounding the theme music of the feature, 'Miami Vice', written and produced by Jan Hammer. The issue here is the argument put forward by percussionist David Earl Johnson that he deserved royalties from the work, because Hammer had prominently used a sample of Johnson's congas, as played by Johnson, in the theme. The sample taken during a live studio session, was stored in the form of digital code on an unpublished floppy disc. Since Johnson claimed that the instruments as well as his playing style were unique, he demanded compensation from Hammer for their inclusion in the theme.

The question of the ownership of a sound is part of a larger issue of creativity that has plagued the world of art and culture for the past century or so. It is predicated on the romantic notion of an isolated creative genius plucking beauty out of thin air in an inspired act of the imagination. And it is this romanticism that justifies the notion of copyright or exclusive authorship or ownership of the creation. However, the detractors of copyright are asking the question: Does any interaction with a text itself create a new text—that is to say, a creative production? 'If a text exists in some form in some public venue, as sound exists in air, are individual uses of that text unique creative acts? An older aesthetic would say no, that creative acts are those which produce new texts. After (Michel) Foucault, it is hard to imagine how any particular instance of interaction with a text does not itself create a new text (thus satisfying the conditions of the older aesthetic anyway), which is why the author is a spurious category for Foucault (1977), and why the sampler's physical and functional fusing of documentary and reproductive capabilities—which serves to throw the authorial producer of sound into a binary electronic limbo—has so thoroughly frustrated a legal model of copyright which is based on assumptions that one can clearly separate producers from consumers and texts from their readings' (Porcello 1991: 77).

Interestingly, this quotation seems to imply that the practice of plagiarism is to be viewed not in pejorative terms, but as an act of creation. What is curious about the Hammer–Johnson dispute is that the case has had several informal precedents involving lesser-known musicians, who have sampled each other's work within a relationship of casual reciprocity. This case acquired legal dimensions simply because it involved a superstar producer sampling from a musician lower down in the hierarchy. The fact of the matter is that,— with so many samples now available on public domain compact discs and 'shareware'—sampling of live musicians in the studio, as happened in the Hammer–Johnson case, will soon become irrelevant or rare.

Grey Zones of Copyright in India

In developing countries like India, copyright infringement may not be as serious a problem as it is in the West, simply because the enforcement mechanisms—when it comes to protecting intellectual property—are necessarily weak.

In 1908, the British-owned Gramophone Company of India had established its factory in Calcutta, and managed to dominate the music market. The supremacy of the Hindi film music and the monopoly of GCI continued well past Indian Independence.

The development model adopted by the Nehruvian state emphasised policies of over-taxation and encouraged the permit and license *raj*, which rather inhibited the consumer electronics and related industries. By the late 1970s, however, large numbers of immigrant workers to the Gulf countries were returning home (India) with cassette players, the ubiquitous two–in–ones, which became coveted objects of desire in the middle-class household, and this epoch saw the emergence of a clandestine grey market for pirated cassettes of film music.[7]

Certain significant developments in this period helped to create a mature market for the consumer electronics industry. The reduction of duties enabled Indian manufacturers to import selected components for local manufacture of cassette players. New policies encouraged foreign collaborations in the field of consumer electronics including magnetic tape production. Tape coating became big in India between 1982–1985; at the same time, record dealers switched to cassettes and by the mid-1980s, cassettes came to account for 95 per cent of the market.

Sales of cassettes went up from $1.2 million in 1980 to $12 million in 1986 and $21 million in 1990. Export of Indian made records jumped from 1.65 million rupees in 1983 to 99.75 million in 1987. By the end of the 1980s, Indian consumers were buying around 2.5 million cassette players. This is the phase that saw the swift decline of GCI (Gramophone Company of India) and HMV (His Master's Voice) as the dominant players in the industry, and witnessed the emergence of a handful of large players and over 500 small music-producing companies. Between 1987–1990, India had become the world's second largest manufacturers of cassettes and was marketing 217 million cassettes. This marks the beginning of the rise of the grey market in electronic goods, ranging from smuggled electronics to indigenously manufactured but unlicensed products and components. By the late 1980s, T-Series—the brainchild of two brothers, (the late) Gulshan and Gopal Arora—emerged as the clear market leader. Currently, it has a set-up worth over $ 120 million. Using a provision in the fair use clause of the Indian Copyright Act which allows for version recording, T-Series issued thousands of cover versions of GCI's classic film songs, particularly those which HMV itself found to be infeasible for release. Despite the fact that T-Series has been involved in straightforward copyright infringement in the form of pirated releases of popular songs, ironically, today it is one of the most aggressive enforcers of copyright in India.

Can Culture be Copyrighted?

It is perhaps easy to oppose the ideology of copyright when it is viewed as an extension of the private property debate. How do we look at the question of copyright when it pertains to cultural groups— rather than to superstar musicians, or even to down–and–out artists and *bazaar* tricksters?[8]

Analysts are now beginning to worry about the possibility that providing research workers unrestricted access to documents describing traditional beliefs and ceremonies violates the privacy of tribes and other cultural groups. The insider–outsider conundrum is a perennial source of conflict in anthropology, and the explosion of information technologies, which makes access to all kinds of data extremely easy, has exacerbated this problem. Since intellectual property regimes fail to recognise either the community ownership or spiritual significance of traditional knowledge, it is fairly easy for researchers and other outsiders to appropriate traditional knowledge, apply for a patent, and thereby claim to have invented a new product.

The 1990 United States' government museum-related legislation, namely, Native American Graves Protection and Repatriation Act (NAGPRA), was enacted with a view to protecting the Hopi and Apache tribes from the prying eyes of 'outsiders' and according them exclusive decision-making power and control over their customs and traditions. What this means is that a whole range of activities by 'outsiders'— like taking ethnographic field notes, making feature films, recording historical details—may be forbidden by these protected cultural groups, unless they are compensated for these. In other words, the Hopi and Apache tribes have copyrighted their cultures, and already there are demands for similar copyrighting from other tribes in South America, Australia and the Pacific region. Copyrights and trademarks are used for traditional art in Australia and Canada. Recently, the

South African government promised to share with the San Bushmen the proceeds from medicinal drugs based on their knowledge.

The General Assembly of the World Intellectual Property Organisation (WIPO) established an Inter-governmental Committee on Intellectual Property and Genetic Resources, Traditional Knowledge and Folklore in October 2000. WIPO is reviewing mechanisms for protecting traditional knowledge while increasing the participation of indigenous people. Traditional communities are now demanding patents and copyright protection for their knowledge systems.

There are, however, several ethical problems with these demands. First, the notion of copyright arose in the context of 19th century industrial capitalism, which upheld the principles of individualism and private property. The identification of inventiveness with a solitary individual cannot be reconciled unproblematically with the collective production of indigenous groups. Second, copyright is a kind of limited monopoly given to an individual for a limited period of time, in exchange for an eventual dedication of the work to the public domain. Culture, on the contrary, has no predetermined life span, and copyrighting culture will reify it as a fixed or corporal *thing*. Third, according cultural groups exclusive control over their affairs is likely to be undemocratic and lead to the creation of oppressive hierarchies within the groups themselves.

The truth of the matter is that researchers and others may be treating traditional knowledge as part of the public domain, where intellectual property protection does not apply. If one were to take the claims of minorities seriously, they would be assessed with the same thoughtful deliberation that we insist upon in matters relating to the cultural mainstream. After all, private property and copyright are seen as invalid proposals for the mainstream. They are equally likely to be so for the marginalised.

Notes

1. This is a greatly modified version of my paper presentation Rajan (2004) during a seminar on 'Information Technology and Social Science Research' organised under the Malcolm Adiseshiah Chair on Policy Studies, MIDC, Chennai.
2. The point that the Copyright law makes no distinction between duplicating software for sales or for free distribution is important because it has been the basis for litigation all over the world. For instance, in the year 2000, Napster.com which claims to have 38 million users incurred the wrath of

the music companies because its software enabled people to download music free of cost.
3. For an elaboration of this point, see Helmreich (2000).
4. For a general discussion of Locke's justification of private property, see Plant (1991: 122–35).
5. Negative freedom is defined as the maximum opportunity accorded to individuals to pursue their own plan of life independent of the constraints and interferences of others. Positive freedom is defined as the maximum number of appropriate resources and opportunities accorded to individuals to pursue their plan of life.
6. This is a summary of the argument of Porcello (1991).
7. My own source of information on this subject is Liang (2005) whose article on this subject is to be found in my edited volume. See also Manuel (2001).
8. For an in-depth analysis of this issue, see Brown (1998).

References

Benjamin, Walter. 1936. 'The Work of Art in the Age of Mechanical Reproduction'. *http://www.marxists.org/reference/subject/philosophy/works/ge/benjamin.htm/*.

Brown, F. Michael. 1998. 'Can Culture be Copyrighted?', *Current Anthropology,* 39(2): 193–206.

Foucault, Michel. 1977. *Language, Counter–Memory, Practice.: Selected Essays.* Trans. by Donald F. Bouchard and Sherry Simon. Ithaca: Cornell University Press.

Hegel, G. W. F. 1821. 'Elements of the Philosophy of Right'. *http://www.marxists.org/reference/archive/hegel/works/pr/property.html/*.

Helmreich, Stefan. 2000. 'Flexible Infections: Computer viruses, Human Bodies, Nation-states, Evolutionary Capitalism', *Science, Technology and Human Values,* 25(4): 472–91.

Hoffman, Lance (ed.). 1990. *Rogue Programs: Viruses, Worms and Trojan Horses.* New York: Van Nostrand Reinhold.

Locke, John. 1690. 'Second Treatise on Civil Government'. *http://www.constitution.org/jl/2ndtreat.htm/*.

Liang, Lawrence. 2005. 'Porous Legalities and the Dilemmas of Contemporary Media', in Nalini Rajan (ed.), *Practising Journalism: Values, Constraints, Implications*, pp. 155–71. New Delhi: Sage Publications.

Lundell, Alan. 1989. *Virus! The Secret World of Computer Invaders that Breed and Destroy.* Chicago: Contemporary Books.

Manuel, Peter Lamarche. 2001. *Cassette Culture: Popular Music and Technology in North India.* Delhi: Oxford University Press.

Nozick, Robert. 1974. *Anarchy, State and Utopia.* New York: Basic Books.

Plant, Raymond. 1991. *Modern Political Thought.* Oxford: Blackwell.

Porcello, Thomas. 1991. 'The Ethics of Digital Audio-sampling: Engineers' discourse', *Popular Music*, 10(1): 69–84.

Rajan, Nalini. 2004. 'Information Technology and the Constitution of "Theft"'. Paper presented at a conference on 'Information Technology and Social Science Research', Madras Institute of Development Studies, Chennai, 18 September.

Rousseau, Jean–Jacques. 1762. *The Social Contract or Principles of Political Right*. Trans. by G.D.H. Cole. *http://www.constitution.org/jjr/socom.htm/*.

UNDP. 2001. 'Human Development Report', 40. *http://hdr.undp.org/reports/global/2001/en/*.

12

Acting among the Shadows of the Screen[1]

Charlene Rajendran

Staging the Realities of Screened Existence

Screens have become pervasive in urban contemporary environments. Within both private and public spheres, screens appear in large and small sizes, with active and passive capacities, as background and foreground presences. From televisions in living rooms to digital phones in pockets, neon billboards along the super-highways to portable laptops at roadside stalls, screens inhabit significant spaces and occupy considerable attention.

Inevitably, learning to manage the screen's omnipresence entails ignoring most of what it tells us. In order to deal adequately with what it means to watch, view, read and remember, only a selection of the screenings can be allowed to matter. Not to do so would result in an instant crisis of overload.

The screen can then be seen as a site for projection as well as a projection of sight since the underlying power of the screen is unequivocally linked to what it actually conceals. With each screen comes a frame that excludes more than it includes. What is on-screen effectively signifies an ongoing relationship with what is off-screen. In order to make sense and make meaning in ways that will entertain, engage and entice, the screen projects a reality by leaving 'reality' out. This then frames what is being 'screened' with all that is being 'screened' out. How we view is framed by what we view, and how we frame what we view is affected by the lens and equipment we employ. How does this pertain to theatre?

In urban contemporary theatre, the presence of the screen on stage is no longer unusual. The integration of screen technology with live performance is simply another extension of sound amplification and illumination—an ongoing mediatisation of theatre performance. It draws on available resources to enhance performance whilst engaging with the issues that arise when live performance is mediated by projection. Staging becomes a form of screening, and the process of viewing is moderated by negotiating between the screen and the stage. This effectuates a 'media epistemology' (Auslander 1999: 32) through which the theatre is apprehended.

Theatre's struggle to stay viable amidst society's escalating fascination with digital technology, television and hyper-reality, has led to an increased need for live performance to integrate with these elements. Interventions from digitised reality are often woven into performance by creating a range of screens (conventional and otherwise) on stage and deploying them as 'performers' in the process. At times the live performance is peripheral and the screen becomes a central site for expression and articulation, not simply a means of refraction. The screen can then become a 'player' in the production.

The screen can also become a site where what is otherwise kept off-stage, finds a space on-stage, visually and aurally, and not just referentially. This enlarges the canvas for the stage whilst also making possible a greater propensity for fragmentation and deconstruction. The way in which the screen recontextualises the live becomes a comment on the live presence of the audience as well. The viewer can become conscious of being viewed through a camera and projected on stage without having to physically switch spaces. This could produce a reflexive yet provocative intervention, which inadvertently dissects the bodily self from the screened self. Whilst drawing on the resources of technology to enhance the craft of making of the theatre, it becomes inevitable that mediatised productions begin to provide fresh insight into the idiosyncrasies and problems that prevail in a socio-political and cultural terrain that communicates increasingly via the screen. As Auslander points out,

> 'the incursion of mediatisation into live performance is not simply a question of the use of certain equipment in that context. It also has to do with approaches to performance and characterization, and the mobility and meanings of those within a particular cultural context.' (1999: 33)

This article considers the use of the screen on stage in three postmodern multi-media theatre performances devised by The Necessary Stage, a theatre company in Singapore, and comments on how the presence of the screen is a reflection of contemporary urban culture and how it affects the process of experiencing live theatre.

Whilst the screen can be seen almost everywhere in Singapore, the stage is rare. The platform for live presence is not as pervasive nor as reproducible. Thus placing the screen on stage makes a tangible link between two often separate styles of viewing within a shared space.

Even though watching the stage is often less convenient and less available, it tends to compel a viewer more intensely than the screen. The shared space of audience and performer becomes a shared reality albeit from different sides of the platform. Although television is often associated with the qualities of immediacy and intimacy—by enabling its audiences' proximity with 'live' events—when the televisual screen appears alongside the live performance, the nature of being 'live' and the idea of being within the 'intimate' and 'immediate' space are challenged.[2]

Whilst on the one hand, the notion of the live performer has a certain 'symbolic capital' and the live performance has grown to depend on the 'mediatised' to make sense, this 'relation of mutuality' is not merely about including the screen onstage (Auslander 1999: 80–85). It involves devising a means of using it that is dynamic and cuts through our comfort zones of perception to provoke a transformation of the theatre experience and the practice of viewing theatre. How does the 'live' stand alongside the projected and lead to viewing differently and not just viewing different things?

It is the inherently voyeuristic nature of viewing the stage that lends itself to a potent collaboration with the screen. In a context like Singapore, where there is persistent policing of the public space and the pervasive gaze of the State into the private space, the co-presence of the screen with its stage window into reality could be a potent metaphor of current existence. The staged presence of commonly unobtrusive surveillance modes draws attention to the camera's silent yet intrusive gaze and reckons with the prevalence of an ongoing 'silent screening'. The 'noisy stage' becomes a site for reversing the gaze by putting the state on view, and staging the politics of the screen.

In South-East Asia, the screen has been an important part of local performance culture for several centuries. Shadow puppetry is a traditional art form that is still popular in several parts of the region that extend from Indonesia to Thailand, Cambodia to Myanmar, albeit hardly so in Singapore. Despite having to contend with the digital and electronic screen, these traditional theatres still continue to find contemporary relevance and popularity.[3]

The oil lamp or naked bulb hanging behind a stretched translucent white cloth held by a wooden or bamboo frame transforms the sheet into a screen. This then becomes a site for epic battles and courtly romance, often based on the *Ramayana* and *Mahabharata*, constitutive Indian epics that have a profound influence in South-East Asia. As a flat surface that comes alive with the shadows at play and the imaginations of audience and puppeteer, the life on screen mesmerises its viewer through transport to another world. It becomes a site for social satire and political comment, enacted by the shadows of characters, often carved in leather and animated by the revered puppeteer.

Performed in open spaces, sometimes through the night, shadow puppets entertain and engage their audiences for several hours at a stretch, crossing from one world into another, spanning the sacred and the secular, the court and the street. Thus, the contemporary screen takes off from the traditional screen in becoming a recent participant in the performance and reflections of culture. In the shadows of the puppets, as with the projections on screen, the images occur within a landscape of culture and the imagination. Screens are not simply surfaces on which images are thrown. They become sites for the performance of culture and the culture of performance. Much like the stage its presence is 'alive' but it detracts from the 'live' in order to scrutinise what 'lives'.

In most forms of shadow puppetry, the audience is free to walk round the screen to watch the live performers at work. The artistry of the puppeteer bringing intricately crafted puppets to life and the synchronicity of a live ensemble of musicians[4] as they respond spontaneously to his every cue, are as much an available part of the performance as the shadows on screen. In Cambodia and Thailand, there is also a tradition of the puppeteers emerging from behind the screen to perform in stylised movement sequences in front of the screen, thus bringing together the 'live' and the 'screened' onto the same 'stage'.

The screen on a theatre stage that places the live performer alongside a mediatised presence is a potent way to integrate a way of viewing that draws on a conscious acknowledgement of the difference between projections of persons and their physical presence. This process demands making connections between how we watch the screen and how we view live persons—the shadows of our selves on the screens that we create. Something we do perpetually, but not consciously in the public and private arena of living in the urban centres of the 21st century, in the quest to upgrade.

Upgrading the Stage View for Screening Viewers

Upgrading socially and materially has become a central tenet of the consumer market. Subscribing to the 'passion for more' and the 'desire to move up' is a regular part of urban living, especially among middle classes. This is particularly so in a city state like Singapore, a notably wealthy capitalist nation with very high standard of living in comparison to her South-East Asian neighbours. The Singaporean desire to upgrade has been described as a 'national urge', and whilst affluence affords a perpetual move to improve material comfort with technology, this 'comfort is achieved through control' and in many ways relies on 'selfish technology' for 'effective insulation' (George 2000: 194, 16–17). The surrender of freedom in exchange for a notion of stability that comes with fiscal power breeds inertia towards the repression of expression and curtails the questioning of imposed practice and ideology.

In a largely depoliticised society with a crying need for improved civic consciousness, the unsustainability of this practice is hardly a conscious cost or a nagging worry for most. Autonomy as a consumer is more of a priority, and the increasing facility to purchase pleasure and culture are welcome compensation in the confiscation of socio-political power. The sinister effects of political repression are easily ignored when material comforts lure the buyer into a numbness that can be so convincingly sugar-coated with contentment. The product that promises an upgrading of critical consciousness leading to discomfort and discontent is certainly not going to be a popular sweet to buy.

Theatre that seeks to empower an audience in critically reviewing its passive attitudes and encourage critical awareness must then attract by other means. The 'limitless seduction' of technology could prove effective (Baudrillard 1983). The use of a screen as a major element in a theatre production can be seen to 'add value' to what can otherwise be regarded as 'raw' or 'simple'—not state–of–the–art. Rather than prescribe a bitter pill without appeal, the use of technology can provide the effects of an 'e(lectronic)-pill' whilst prodding the consciousness still.

Birringer argues that the impact of technology on viewing has led to a 'dislocation of the actor–in–performance' due in part to 'a post-modernist trend toward a fetishisation of surfaces' (1991: 170–80). In many ways, the nature of the lit surface with a light source behind or within draws the attention of the eye as a very natural instinctive reflex. Thus, flashing images on a stage that has been dimmed in order to increase clarity on screen is one way in which the compensation may work against the performer.

Has this fetish compelled the viewer away from the live performer because the screen has a more glitzy and snazzy presence? Or has this deflection been due to a less grounded, less charismatic live performer on stage? Is it possible for the screen to have its own character, which thereby enriches the presence of the live actor? Or is the live actor able to collude with the screen to create a seamless consciousness of surfaces that frame and reflect, projecting and processing images, ideas and sensibilities?

The screen on stage need not reduce the importance of 'character' by shrinking the notion of self from a three-dimensional presence to a two-dimensional one—flattening the live and keeping the screen flat. The presence of a two-dimensional image demands that a screen be available. But the space for the surface is itself a third dimension that can come into play. It need not remain flat.

A socially critical theatre company such as The Necessary Stage (TNS) has sought to integrate the screen to cultivate a form of theatre making that is identifiable for its conscious reference to local vocabularies of expression and ongoing technological developments of cultural life. The screen–on–stage also marks the company's 'upgrade' and capacity to move with the times. It signifies a more sophisticated engagement of culture by 'staging' the presence of the digital image and the technological sense. It brings into focus the fascination with technology and employs that nerve to stir the theatre 'viewer'. From the TV screens that project a parallel text to the projection of 'live' images obscuring the 'live' performer on stage, an audience is prompted to view and re-view the issue at hand through the disruptions and dislocations of a regular viewing process, thus 'upgrading' the viewer's theatre experience as well.

The Necessary Stage: Producing Live Realities alongside Projected Worlds

The Necessary Stage (TNS), is a non-profit theatre company that was formed by Alvin Tan, the current artistic director, in 1987.[5] It is committed to creating local theatre based on current issues and social concerns. The company is best known for its inclusion of youth and community theatre events, whilst continuing to develop works that are experimental and attempting to forge fresh and relevant theatre vocabularies.

Since 1997 TNS has devised productions incorporating a range of screens with live and recorded projections to create theatre performances that demand a change in the practice of 'viewing' theatre by negotiating live realities alongside projected worlds. This is a significant reflection of contemporary living in Singapore, which is a technology savvy culture familiar with fast-paced electronic change. Many TNS productions are based in urban Singapore and draw on vocabularies of sound, movement and image that are distinctly Singaporean but not without resonance for other urban, materially affluent and politically stifled environments in post-colonial, cosmopolitan and plural societies. They are codes that become more accessible the more one learns to read Singapore, but they are culled from a range of sources that are not limited to the geographical boundaries of this small but diversely influenced nation.

The use of the screen in the expression and representation of a highly stressed and often deeply distressed human condition in Singapore seems to have preoccupied much recent theatre making of TNS's. By working with the devised play approach the screen on stage has become a site for a range of symbols and metaphors reflecting concerns and preoccupations from repressed sexuality and obsessive materialism to intense loneliness and political oppression. By reflecting a particular stage of thinking and feeling, the screen becomes a site for the articulation and simulation of these ideas and the ensuing expressions of dissent, despair and dejection.

The setting up of The Orange Playground (TOP), described by TNS as a 'Design, Research and Development Unit housed within the company to experiment, research and construct ideas in Space Design, Multimedia and Object Design, with the aim of developing innovative ways of art-making in a multi-disciplinary approach' is clear recognition that there is a need for work of this ilk to evolve through studied and reflective practice (BOTE programme notes). It marks the commitment of the company to provide space and opportunity to nurture the desire and need for the reflective and interrogative developmental practice.

The company's decision to invest in the research and development of media technology (such as making the costly choice to purchase equipment like high-powered video projectors) has enabled the process work of TNS to integrate multimedia more intrinsically into the conception, improvisation and rehearsal process. The intention is to improve the quality of design by working with the media more intricately and dealing with the problems of inter-media at close hand. This should effectively challenge the aesthetics of the creative team and ideally propel a theatre-making process that results in a more seamless consciousness of the stage and screen.

'Upgrading' must involve a will to read and write theatre, such that the links between the screen and stage also 'upgrade' the process of perception or theatre literacy. Unless this occurs, the theatre will not raise a critical consciousness of the character of screen and stage that provokes a questioning view of the 'screening' and 'staging' that we do. In the productions where this has begun to happen, and the screen has moved towards becoming a character with a role to play and not just a surface for projection, a valuable intervention in local theatre-making has resulted.

BOTE: Reconstructing the Worlds of Deconstructed Living

BOTE: The Beginning of the End was staged in April–May 2002, conceived and directed by Jeff Chen, then Resident Director of TNS. It examines the tyranny of normalcy and the psychosis of social respectability in the 'living' room of a fictional family whose 'deathly' lives are theatrically framed within an expressionistic collage of styles that mix realism with vaudeville, absurdism with Artaudian cruelty. A mother, her two adult children and her immigrant daughter-in-law are presented as frustrated and indolent characters, who share the same space, but are unable to connect. The relationships between them are cold, terse and indifferent, broken only by violent and catatonic outbursts of exaggerated feeling when they can no longer contain their repressed emotions.

The story begins on screen and continues on stage. Using a living room set, designed in retro–1960s style, as the screen and stage set, the production forces a connection between how we view live persons in relation to how we view their recorded selves. Characters initially appear in projection on the back wall of the stage set, which is identical to the set on screen. The audience is first introduced to a seemingly normal, then later evidently dysfunctional family as projected beings, who then materialise on stage.

As characters who are initially presented as enlarged images and amplified sounds, their actual physical appearance on stage seems dwarfed by their prior presence. Their voices now seem reduced and their bodies appear smaller than when we first encountered them. Their desperately painful existence on screen is now physically present in a shared space with the audience, and although we view them and sense them in the same room, we know theirs is a fiction from the screen onto the stage, and vice versa. The screen has framed them as persons living projected lives. This transforms their physical presence by making them both live and recorded—a complex mesh of the two. The recorded image, when conflated with the live, questions the assumed notions of 'pressure' and 'liveness'—projecting them as further 'screens' in the process of apprehension.

The relationship between screened and live presences continues through the production. It unleashes the potential tyranny of the screen in reducing what is off-screen to a pale imitation of the screen 'reality'. But it also realises that the staged 'live' can feed the screen, making both realities converge and diverge. In one segment, a live camera feed projects the face of the mother who is seated on a chair in the middle of the stage, with her head upturned to the ceiling. A close-up of her face is projected on a sidewall, and we realise that a bird's eye view is being given to us from our seats, but it feels more as if we have entered her head. The effect is an eerie dislocation of her body from her presence. She is seated on stage, but we are drawn to look at her enlarged face projected onto a screen located on another side of the stage where her body is not present. This dismembers the live performer and enlarges what the camera chooses to project, rendering ineffectual the rest of her body.

BOTE uses the projections on these staged screens to deconstruct and reconstruct realities lived on stage. The screen has not only projected character, it has also sought to become a character of projection; a point of entry and exit; a blurred boundary between live and recorded; a porous surface through which we see the outside, sometimes disrupting what lies on the inside. And vice versa.

The performers step onto the stage and exit through the doors, which are built onto the background wall of the set. Life-size projections of the doors are then technically executed to fit the exact size and positions of the stage doors. Recorded sequences of performers going in and out of doors are projected, interspersed with live performers making entrances and exits, timed perfectly so that it is in sync with the projection. The performers become flat and full-bodied simultaneously, and they become almost indistinguishable from their virtual selves.

The images on screen now inhabit the 'live' space. The screen that began the action is not a separate sphere. Its porous presence has blurred the difference between on-screen and off-stage, on-stage and off-screen. In some scenes the performer exits the stage and appears on screen, emerging in a space outside the stage and beyond the actual building. It stretches the stage to include what can be screened, linked by the performer, recorded and live. The pain and despair is then pushed beyond the fictional space of live theatre, to encompass the world outside, albeit through the lens of a camera.

This breaks into the viewer's comfort zone of distance and indifference, to bleed into the psyche of inertia. The screening offers initial safety from the violence of desperation, and then the staging pierces a hole through the wall between 'us' and 'them' to incriminate us all in the same present, to jolt us out of the non-presence through the recorded, projected, televised persona made live, to come alive, in the same deathly 'living' room.

The switching of surfaces and moving between platforms of action, from stage to screen—simultaneously and in sequence—makes demands on the reader and writer of theatre to consider how varied media are at work (and play) in the constructs of reality and illusion. The screen is no longer a simple part of narrative, but a player in the disruption and displacement that come with a more post-modern type performance. In BOTE, this strategy underlines the dysfunctionality of seen and screened lives as pathetic reminders of the futility of images that are mere illusions of hope as well as desperation.

Godeatgod: Conflating the Live Screen with the Flattened Stage

Godeatgod created as a response to the events of September 11, 2001 was conceptualised by Alvin Tan and Haresh Sharma and performed in July–August 2002. The play weaves separate stories of sickness and death whilst questioning the role of religion in purportedly offering peace and healing. It points at the cruelty and the violent instigation of 'gods' in a sequence of scenes and songs performed by an ensemble of actors who are costumed in the same fabric to indicate they are in fact variations of the same—mortal and immortal. Spontaneous and scripted dialogue raise issues of civil society that include the decline of moral values, the need for censorship, the paradox of religiosity and the inevitability of human suffering within the meaning of life and the life of meaning.

The set is staged like a screen, a tabula rasa—a white space in the surrounding dark space of a Black Box theatre. It is occupied by a long white movable platform, a scaled model of the set on one side and a microphone on a white rostrum on the other side. Three white screens form three elevated walls facing the audience. Embedded in the movable platform is a television screen, visible to the audience.

Several texts are written into the empty white space. Images— live and recorded, moving and still—are played on screens. Music— live and recorded, background and foreground—is played into the space. Words, sentences, questions—spoken and projected, strung together and ripped apart—are played across the screens. Interwoven media and text are projected and played across the tabula rasa.

Performers enter as 'themselves' and move in and out of the white space; seated at and on the platform, facing the audience, they are relaxed, casual, natural—or simulations of these on stage. The playwright Haresh Sharma, then enters in seeming non-performance mode, speaking to us as 'himself'. He introduces the idea of religion as the focal material for the performance and proceeds to 'preach' the need to be good and believe in god (or gods). After advocating the need to value our comfort and improve our charity, he tentatively proceeds to make a 'heartfelt' attempt at spontaneous dialogue. When this fails, he proceeds to share letters written by religious leaders in Singapore that are read aloud by the writer and other performers. Then he announces that all else that is about to happen is 'art', and proceeds to leave the stage and join the audience on the 'dark side'. The 'screen' is then framed by the text as a space for art, and the stage is transformed into a screening space. The audience remains off-screen, the performers only play on-screen. The audience 'face art' on screen, whilst the performers 'make art' on screen. One side is framed as fictional, the other is more factual. Yet, the process of 'being art', is led towards a questioning of what is 'real'.

Two of the performers in the ensemble, Patricia Mok and Norleena Salim, are well-known media personalities. In some sequences, they play their screen personalities as characters on stage. Sometimes they are their private selves and at other times they are reproductions of their public selves. On this staged screen, they become a fusion of the two.

They engage in humorous banter about a range of issues that focus on moral values and civic consciousness in Singapore society. They consider what they should do, and how they can intervene. They intersect their comic routine with comments on each other and expose their seemingly vulnerable and private selves in spontaneous and easy-going discourse. They seem natural. They are not contrived. They appear relaxed, and there is no stylised gait.

In these sequences, they are incomprehensible except as well-known media personalities, shedding their screen skin, becoming more accessible, stepping out of the screen on to the stage. A deflection of their public persona is also a deflection of their private person; who they really are is immaterial after all.

Paradoxically, the other performers in the ensemble become 'staged' presences. Unknown except as stage actors, who do not have a presence on the public screens of mass media, these characters seem more fictional than real. Hence, the media characters have become more 'real' despite originating from the 'unreal' world of the screen through the 'immediacy and intimacy' of their being 'screened' in public. The 'gods' of this world are presented as voices, texts and presences that are continually asking questions and giving instructions. Characters interrupt each other when they speak, giving orders about how to change and improve what they do. Screened texts interject the meaning of stories by devaluing one reality with another. The power of the 'gods' appears to lie in their attempt to control perception, yet their orders are recurrently disobeyed and deemed futile by their ineffectiveness to actually help alleviate suffering or heal sickness.

During the performance, varied images appear on three elevated screens. Among them are words, questions, statements and definitions, which are sometimes blown apart, showing letters moving up and down the screen. The soundscape that accompanies the disarray of words is that of an air-raid and the screen becomes the site for meaning to be blitzed. There is a war *on* words with the 'sacred text' being destroyed on a disruptive screen, and the meaning is visually pulverised.

Towards the end of the performance, the projected text appears more staid: this is when pronouncements, conclusions, resolutions and decisions are declared. These statements are never spoken, but lived through the screened word. By then we have begun to 'screen' all that is said as projection and simulation, no longer as pronouncement and declaration.

A simulated child-like voice that speaks with a god-like authority produces the writing on a wall that cannot be inscribed. The spoken word, like the live character, now has a partner on screen: neither can claim permanence and both thrive on transience. At the intersections of their presence, the theatre has simulated the screen in the live performance. The collusion between stage and screen is made blatant in the repeated refutations of permanence and challenges to 'truth'—both sacred and sacral. In depicting the manifold crisis of belief and faith, the collaboration between screen and stage (decreasingly distinct) produces a space where the screens have come a-live just as much as the stage has been flattened.

Boxing Day: Moderating Realities through Sensationalised Screenings

Boxing Day : The Tsunami Project was developed as a response to the tsunami that devastated several parts of Asia on December 26, 2004. It resulted in a devised play performed in May 2005, directed by Alvin Tan and written by Haresh Sharma, in collaboration with a cast of performers from Malaysia, Thailand and Singapore. The play draws on stories and experiences from Indonesia, Thailand, Sri Lanka and Malaysia that collected by the ensemble whilst conducting research in a few communities that were affected by the natural disaster. It also includes the perspective of the Singaporean as an outside observer and commentator. The actors play a range of characters: some based on real life figures and others being part of the frame through which their encounters are viewed.

The stage is bare except for several movable platforms, which become the building blocks for several landscapes. The actors wheel these sand-coloured wooden surfaces as they reshape and reconfigure the space. At one point, the movement of these platforms appears to represent the shift in tectonic plates whilst the images of large waves are shown crashing down repeatedly on the screens above.

Large screens stretch across the top of the stage and these are used diversely and severally, but primarily for the display of subtitles when English is not being spoken. The multilingual performance, using English, Malay, Chinese, Thai and Indonesian languages, is then viewed in much the same way one watches the news on major broadcasting channels in English. With the translation on screen, the speaker is refracted through the interpretation of spoken text into projected words. The subtitles appear above the actors, literally locating the speaker beneath the translation, putting the person under the dominance of how she/he is translated.

On several levels, the performance questions within the theatre space, how the news informs our views. The screen is used to frame the stage by placing 'live' events below it and moderating the meaning of these events through what is projected. It references the realities of the actual tragedy through interviews with actual victims of the disaster. But it also points to the processes that reconfigure how the event is perceived by the outside by moderating the information through several kinds of translation. The notes given in the pro-gramme explain that 'The Verbatim Theatre method—using voices of people involved in the tragedy—will bring word for word, thoughts and experiences direct from them onto the stage.' Then the use of the screens to deconstruct how these words are communicated through the media occurs on a few levels.

In some instances the screen is also used to project 'live' images of actors playing tsunami victims who are responding to the character of a journalist asking questions. The screen is divided into three parts: the right and left screen show two 'victims' of the tsunami, whilst the middle screen projects notes being typed by the journalist keying onto her laptop. The reportage is clearly skewed towards sensationalising the information to make 'headline' news. It slaps a dark humour across the plight of the victims, highlighting how what they say is of secondary interest, compared to how they can 'be sold' as the news.

The epistemology of theatre is affected by the news room scenes, in which we hear about the tragedy through the victims but we are also made aware that their story often reaches us through a moderated means. The screen makes evident the multiple reality of how perception and reception occur. There is no singular narrative, nor is there a primary text. They compete for attention, often having lost out to dominant contextual media. A reportage, which even the theatre is part of. None of the performers are 'victims' themselves. They too are reconstructing after deconstructing. Perhaps not for journalistic intent, but certainly for theatrical value—screening as they do.

Rethinking the Play of Screens and Stages

The use of the screen to enhance the capacity for socially critical theatre has involved a re-thinking of how viewers will engage in theatre literacy and the impact of mediatisation in self-apprehension. It modifies the role of the screen from a didactic and instructional device towards a more porous and refractive intervention. Whereas in earlier productions by TNS the screen on stage was often relegated to a background presence as commentator or illustrator, the more the company has experimented with this media, the more it has moved towards using the screen as an interactive player with disruptive and provocative purpose.

Questions still need to be raised about how the performers on stage are prepared and directed towards a consciousness of this shift. Perhaps due to the use of screen entering the rehearsal process at a late stage, their engagement with the mediatisation of their presence seems thin. Perhaps the collaboration with the 'screen artist'[6] is not as central as it needs to be, thus resulting in the performers being less able to integrate the character of the screen into their performance sensibility.

Whilst the screen has been employed as a porous player on stage, the live performer has not been sufficiently pervious to this presence, but somewhat blocked, impermeable and at times two-dimensional. This signals a need to examine the surface of bodies as screens and to see how the performer's consciousness of this can transform the framing of the self towards a more engaged interaction with the more conventional rectangle of a screen.

In Singapore particularly, where several social realities are constructed through the highly controlled and manipulative media to facilitate comfort and convenience, the screens that embody these energies—from televisions and computers to thermal-screens and security scanners—signify a mutuality in daily life that cannot be ignored. This weaves an ongoing simultaneity of simulated truth and staged reality: projected, performed and present; recorded, reproducible and original; screened and screened off.

To work intelligently through this dimension of collaborative theatre making, the integration needs to come not merely from the directors or designers but from the performers as well. That stage in the process does not seem to be prevalent. When performers participate more proactively in the staging of screens and engage more deeply with their own screened presences, the screen and stage will become more resonant and dynamic as co-existent sites for reflection and refraction. At this juncture performers should become more able to feed off the presence of the screen rather than merely co-appear.[7]

When the performers can *play off* and *play with* the screen by enacting an awareness of the media in the staged play, the viewer will be prompted towards a heightened consciousness of the process of viewing. The visual and material transformation of persons becomes a conscious and an active screen of sorts—a more critical and powerful upgrading of perceptive screening.

We live with the screen, and we work within its frames. We screen our worlds and project several realities onto diverse stages and surfaces. These realities are a combination of tangible three-dimensional presences, as well as shadowy two-dimensional projections. Just as the puppeteer constructs his story from the sounds of the musical ensemble, the shadows of the puppets and the voices with which he articulates their tale, the contemporary theatre maker is clearly being called upon to weave the screen and the stage into a thinking texture of play and performance that characterise the concerns of society and art.

The screen on stage represents more than a site for projection. It becomes a reflection of how we view and the frames with which we view. To challenge the viewing process entails getting under the surface of the screens—getting under its skins—to disturb the pores and nerves grown numb with the comfort and insulation of our screened apprehensions of the human condition. It demands playing with shadows as much as shadowing the reality of our existence.

For TNS, the screen as a porous character of projection and simulation has prodded the audience towards becoming critical meaning makers and active viewers while the gaps between media have offered a stirring presence that stimulates and provokes through discomfort and resonance. If the disturbance occurs without a corresponding vibration that prods reflection, it only leads to a numbing effect and not a stirring one—one in which the device of shifting surfaces is reduced to a powerless gimmick, unable to tease or elicit response. The screen needs to be relevant as well as resonant. We do not need screens that remain as flat characters without any roles to play. We need screens that intervene and upgrade how we see. Flatly.

Acknowledgements

I am grateful to Ashim Ghosh, C.J. Wee Wan-ling and Madonna Stinson for their valuable comments and discussions in the initial stages of thinking through ideas for this article. I also thank Alvin Tan and Haresh Sharma for the opportunity to write about this area of their work at TNS.

Notes

1. For a modified version of this article, see Rajendran (2004: 151–64).
2. For a thorough discussion of how live events and mediatised representations have had an impact on each other, particularly with the increased importance of television in society, see Auslander (1999: 10–60).
3. For examples of how shadow puppetry is still used in contemporary workings of culture and as socio-political responses to issues in the community, see Dowsey-Magog (2002); Sedana (2005). These instances of contemporary shadow puppetry in Indonesia and Thailand highlight the integration of current events and available technology, whilst retaining crucial cultural dimensions of the form.
4. The ensemble of musicians is usually seated behind the screen, where they are able to watch and take cues from the puppeteer. They play an assortment of percussive instruments such as drums (made with wood and animal skins) and metal gongs. This sometimes includes a couple of wind instruments such as flutes and pipes.
5. For more details on The Necessary Stage, see *www.necessary.org/*.
6. In all three productions discussed, the collaborating multimedia artist for the TNS productions was Brian Gothong Tan. Tan has worked with a range of theatre artists in Singapore and is currently studying at the California Institute of the Arts on a Shell–NAC Arts Scholarship.

7. For discussion of strong multimedia integration in theatre, see Hood (2003) which discusses the work of *dumb type*, a Kyoto-based arts collective.

References

Auslander, Philip. 1999. *Liveness: Performance in a Mediatized Culture*. London: Routledge.

Baudrillard, Jean. 1983. *Simulations*. New York City: Semiotext(e).

Birringer, H. Johannes. 1991. *Theatre, Theory, Postmodernism*. Bloomington: Indiana University Press.

Dowsey-Magog, Paul. 2002. 'Popular Workers' Shadow Theatre in Thailand', *Asian Theatre Journal*, 19 (1): 184–211.

George, Cherian. 2000. *Singapore: The Air-Conditioned Nation: Essays on the Politics of Comfort and Control, 1990–2000*. Singapore: Landmark Books.

Hood, Woodrow. 2003. 'Memories of the Future: Technology and the Body in Dumb Type's Memorandum', *Performing Arts Journal*, 25 (1): 7–20.

Rajendran, Charlene. 2004. 'Viewing the Necessary Stage Screen on Stage: A Flat Look at its Character', in Chong Kee Tan and Tisa Ng (eds), *Ask not: The Necessary Stage in Singapore Theatre*, pp. 151–64. Singapore: Times Editions.

Sedana, I. Nyoman. 2005. 'Theatre in a Time of Terrorism: Renewing Natural Harmony after the Bali Bombing via Wayang Kontemporer', *Asian Theatre Journal*, 22 (1): 73–86.

Digital Cinema in India: Apparent Horizons

K. Hariharan

Do films tell us a story or do they write one? Are they images of a dreamscape or are they narrating imaginings of a reality? Do dreams have sounds in the same way as those that we play or hear while awake? As film scholars question such issues, the world of cinema has a sense of gloom on hearing the news that its dream factory Eastman Kodak has to lay off over 3,000 workers in the wake of sharp predictions that celluloid cinema is going to disappear to give way to the digital domain, in the guise of a 4K resolution digital imaging chip and projector. The 'Cinematograph' recorder-cum-projector of 1895, ushered in by the Lumiere Brothers, would never have anticipated such an early exit and it is even less than a hundred years since our first film *'Raja Harishchandra'* (1913) was delivered by Dadasaheb Phalke onto the Indian screen. Is the new 4K technology going to reverse everything done by the intermittent Maltese cross which has been flickering frozen metaphors on the big silver screen throughout the 20th century? Will everything that is analogue really come to an end because of the digital empire?

As a practicing filmmaker and pedagogue, the impending extinction of the celluloid format confronts me as a nightmare and a relief at the same time. And it is not because Hitler's warhorse—the legendary whirring Arriflex camera—is going to breathe its last whilst leaving in its trail a slim flash card that can store hours of digitally recorded sounds and images. It is a nightmare because the world of imaginary signification looks like being throttled by a sterile world of metallic sounds and tinny images that can easily let Keanu *Matrix* Reeves escape a shower of bullets or can, at best, permit Tom *Gump* Hanks to grab a bottle of soda from the hands of late President John Kennedy! Relief comes from the fact that the vision of the ubiquitous digital camera and the mini DV tape has truly become the 'Vox Populi', helping voice and image to simultaneously converge and become chaotic like never before! There is a touch of frustration when James Monaco (2000) notes that our intoxication with our new power to produce and to distribute media renders us indifferent to the ownership of the old-fashioned media. A.J. Leibling (see Monaco 2000), a great press critic, noted four decades ago that freedom of the press belongs to those who own one. Today, we are nearly at the point where we all own the media, thanks to the radical possibilities of the digital revolution.

While re-examining the state–of–the–art digital condition, it is untrue that the soon–to–be–old world of celluloid cinema has been completely analogue in its production methodology. Rarely do filmmakers shoot or edit their films in a linear or continuous manner. In fact, film technicians have truly perfected the art of assembling images in the most optimum and efficient ways—whether on location or on a Steenbeck editing table—through a complex 'digital' arrangement of shots and sounds. Long time associate and editor for Steven Spielberg, Michael Kahn says: 'I still love cutting on film. I just love going into an editing room and smelling the photochemistry and seeing my editor with mini-strands of film around his neck. The greatest films ever made were cut on film, and I'm tenaciously hanging on to the process.'[1]

On the other hand I realised the cumbersome art of analogue editing only after the advent of videotape that was often digitally recorded upon. The Digi-beta tape was for all practical purposes an analogue mechanism. So, while the acrid debate on the efficacy of digital over analogue wages, I choose to pause and think of some of the epistemological issues involved in this transition.

There is a notion that digital cinema manifests itself due to it being recorded on a digital video camera, processed on a non-linear computer editing system and transmitted through LCD/DVD projection systems. The digital domain should be seen in its entirety of acquisition, processing and dissemination. I would like to state here that acquiring plots and stories, finalising actors and locations, editing and projecting the final mixed film, happen in the most non-sequential manner, especially in a country like India. A motion picture project could commence just because an actor has some free dates; a couple of catchy songs have been recorded, or even because some black money needs to be re-circulated! What appears to the Western, modern eye as the most disorganised and unprofessional manner of functioning ends up, in fact, ironically, with India producing the world's largest number of films with the tiniest budgets and with all the latest in technology.

Disparate song and dance numbers and comedy sequences flow around seamlessly into an oft-repeated narrative of love, revenge and reconciliation. Stars look almost the same in all their films, singing songs rendered by even more famous playback singers, and sometimes even mouthing lines which could ultimately be dubbed by someone else altogether. And to top it all, the viewer is perfectly aware of this production strategy and finds nothing inauthentic about this at all. To an outsider, this must be bizarre and almost hallucinatory, reminiscent of the Beatles singing 'Strawberry fields forever, where nothing is real'. But fragmented structuring is the key to understanding the narrative in Indian cinema as much as it would apply, although for different reasons, to the highly anarchic methodology as evinced in the modern movements displayed by the French *avant garde* or in the experimental works of scores of independent filmmakers all over the world.

A strong case for exploring this idea is made by the recent Bollywood success of *Rang De Basanti* ('Paint it Yellow') directed by Rakyesh Mehra. The film combines history, media, popular culture, urban angst and investigative journalism into one complex discourse. It is an inquiry into its own narrative method, while creating another one with the aid of sophisticated digital intermediate processes, thereby requiring the viewer to access the story in multifaceted 'digital' ways. The film cuts back and forth between period footage, recreated history, flashbacks, and the contemporary, challenging the audience in extremely baffling ways, while simulating a similar challenge into its own story-telling scheme. Undoubtedly, this is no ordinary film— more so when you hear that the film is a major commercial success cutting across a variety of viewers in a reasonably diverse democratic nation like India!

The fragmented world and the random access of the digital process will soon come to stay, and this is not solely due to the recent launch of computer technology. So what could have made films like *Rang De Basanti* and its ilk such huge successes? I am trying to argue here that the world of digital comprehension is located in a semiotic zone, rooted in the 'oral' tradition, where narrators spin out long stories based on thin hairline plots. Therefore, be it the narration by a *Harikatha*[2] exponent in South India or the *Bengshi*[3] on a Japanese stage, this unscripted 'oral' style plays upon the unique ability of the *'Rasik'* or the 'benevolent appreciator' to combine a complex amalgam of body-language, poems, scriptural quotations, jokes, music and even some dancing into one 'totalised' narrative.

This seemingly disconnected random experience gets integrated into a 'proper sequence' of events, largely due to an amazing socio-cultural interface with memories, legends and assorted folktales. While in traditional Indian theatrical narration, this unification was made possible by a benevolent jester called the *Sutradhar*,[4] in modern digital technology this interface happens, thanks to a friendly instrument called the 'mouse' or the 'remote'. One can therefore safely conclude that any medium becomes digital when it allows dynamic levels of 'interface', in order to empower the participant observer to negotiate the narrative through highly individualised protocols. Watching home movies on DVDs today has almost replicated this experience and one can access the final work with multiple layers of representation in a completely free and unrestrained manner.

I am proposing here a rather unsubstantiated reflection and, in its tenuous positioning, a truth exists somewhere, I believe, which may help us unravel this digital versus analogue dilemma. I feel that there are two kinds of film making and watching experiences: there is a 'spoken' film and there is a 'written' film. There is a film that 'tells' a story, relying largely on the semiotic level, and a film that 'scripts' a forward movement depending totally on the transparency of its semantic construction! I said that this argument is tenuous because the viewer can always turn his or her perception of the cinematic image around to see the 'written' as spontaneously 'oral' or vice versa. This argument for a semiotic understanding can become relevant only if we avoid comparing the picture concept of the 'written' to the writer's usage of the 'word'. As Christian Metz has pointed out, the image or shot is a unit of discourse, with an outside reference. 'It is unlike the word, which is merely a lexical unit, but like a statement, which always refers to an objective reality'(1982). So while the 'written' film locates the discourse into a very specific reality to the extent of inhibiting any other form of representation, the 'oral' film spreads itself in highly interactive ways to denote other realms of signification. In some ways the 'written' film gets registered into the specifics of 'Realism', as evinced in some of the films made by Satyajit Ray or in the logical world of a Shyam Benegal, while 'oral' films manifest themselves in the non-rational narratives of Manmohan Desai, Mani Ratnam or a Rakyesh Mehra.

Looking back we realise that it was the 'written' novel that actually converted the oral narration into an analogue experience for the first time. It introduced a definite spatiality to the narration in terms of sentences, paragraphs and chapters spread over a specified number of pages, quite like the way that cinema would do many centuries later within a very finite spatial–temporal parameter.

Would such a specifically prescribed format of the book inhibit a non-analogue form of reception? Certainly not! The reader can skip pages or chapters and access the unfolding of the narration in any manner. Whereas the book was written with the intent of being followed through line by line, the reader can browse through and derive his own form of decipherment. The strength of cinema, on the other hand, so far, has been its complete control over the mechanical process of projection, which demanded a certain order of reels to be projected in its entirety, before it could unwind to its end within an unchangeable, specified time format. It is this tyranny of narration which rebels like Jean-Luc Godard and Francois Truffaut sought to contest as they launched the *avant garde* movement in the early 1960s. Their cinema was virtually crying for a radical interface that could allow them and their viewers total freedom over the narrative process. In the famous lines attributed to Godard (in conversation with a more conventional-minded filmmaker): 'Cinema should have a beginning, middle and an end, but not necessarily in that order!'

With all reverence to the irreverent Godard, I would like to submit that a lot of Indian mainstream cinema gets constructed on such random lines, be it at the level of scripting, producing or distributing. While many cineastes would perceive such cinema as melodramatic and kitschy, I see in it, an approach which subconsciously reflects an 'oral' tradition full of lateral thinking, capable of being restructured in as many creative ways as possible. In the global context today I am convinced that Indian cinema and her filmmakers can deftly handle the digital transition and that is, if all goes well!

Looming on the horizon in the guise of huge amounts of FDI (Foreign Direct Investment) and the opening up of 'free' markets, we are at the threshold of welcoming a completely stagnant Hollywood system which has had not moved beyond the aesthetics of the 1970s triumvirate of Steven Spielberg, Francis Coppola and George Lucas. It has been a cinema of Stars and Wars all the way! Science fiction and corporate dilemmas have been the staple diet of a people, who have had hardly any energy to lift their heads out of a quagmire of an overpriced economy and uninspired leadership. While serious post-modernists believe that the time is ripe for Hollywood honchos to let some eastern breeze sweep their prairie fields, we should also hope that our Indian filmmakers revisit the narratives of their great bards, who have always made it their business to encounter modernity in creative ways. The spurt of multiplexes all over India and their readiness to gear up for digital 4K projections reveal the enthusiasm of filmmakers to try out the new HD digital cameras and embrace newer forms of cultural politics. At the same time, a robust population of youngsters are willing to watch altered forms of their self identity usher in the new digital era with the fanfare that it richly deserves.

Notes

1. For more information on Michael Kahn, see *en.wikipedia.org/miki/Michael Kahn*.
2. *Harikatha* is a traditional oral Indian form of narrating myths and legends
3. *Bengshi* is the interpreter on the classical Japanese stage
4. *Sutradhar* is the interpreter in folk and classical Indian theatre

References

Metz, Christian. 1982. *The Imaginary Signifier.* UK: Macmillan.
Monaco, James. 2000. *How to Read a Film: The World of Movies, Media, Multimedia: Language, History, Theory.* New York: Oxford University Press.

14

Radio Daze: A Medium in Churning

Bindu Bhaskar

The message and the medium seem to be on a steep curve. Radio has been steadily pushed away from the centre-stage in all cultures. Even so, its role and status in a mediatised society cannot be perceived as peripheral or marginal. A range of identities associated with radio—personal, mobile, global and local—comfortably fit into a digital frame.

At the individual level, a digital interface can be empowering, reducing the technological divide between the receiver and the transmitter or the listener and the producer. In a simple sense, a digital audio system permits a single operator to compose, produce and edit. A cocktail of music, talk and sound effects, segmented according to individual preference, completes the auditory experience, while digital technology steadily improves clarity and access. A medium is always a complex network. An array of platforms, short-wave, microwave, AM (amplitude modification) and FM (frequency modulation), satellite and digital have expanded the reach and quality of radio. 'Churn', a term that describes the rate of subscriber turnover or the number of subscribers who disconnect from a cable system, appears appropriate to describe a medium that changes mode frequently. The signals are hard to miss as radio redefines itself as a legitimate and vibrant digital era participant. Digital technology breaks down pictures or audio into data bits, which can be sent in a stream and then recombined by a computer into sound or picture. Initially developed in Britain by BBC (British Broadcasting Corporation) engineers in the 1970s, Digital Audio Broadcasting uses new high-frequency bands, with several services carried in one block of frequencies called the multiplex. Radio can be viewed both as a personal and as a background medium. Of all the media, radio has not confined the individual to a certain location. The portability of the radio receiver ensures mobility. The radio listener is never restricted from doing something else. As an exclusive medium of sound, its range has been random, allowing for unlimited movement and choice. The absence of the visual saves the radio from the hindrance of light.

Radio's apparently dynamic mode, fashioned by technology and policy, make it incapable of prolonged stasis, political, economic, social and cultural. Compulsions of fluctuating international and national markets have transformed radio and other competing forms of mass media from being a static presence in fixed zones to fluid essentials in flexible zones, almost inevitably challenging established notions of media time and space.

Even major players such as the British Broadcasting Corporation 'who have been nimble in adapting to the rapid pace of change', according to a statement made by BBC World Service Director Mark Byford in 2002, are witnessing dramatic changes in audience habits, increased competition, deregulation of markets, shifts in technology and greater listener choice. The BBC World Service surveys people in 130 countries over a three-year period and looks at a third of that sample over one year to work out an annual listening figure. The figure for 2000 was 153 million, with 151 million listeners in 1999 recorded during 1999 and 143 million in 1998. BBC's short wave transmissions to the United States, Australia and New Zealand ended on July 1, 2001. Cuts to the short wave broadcasts were compensated elsewhere. FM audiences for the BBC World Service had trebled from 1996 to 2001 and accounted for a third of listeners, and justified the World Service's commitment to further FM expansion. The BBC upgraded transmitters to those areas where short wave listening will continue to be the only viable means to receive BBC services for years to come. The 'overwhelming majority' of the survey measuring how many people listen to the service was completed before September 11 and audiences in areas such as Afghanistan, Iraq and Somalia could not be measured.

In an article on declining radio listenership, Julia Day (2002) writes that the BBC World Service lost 3 million listeners in 2001, its lowest listening figure since 1998. The BBC lost 12 million listeners in India. The massive drop in India, where the World Service has been held in high regard for decades, was made up by growth in listenership in Africa, Australia, Europe, Bangladesh, Ukraine and the United States. The BBC lost millions of listeners in Pakistan, Indonesia and Poland.

The reason offered for the World Service suffering in India was that people were switching off the radio and turning on television. Radio listening in India had fallen from 53 per cent in 1991 to 25 per cent in 2001, according to national surveys. With news and current affairs banned from FM radio, people favoured television over short wave radio transmissions.

Sylvain Lafrance, Vice-President, Radio de Radio–Canada, addressed the issue of altered priorities, in a speech on 'The Role of the Media in the Dynamics of Cultural Diversity' delivered at the Radio Development Forum on October 25, 2004, in Beijing: 'Even before the events of September 11, 2001, we had begun to feel very clearly Canadians' growing interest in international affairs. Our radio services therefore adopted an action plan.... The first thrust was *openness to the world*, seen as a way of describing to Canadians the big issues at stake in the world in an age when ignorance and misapprehensions among peoples can lead to great upheaval' (2004).

Radio–Canada, rethinking its place as a public broadcaster in an international context, developed a fresh approach by launching a new radio network, Espace musique, in September 2004, dedicated to diversity that would allow it to play a strong role. By contrast, private radio stations limit the number of songs in their playlists and stick to a narrow range of musical styles, which reduces the diversity available to audiences.

While the compulsions of operating in mature media markets force a rethink on big players, the medium has been evolving in small spaces, adding imaginatively to democratic or revolutionary discourse. The most illustrative examples arise in the context of developing countries. Community radio has captured the public imagination from Latin America, Africa to South Asia. Land-locked Nepal has become a crucible for political change and its airwaves have contributed to this process in no small measure. According to Sumit Pradhan (2006), 'Nearly four months after successfully pushing the fight against royal dictatorship, community radio stations in Nepal are at the forefront of another revolution—turning the airwaves into an educational medium for constitutional reforms. Several stations in Kathmandu and outlying areas have been broadcasting programmes aimed at raising awareness about constitutional issues. The aim is to positively influence the Constitution-making process for an inclusive and democratic Nepal, say station managers.'

In the developing world, India stands apart as a large and functioning democracy, but it is also an arena where radio's political power remains diminished. The era of state control, which allowed for a major terrestrial expansion, also meant a tight grip on the nature of news disseminated. While the state has allowed alternatives to emerge, its reluctance to grant any extra-governmental entity permission to broadcast news on the radio limits the scope of the medium. Worse, radio takes off in another direction with a skewed set of priorities.

In India private radio has come more than a decade after private television. The Central government has treated radio as a special child that needs protection. While the other media, print, television and the Internet kept pace with international changes in hardware and software, radio was left behind. Unnatural concerns about censorship and misuse by political rebels meant that the medium found limited outlets.

Government decontrol over domestic radio in 2004–2006 also set off some dramatic changes. India's FM radio broadcasting band lies between 88 and 108 MHz; and international practice designates this radio spectrum as suitable for FM broadcasting. Out of this, 100 to 108 MHz is informally reserved for the state-run All India Radio and 88 to 90 MHz for community radio. The only part of the band available to private operators is 91 to 99 MHz. That explains the small number of frequencies being offered in each town and indicates assured appreciation in value. Couple this with the flexibility of capital and operating expenses involved, and media houses, big and small, national and international, are developing business plans to occupy this space.

Sunil Kumar, Managing Director, Big River Radio (India), pointed out in April 2006 on *exchange4media.com*, a portal tracking Indian media policy and management issues: 'Radio has a huge market: It will be worth not less than Rs. 1,300 crore (roughly, $300 million) by 2008. Today the share of radio in the Rs. 12,000 crore (roughly, $2700 million) advertising market (adspends) is not more than 2 per cent, which is much lower than the global average of 6–7 per cent. Even in Sri Lanka it is a huge 14 per cent. With over 600 stations (250 All India Radio and 350 private) in 100-odd cities up and running by 2007, adspends growing at the rate of 20 per cent to Rs. 20,000 crore (roughly, $4,440 million), and the radio pie taking on international shape and size, the market size for radio is certainly going to meet any analyst's forecast' (2006).

Radio in India has moved from one extreme to another, from state control to market control. The entry of private domestic and foreign investors into the FM radio space has made it a lucrative commodity. The two phases of bidding for radio licences have been keenly contested with major Indian and foreign media brands playing for high stakes. Channels vie to keep the masses happy in a time-tested fashion. The multi-city Radio Mirchi stations play Hindi or regional film music interspersed with chat, movie gossip, teenage love problems and game shows. Their jockeys speak in the local language and avoid English tunes. Radio City, on the other hand, has targeted the upmarket crowd by adding Western pop. The jockeys speak mostly in English with a smattering of Hindi, but no regional language. However, in Indore city, which was the first station of Radio Mirchi to go live in Phase I, the local taste for *ghazals* and old music was adopted, even though it was also a Hindi market. The current buzz around private radio has also made it look and feel like a medium for the post-liberalisation generation. Brands being advertised seem to suggest that. Cars, music systems and cell-phones are coming equipped with an FM receiver and with no major subscription costs.

The legacy of the public broadcaster All India Radio, exemplary as it has been in the Indian context, may prove inadequate in the changed but charged circumstances. Private ventures will ultimately be narrowly self-serving. The developing world abounds with examples of successful community radio ventures. India should encourage people's radio to offset any rural–urban divide that might emerge in the new complex interplay of transnational and domestic commercial forces.

No form of the media can afford a singular identity. Degrees of separation are becoming unspecified and flux within specified spaces unstoppable, making descriptions hazy and definitions harder. While those with free-flowing capital and influence have found their niche in the competitive radio spectrum, some home-grown innovators still find their options and outlets limited. The following illustrations, taken from private Indian television news capsules, point to an explosion of problems:

(1) In April 2006, Raghav, a radio mechanic in Mansurpur village in Muzaffarpur district of Bihar State in India was in the news for his entrepreneurial radio station, but later the government seized it since he did not possess a licence to run it. He ran his venture from an electronics-spare parts shop, with nothing more than a

transmission kit and an antenna mounted on a bamboo pole. Raghav, who abandoned his studies due to poverty, used to handle cordless mikes while working with an orchestra and based his radio station on that principle. His station played film songs, broadcasted public interest messages on AIDS and polio, and even offered snappy local news from a 10-km radius for 12 hours at a stretch. He had been working very hard at running this radio station for three years. Unaware that he needed a government licence to run an FM station, Raghav was happy to provide news and entertainment to his village. Many felt that the radio station had given Mansurpur a special identity. The local people thought him talented and his radio station was popular in and around the village. He made no money from the initiative. With a little help from the government, this grassroots enterprise should have unleashed a string of small radio stations.

(2) The son of a politician in Mugrahiya panchayat was also running a similar kind of radio station. The station was being used for electoral campaigning, causing anger among the other candidates, who believed that campaigning via a radio station was a breach of the Election Commission's code of conduct. The district administration, on its part, could not immediately offer a conclusive solution and allowed the station to function.

(3) For many years before the advent of the television, radio commentary was the only way link between cricket and its enthusiasts. In the Nagpur Test against England in April 2006, a record was set—for the first time a Test match played in India had not been beamed widely through radio. Nimbus Sports, which bought all rights for cricket in India, managed to sell the radio rights to BBC in the United Kingdom, to ECHOSTAR in the US and to ARY Digital in West Asia. But it failed to find a major partner in India. The problem was that All India Radio (AIR) and Nimbus Sports could not work out a deal on how to share revenue. Nimbus sold the rights to a private FM channel, but that left millions of listeners across the country disappointed.

These isolated incidents from one country reflect the volatility of the possibilities that arise. This is true of media outlets across the world. Radio-casters around the world face the challenge of trying to reflect regional realities within distinct territories, but retain the fundamental role of acting as a link between cultures. The advent of new distribution channels is always exciting but growing concentration of ownership is worrying. Private enterprise does not mean the end of an effective public policy response. A grassroots revolution in radio that is allowed to sprout in remote pockets through local initiatives would represent an appropriate outcome of the digital era.

References

Day, Julia. 2002. 'BBC Loses 3 Million Listeners', *Guardian Unlimited. http://www.guardian.co.uk/*. April 16.

Kumar, Sunil. 2006. 'Time to Tune in Folks! Here are Ten Reasons to Invest in Radio', *Macro View. http://www.exchange4media.com/*. April.

Lafrance, Sylvain. 2004. 'The Role of the Media in the Dynamics of Cultural Diversity', speech delivered at the Radio Development Forum, Beijing, Radio–Canada. *http://www.cbc.radio-canada.ca/speeches/20041025.shtml/*. October 25.

Pradhan, Suman. 2006. 'Nepal Radio Stations to Help Bring About Social Change: Community Radio Stations Use Airwaves to Shed Light on Constitutional Issues', *Dawn. http://www.dawn.com/*. August 10.

15

The Internet and the Bully

Valerie Kaye

My close friend Jenny, now in her mid 50s, recently confided in me some disturbing facts. Like many other children, she had been bullied at school. Margaret had been a good friend of hers before going to secondary school, and they started at the new school as a close unit. They messed around together, got told off by the teacher together, hung around at cafes out of school together, and did the usual things pre-pubescent girls do.

What went wrong? My friend Jenny never knew. As she remembered it, 'One day we were friends and the next day we were not, and I never knew why'. What happened next has been verified by a couple of women who were in the same class in that suburban school in the early 1960s.

'Well, Margaret started to hate Jenny,' one told me. 'We never knew why. We just knew that they had been friends but that was over. And Margaret was such a strong character. When she told us to do something, we just went along with it'.

'Going along with it,' meant, in this case, that Jenny spent two or three years being ostracised by the whole class, apart from one or two exceptions. When they were not ostracising her, they were name-calling or indulging in other childish yet damaging behaviour all designed to demean Jenny.

Jenny never told her family about this even though it went on for years. Of course she never told the teacher. As soon as she could, at the age of 16, despite being very clever, she did not want to go to university and left school determined to join the adult world and get as far away from the unhappiness of the school environment as she could. It is true to say that her experiences in school of being bullied changed her life.

Today Jenny is the mother of a young child, and seeing the occasional unkindness of children in the school playground has brought her own childhood experiences to the forefront of her mind. She told me, 'I don't want revenge in any way. I just want to know why'.

I have been her close friend for many years, since childhood, and although she had never before told me the story of the bullying, I found that Jenny's behaviour changed around the age of 15. She became less accessible to me and her boundaries were very firmly in place. In many ways, she became a harder and more inflexible person. I can see now that much of her behaviour was a direct product of her unhappy experiences in the classroom.

And here we get to the power of the Internet. Jenny hates computers and has never mastered email or the Internet, until now…

Jenny knew enough to be able to bring up one of the search engines commonly used to find out information. There are so many of them now, including *Google, AskJeeves,* and *Yahoo.*

She entered Margaret's name on to one of the search engines and pressed 'Enter'. She had to sift through a few pages to get to the only likely candidate, a woman with the same name (luckily a fairly uncommon one) who had founded a cosmetics company based in Canada. Jenny knew enough by now of the workings of the Internet to be able to bring up the home page of this company, and there she recognised her old adversary, albeit aged by over 40 years since they had last met.

What to do now? It seemed to Jenny that the powerful tool of the Internet had given her a unique opportunity that had never existed before in history. She had in just minutes, at the click of a mouse, been able to track down someone living on the other side of the world who had been such an important influence on her life. She could not pass up this opportunity to find the answer to the question that had been nagging her all her life. Why?

She wisely decided against sending a hard-hitting accusatory email. The main purpose here was to get answers, not to fall onto stony waters. So firstly, she sent a brief exploratory message, 'Are you the same Margaret who was at such and such girls school in the early 1960s?'

To her shock and elation she immediately, allowing for the time difference, received an email back. 'Yes it is me. How extraordinary to hear from you after all these years'.

Jenny ventured a bit more with each email, yet gingerly so as not to scare off her correspondent. 'Do you remember those days when we were friends? Do you remember going to that pop concert?' There were more innocuous reminiscences both women exchanged, and Jenny felt in spite of herself that she was warming to a person who was clearly intelligent and thoughtful. Then she wrote, 'We were friends and then not. Do you remember why?'

Back came a disarming reply. 'I remember clearly that we were friends in those early days at school. I enjoyed your company and we had fun being "the bad girls" for a time. However, I was always insecure, and I felt that you were in a group of girls that was a bit more upmarket and cliquey than me. One day I went to your house for tea and soon afterwards, you came over to mine. I remember that our carpet seemed rather threadbare and there was a stain on it I had not seen before. I felt embarrassed. Next day in school you commented on the carpet, and I felt even more embarrassed. I threw a netball at your head in a temper.'

Jenny has no memory of either incident but undoubtedly it was at that time the feud started. Since then, various emails have been exchanged. What is clear is that Jenny's memory of what happened and why the feud started is very different from Margaret's recollections. Margaret remembers that she herself was ostracised in school, which is something Jenny questions.

Margaret appears to have spent some years in therapy and freely admits that she felt very insecure at school. She seems a very different person from the one Jenny remembers, indeed, someone that she would be keen to meet now as the two women have a lot in common. In fact, they have a meeting planned for later in the year when Margaret is to visit England.

The correspondence is going on and is proving fruitful in giving both women a chance to air their feelings of hurt, to review the past and see that memory sometimes does play some tricks, and all this mediated by the Internet, the extraordinarily potent device that the tail end of the 20th century threw up to make these world-wide connections possible. Now it is my turn to trace my own bugbear from the past. Heather Blakely, please come forward.

Notes on Editor and Contributors

Bindu Bhaskar is Associate Professor at the Asian College of Journalism, Chennai. She has worked at *The Economic Times*, was selected for an international journalism fellowship in New York in 1989, and wrote on socio-political issues for *Frontline* in the 1990s. She has authored *My Vote Counts*, 2000 and scripted-produced a video documentary (2002) on livelihood issues in Kerala.

Dilip D'Souza was formerly a software professional, and is now author of *The Narmada Dammed: An Inquiry into the Politics of Development*, 2002 and *Branded by Law: Looking at India's Denotified Tribes*.

K. Hariharan is filmmaker, Visiting Professor in India and the USA, and Director, L.V. Prasad Film and TV Academy, Chennai.

Valerie Kaye has been a producer with the BBC, London, made a few well-acclaimed documentary films, and has a Master's degree in Chinese Studies from SOAS.

André Lemos is Professor of the Communication Faculty (Facom) at the Federal University of Bahia (UFBa). He has a doctorate in Sociology from the Sorbonne, Paris. For more information, see *http://www.facom.ufba.br/ciberpesquisa/andrelemos*.

Ashok Panikkar, a professionally trained mediator, works as a teacher and consultant in the areas of conflict management, cross-cultural engagement and critical and creative thinking. He is the founder of Meta–Culture, a Bangalore-based integrated dispute resolution centre that works with both businesses and communities. He is passionately interested in exploring the intersections of technology, culture, human values and social behaviour. He can be contacted at *ashokpanikkar@meta-culture.in*

R. Radhakrishnan is Professor of English and Comparative Literature and Chair of the Department of Asian American Studies at the University of California, Irvine, and author of *Diasporic Mediations: Between Home and Location*, 1996; *Theory in an Uneven World*, 2003 and *History, the Human, and the World Between*, 2007.

Nalini Rajan has a doctorate in Social Communication (specialising in political philosophy) from the Catholic University of Louvain, Belgium. Her academic publications include *Secularism, Democracy, Justice—Implications of Rawlsian Principles in India*, 1998, and *Democracy and the Limits of Minority Rights*, 2002. Her edited volume, *Practising Journalism—Values, Constraints and Implications* was published 2005. Another edited volume, *Twenty-First Century Journalism* was published in 2007. Her fictional work, *The Pangolin's Tale* is to be published in 2007. Dr Rajan is Associate Professor at the Asian College of Journalism, Chennai.

Charlene Rajendran, a Malaysian theatre practitioner, directs, teaches, writes and performs. She currently teaches theatre at Nanyang Technological University, Singapore.

Sandhya Rao is editor with Tulika Publishers, a leading children's books publisher based in Chennai. She is a writer and translator. Her *My Friend, the Sea* won a special prize at the Berlin Children's and Youth Literature Festival, 2005, and she has translated Astrid Lindgren's *Pippi Longstrump* into Hindi.

Rahul Srivastava has studied anthropology in Mumbai, Delhi and Cambridge, England. He has conceived many pedagogic activities involving urban history and architectural heritage. He writes a weekly column on urban issues for a Mumbai daily and contributes regularly to mainstream and academic publications on topics like environmentalism, cities and tribal history.

A. (Aravamuthan) Srivathsan received a degree in M.Arch. from the School of Planning and Architecture, New Delhi, India, and a Ph.D. from the Indian Institute of Technology, Madras. He has been a Fulbright Fellow at the University of California, USA, and Assistant Professor at Anna University, Chennai, India. Presently, he is assistant editor at *The Hindu*, and is a consultant architect.

Julio Valentim (UOL/Cnpq) is doctorate student in Contemporary Communication and Culture at Facom/UFBa. He was sponsored by UOL (*www.uol.com.br*), through its UOL Bolsa Pesquisa programme, process number 200503191556. For his research, see *http://www.smartmobscibercidades.blogspot.com/*.

A.R. Venkatachalapathy took his Ph.D. in history from the Jawaharlal Nehru University, New Delhi, for his dissertation on the social history of book-publishing and print culture in colonial Tamil Nadu. He has taught at Manonmaniam Sundaranar University, Tirunelveli, the University of Madras, and the University of Chicago.

Presently he is Professor at the Madras Institute of Development Studies, Chennai. Apart from his scholarly writings in English he has written/edited over 15 books in Tamil. His most recent publication is *In Those Days There Was No Coffee: Writings in Cultural History*, 2006.

A. Vishnu is IT and Lifestyle correspondent with *Mid-Day*, based in Bangalore. Earlier he anchored the 'Insite' technology column of *The Hindu* MetroPlus for four years.

Felix Wilfred is Professor and Head, Department of Christian Studies, University of Madras. He has written widely on issues related to religion and post-modernism.

INDEX

For Product Safety Concerns and Information please contact our EU
representative GPSR@taylorandfrancis.com
Taylor & Francis Verlag GmbH, Kaufingerstraße 24, 80331 München, Germany